Prais

Who Says?

"Lisa Zeidner's *Who Says?* is as captivating as it is instructive, an enormously useful craft book that is also, miraculously, a page-turner. Witnessing how Zeidner constructs her own erudite and hilarious point of view is a class in itself. An essential resource for teachers and students, writers and readers."

—Karen Russell, author of *Orange World and Other Stories*

"As an experienced teacher and witty, engaging novelist, Lisa Zeidner has a real understanding of what makes fiction tick, and from whose perspective that ticking might arise. Her book will surely be a good resource for anyone setting out to understand the complex and all-important topic of point of view."

—Meg Wolitzer, author of *The Female Persuasion*

"Zeidner's book is a joy. Usually books that claim to be about the craft of fiction leave my mouth, eyes, and room full of dust, but this work is actually fun. It's also full of erudition, wit, and insight. And it is wonderfully accessible, a helpful text for any writer at any stage of their career."

—Percival Everett, author of *Telephone*

"Lisa Zeidner's terrific book on point of view is lively and insightful, an indispensable guide for writers of all levels. No small part of the pleasure of reading it is the way she makes you think anew of many of your favorite novels and stories. Highly recommended."

—Ann Packer, author of *The Children's Crusade*

"As a novice teacher thirty-something years ago, I realized that the biggest obstacle for most beginning writers was complete ignorance of how to manage point of view in fiction. I've been teaching to that insight ever since, which means that I agree with Lisa Zeidner! Not only on the importance of the topic but also on the key points she makes about it in *Who Says?* To have such a well-organized manual on point of view is a tremendous asset, especially with the thousands of examples found here, deployed from Zeidner's almost intimidating erudition, but softened by her customarily light and witty touch."

—Madison Smartt Bell, author of *The Color of Night*

"In witty, accessible prose, drawing on examples from a vivid universe of fiction, Lisa Zeidner breaks down the science of perspective in fiction writing. This volume articulates with stunning clarity so much of what we feel when we read but struggle to explain, offering gems for the author attempting to gain a reader's interest and trust. Writers, students, lay readers, and scholars of fiction will come away from *Who Says?* with a greater understanding of how to write all of the selves: them, ours, and maybe even yours."

—Asali Solomon, author of *Disgruntled*

"While point of view is the primary subject here, *Who Says?* is anything but narrow in scope. This capacious volume spins tales about tales themselves, drawing us into the heart of storytelling in ways that feel rich and whole, providing along-the-way insights into language, character, voice, and structure. It's a great pleasure to read, and at its core inspirational—useful for new writers and writers made new by their latest project, too."

—Aurelie Sheehan, author of *Once into the Night*

WHO SAYS?

WHO SAYS?

MASTERING POINT OF VIEW IN FICTION

LISA ZEIDNER

W. W. NORTON & COMPANY
Independent Publishers Since 1923

For information about permission to reproduce selections from this book, write to
Permissions, W. W. Norton & Company, Inc., 500 Fifth Avenue, New York, NY 10110

For information about special discounts for bulk purchases, please contact
W. W. Norton Special Sales at specialsales@wwnorton.com or 800-233-4830

Manufacturing by LSC Communications, Harrisonburg
Production manager: Lauren Abbate

Library of Congress Cataloging-in-Publication Data

Names: Zeidner, Lisa, author.
Title: Who says? : mastering point of view in fiction / Lisa Zeidner.
Description: First edition. | New York, N.Y. : W. W. Norton & Company, [2021] |
Includes bibliographical references.
Identifiers: LCCN 2020041066 | ISBN 9780393356113 (paperback) |
ISBN 9780393356120 (epub)
Subjects: LCSH: Point of view (Literature) | Fiction—Technique.
Classification: LCC PN3383.P64 Z45 2021 | DDC 808.3/926—dc23
LC record available at https://lccn.loc.gov/2020041066

W. W. Norton & Company, Inc., 500 Fifth Avenue, New York, N.Y. 10110
www.wwnorton.com

W. W. Norton & Company Ltd., 15 Carlisle Street, London W1D 3BS

1 2 3 4 5 6 7 8 9 0

FOR JOHN

CONTENTS

WHO SAYS?

CHAPTER ONE

INTRODUCTION

"YOU TALKIN' TO ME?"

There is always a ménage a trois when you're reading: you, the author, and the character.

At least a threesome, though in sprawling epics the trio can morph into an immense, tribal, polygamous family.

You're in Paris, or Pittsburgh, in bed, or at a café, holding the book (or your device) in your hand, your lips moving, or not, as your eyes scan the page. Even if you belong to a book club, you read alone. And unless he is James Patterson with a Santa's workshop full of ghostwriting elves churning out thrillers for his insatiable fans, the author is alone, too, when he creates the characters.

Who, basically, don't exist, except insofar as the author Frankensteins them into lurching life. Even if the character is a thinly veiled stand-in for the author himself—a neurotic but endearing nerd with a disastrous dating life, or a veteran adjusting to civilian life after the war that took his legs—the character is by default a chiasma.

But let us agree that the job of the fiction writer is to make us feel something for his imaginary friend, or for the evil twin whispering in his ear that he must do awful things. We can feel sympathy for the character, solicitude, grief for his loss, fervent hope for his success, or even morbid fascination, if the dude happens to be a serial killer.

If you're a Venn diagram type, think of three nice round bubbles, each floating separately and safely in its own enclosed world, labeled "Reader," "Author," "Character"—and then think about how much the bubbles will overlap. It's in that bleeding or overlap between the entities—choose your metaphor, or your ink color—that empathy lives.

Sometimes the author and the reader form their own band of brothers, watching the character coolly from afar, giggling or gaping at him, judging his foibles, watching him fumble. Sometimes the author shows you the world so completely from the character's perspective that you pretty much forget the author is even there. It seems that you and the character are alone together at the empty diner after closing time, bathed in spotlights as in a Hopper painting. Of course you know that is not really the case, because no matter how much you are encouraged to "suspend your disbelief," you are aware that a writer has constructed the tale. But your identification with the character is so complete that all three of you—author, character, reader—might as well be participating in a synchronized swimming routine, or perhaps you crawled directly into the hero's head through the strange little portal on Floor 7½ in *Being John Malkovich*.

Let's say the subject is a nasty divorce. The author can pick a side—say, that of the beleaguered, betrayed wife (Nora Ephron's *Heartburn*). If the major characters are the two warring spouses, the author can serve as a kind of mediator, giving equal time to both spouses' versions of the story and inviting you to be impartial, or to witness the nuptial carnage in head-shaking wonderment. The author might choose a supposedly reliable arbiter to ensure fairness, the role taken by the divorce lawyer in Warren Adler's *The War of the Roses*. Or the author might choose to let the poor kid the couple is fighting over own the story—to show the divorce through her perspective, even though she's too young to understand what's going on (Henry James's *What Maisie Knew*). The choice of point of view, in talking about divorce, basically *is* the story, and if the fiction is successful, it will be neither a court docket full of facts nor an unfiltered screed of lament against the cheating spouse.

If the cast of the novel is large, your author can function as a kind of cheerful party planner, escorting you around to introduce you to the people she thinks you might find interesting, filling you with admiration for the breadth of her vision. She might provide you with a genealogy, so you can keep the characters straight. She might provide you with a historical timeline. Hilary Mantel gives you both a cast of characters and a chart about the evolution of the Tudors at the beginning of *Wolf Hall*. You admire Mantel for doing her homework. Still, you're aware that no matter how assiduous the research, she doesn't really know what Cromwell had for breakfast.

The author is an intermediary. He is a guide and translator— and that is true even (or, as we'll later see, especially) when the story is being told in first person, or involves facts or historical events.

Point-of-view choices involve skillful manipulations in, and modulations of, your alliance with your characters. In fact, I will argue in this book that those manipulations are the very heart of fiction, more central and crucial than plot—that only fiction that challenges your allegiances to author or character ever fully succeeds. And while most of us, when we write, make choices about point of view automatically and instinctively, we can learn a great deal about both our goals and the best ways to achieve them by breaking down those choices, and looking carefully at our options.

We can hate or mistrust a character. A narrator can be anywhere from subtly to riotously unreliable. *But we cannot hate or mistrust the author.* If we hate the author, we hate the book. When the author ushers us to our seats, we trust him to not position us behind a huge concrete pole, where our view of the action is obscured. We don't want to watch a rehearsal, either. We want the players to know their lines and be in costume. There is a huge amount of trust implicit in the contract between author and reader. We do not want to be promised insight into the human heart and instead be given snuff porn. We do not want to be promised a story that is, to use the adjective of the moment, "edgy," and instead wind up in a Hallmark card.

You can think of point-of-view choices as stopping points along a spectrum or sliding scale:

Closeness..........................Distance
Empathy..........................Judgment
Internal............................External
Subjectivity.......................Objectivity

Deciding about point of view requires an assessment about whether you're moving toward your subject, or whether you're moving away. Whether you're going to encourage the reader to bathe in the character's view of the world, or offer a complementary or even competing one.

Here is why things get tricky. Of course a surefire way to school us in characters' feelings is to allow us to gain access to their minds and souls—that is, after all, why we bother to read fiction rather than the newspaper. As Atticus Finch asserts in *To Kill a Mockingbird*, "You never really understand a person until you consider things from his point of view ... until you climb inside of his skin and walk around in it." Much of this book is devoted to methods for achieving that identification with character. But the best route to empathy is not always immersion and closeness. Paradoxically, on some issues, if you get too close, it can be more off-putting than immersive. Sometimes you need to pull back for a wider view to really feel the desired impact. Not all distant, objective observations are necessarily cold and clinical, either. Sometimes they, too, can engender strong reactions.

To talk in cinematic terms for a minute, if you're filming a romantic kiss, you don't want to get so close to the smooching duo that you see the hair in their nostrils. You might build the mood better if you show the lights twinkling in the harbor behind them. But if you do the equivalent of one of those wildly circling crane shots with a suddenly swelling violin score, your audience may be snorting with derision about the cliché rather than sighing with gauzy, romantic satisfaction. It's particularly difficult to get the point of view right with a sex scene, because such scenes almost by default turn the reader into a voyeur—even though the act in question is (at least most of the time) private, and titillation might not be the desired effect. It's also a situation where a writer can seem to be gloating about his own prowess. I use "his" here advisedly: see Norman Mailer or other writers of a certain swagger who are sometimes accused of uncomfortably celebrating their own irresistibility and talent for pleasing the ladies, rather than their protagonists'. Back to our Venn diagrams: the reader then objects that there isn't *enough* separation between character and author, that the author is merely showing off or engaging in some kind of wish fulfillment, in which he becomes Austin Powersesque, a crude parody of machismo. (No, you aren't a dweeb hunched over a laptop! You're a man of action and mystery, Baby!)

Similarly, if you are trying to show the horrors of the battlefield, a close-up of one man's howl as his leg explodes (perhaps in slow motion) might not be quite as effective as a wider shot of the battlefield, with thousands of bodies writhing or face-down in the mud—at least until that image becomes a cliché of "The

Horror of Battle," and makes us feel almost nothing, as clichés are wont to do. If you're trying to show Catherine having finally gathered the courage to escape Heathcliff, walking alone over the moors in the middle of the night in torrential rain, miles from safety, it might be useful to give us a long shot of just how vast and cold those moors are.

Or it might not. The incontrovertible fact about point-of-view choices: *they depend.*

Always.

Look how wantonly Emily Brontë complicates the point of view of *Wuthering Heights*: she tells the story of Catherine and Heathcliff's stormy romance not from either of the lovers' points of view but from that of Lockwood, a nearby renter from cosmopolitan London, who got much of his story from Nelly, a local servant who has known Catherine since she was a tot—who, in turn, got some parts of her story from other servants and observers. Brontë actively keeps you on your toes, makes it difficult for you to trust the version of the story you're getting at any given time, and, in fact, the novel is much less gothic than virtually all of the film versions. If you have stellar graphic design skills, try drawing the Venn diagram on *that* set of relationships.

The effect of so many interpreters and translators is to make the writer seem to almost disappear. If you're not careful, you can lose sight of the fact that *Brontë is making Catherine and Heathcliff up.* To make us feel that we're getting different versions of events that actually happened is a kind of magic trick.

Because they didn't.

Slavery did, however. How to write about its gruesomeness, though, and root us in the horrors of the slave experience? You might choose to entrap us completely, without translation or mediation, in the shame and pain of a man in a chain gang forced to wear a bit in his mouth, like a horse, or locked in leg irons, in a box in the muddy ground, during a raging flood. Give us the full *you are there* immediacy. But then you risk making the reader feel lectured to, or even numb to the pain. That astonishing section about the chain gang in Toni Morrison's *Beloved*, so full of lyrical empathy, comes very late in a novel that is pointedly set after the Civil War, and that offers us a series of very closely aligned third-person narratives showing how disparate characters cope with slavery's legacy. The novel is about how we think and talk about the grief and rage, not solely about the horror of the experiences themselves. Temporal distance can be as important as physical distance in establishing authorial reliability and range. Morrison's characters are richly drawn enough to feel real, but our bond is first and foremost with Morrison herself, with her insight and vision. The novel aims to be both deeply personal in scope and also to have enormous breadth—delivering a story that is, as the flap copy says, "as powerful as Exodus and as intimate as a lullaby."

And yet Cynthia Ozick, in her heart-wrenching short story "The Shawl," pointedly does *not* pull back for that larger view. Rosa is on a Nazi death march to a concentration camp with her infant girl hidden at her breast, behind the eponymous shawl. She is cold, starving, her breasts dry; her daughter, Magda, sucks on the "magic shawl" that keeps her quiet and alive. We are trapped not only in Rosa's point of view, her consciousness narrowing to that one desperate hope, for the safety of infant Magda, but on that secret corner of concealment. Again, we may sympathize with Rosa, but our bond is with Ozick, who trusts us to understand what a prayer shawl is to Jewish religion, thus the story's metaphorical heft; and further to notice that she has crafted a story *seven pages long* that shows the full trauma of the loss of an individual life in the unimaginable scale of the camp's barbarity by forcing total identification with a single character. If you want the big picture, you can go to the Holocaust Museum, or watch *Shoah*. The profundity of Ozick's story is not just in what she makes us feel about Gestapo barbarity (How tragic is even one death among six million deaths, to the one who is dying, or worse yet, to the one losing her child?) but in what she asks you to consider about fiction's relationship to experience: How much pain and grief can a short story contain?

We hear the author's voice in a very different way in a book with a much quieter subject and a less dramatic sweep, like Alice McDermott's *Charming Billy*. We grow to love and care for this Irish family from Queens. They could be our neighbors, whether or not we happen to be Irish or from Queens. McDermott makes us a different kind of promise. She assures us that ordinary lives of quiet desperation matter. We feel grateful to her for encouraging us to move this close. We also appreciate a certain modesty, and selflessness, in the telling. Like a good therapist, McDermott seems to stand back, let the characters come to their own realizations.

Sometimes we get smacked between the eyes with insight as the characters do, concurrently—and sometimes we are encouraged to notice things that the characters don't. We'll talk about foreshadowing and other techniques that allow an author to simultaneously cleave to a character's perception of events, while still signaling to his readers that they must look beyond what the character himself perceives. If the clues are too loud, they're obtrusive. If they're too quiet, we miss them, and don't feel a shock of recognition when we get to the end; we feel annoyance or betrayal. In a story like John Cheever's "The Swimmer," we hop from neighborhood pool to neighborhood pool in the leafy suburbs with Donald Westerhazy, who is drunk and seriously dysfunctional. We've got our wits about us, however, and part of the joy of the story is realizing before Westerhazy does that something is very wrong with his idyllic life. The clues mount. The pleasure is the skill with which Cheever unfolds the revelations. Go back to our Venn diagrams: in this case you and the author are *mostly* doing the breaststroke right alongside Westerhazy, but our circle and his circle don't completely and totally overlap. It's as if you have a kind of peripheral vision— you see outside of the story's ostensible frame.

And then you reread. You savor. The clues mount differently, again. "Spoilers" make absolutely no difference in the appreciation of a good piece of fiction. In fact, the opposite: when you know what's coming, you feel the tension even more acutely. I've reread Flannery O'Connor's "A Good Man Is Hard to Find" many times after I first learned that the characters are all hurtling toward their deaths, and I don't feel tricked, or bored.

Alfred Hitchcock talked about the distinction between surprise and suspense, and why suspense is the more substantial achievement in film. If we see four men at a table playing poker and are bored until a bomb goes off, that's *surprise*. But "if we watch the same scene again with the important difference that we have seen the bomb being placed under the table and the timer set to 11 AM, and we can see a watch in the background, the same scene becomes very intense and almost unbearable . . . that is called *suspense*."

Point of view in movies and fiction differ in essential ways, as we'll discuss in Chapter 8. But Hitchcock's distinction holds for fiction as well. Giving readers the clues they need to fully interpret a scene amounts to a kind of respect for the readers' intelligence and acumen. What this means is that plot itself involves critical decisions about point of view: how much is going to be revealed to the reader, and when.

Here's an obvious but important point about foreshadowing: the very fact of it being there means that *the author knows what's going to happen*. He isn't just making it up as he goes along. The fiction acquires a kind of layered density, and thus can begin to feel less like an artificial convention and more like life, in which a real person exists both before and after the scene at hand.

We are not only engaged right from the onset—as we'll discuss in Chapter 2—but we trust that the engagement is going to go somewhere. That the writer isn't going to keep banging on one note over and over like a bad heavy metal band; that there will be variations, motifs, new combinations to listen to; that, moreover, things will eventually resolve, even if the resolution is to let us see that no resolution is possible.

Great writers know when to move in, and when to pull back. They manipulate the distance. They don't go too vibrato on the heartstrings, because that almost ensures sentimentality. They know when clinical information, even about a plot where facts are critical, becomes too much information—because then you've got a history textbook, not a novel.

But enough about them, the author and character. What about you?

Earlier, I said that the reader—let's call him "you"—is always alone while reading, and though that's true as you turn the pages, it's only partially true. You may feel as if you're sharing the book with like-minded brethren. This can happen when you're reading a bestseller, a sensation—with millions of people plunging into the *Harry Potter* books, it's harder to imagine that J. K. Rowling has created Harry solely for your personal delectation. There are also cult novelists, whose readers share certain traits or beliefs, from the people who are attuned to the God-inflected, gently witty inspiration of an Anne Lamott or single women who appreciate the hardships of the dating scene outlined in Candace Bushnell's *Sex and the City* to those who are tough enough to cotton to Cormac McCarthy's grim dystopian vision. For certain kinds of humor, you may come to the book with ideas about the writer's tone that predispose you to laugh. It's not exactly a stand-up routine, where you have the live audience's collective roar of approval and delight, but the author nevertheless counts on you to embrace a set of tenets about the world's absurdity, which feels almost giddily shared.

As a reader, you expect to be paid attention to, courted—seduced. Here is French theorist Roland Barthes, in *The Pleasure of the Text*:

> If I read this sentence, this story, or this word with pleasure, it is because they were written in pleasure.... But the opposite? Does writing in pleasure guarantee—guarantee me, the writer—the reader's pleasure? Not at all. I must seek out this reader (must "cruise" him) *without knowing where he is*. A site of bliss is then created. It is not the reader's "person" that is necessary to me, it is this site: the possibility of a dialectics of desire, of an *unpredictability* of bliss: the bets are not placed, there can still be a game.

Can we call Barthes's "site of bliss" the part of our Venn diagram where writer and reader are "on the same page?" The feeling that the writer is talking to you—*gets* you—is critical. What does the writer give you credit for? How large a vocabulary, how wide a net of literary allusions or historical frame of reference? What set of experiences, beliefs, concerns?

Even though you're not directly addressed by the writer, you want to trust that he's respectfully aware of your presence, tracking your responses. You don't want to feel like you're being blathered to by the stranger sitting next to you on an airplane. You don't want to be smooth-talked by a snake oil salesman, either (or, updating for our times, pelleted by spam about a penile enhancement product). I often have students complain that some novel that has done exceptionally well is garbage, that they could write a better book blindfolded and skunk drunk. But in fact, it is shockingly difficult—almost impossible—to successfully "write down." Back to that pact with the reader: such efforts often seem transparently insincere. The reader will know that you think the plot or prose is "good enough for them." Oprah believes in the books she trumpets; she never condescends to her audience. Your reader may not have the most refined palate in the universe, but that doesn't mean he'll feel flattered to eat Happy Meals at the kiddie table.

So, you. Yes, I'm talkin' to you. Are you working in earnest on a novel that has grown to five hundred pages but you're not sure exactly where it's going and you're not sure what to cut and also the story is told from two different points of view, one of which is first person and one is third person, and your professor has insisted that you change this, but you don't see why because lots of authors you admire have done alternating points of view, so why can't you? Is the work you're doing pretty much autobiographical (your childhood sexual abuse, exile from your homeland, battle with addiction) and you have a lot of queasiness about revealing some of the things you must reveal to tell the story, but haven't found a way to fictionalize the story, either, at least not convincingly?

I assume when I say, "I'm talkin' to you," that you get the *Taxi Driver* allusion. If you don't, you can google a YouTube clip. While I'll be referencing many works of fiction in this book as examples, I don't want to lard it up with too many long sample stories. If a particular piece of fiction seems particularly relevant to your own writing concerns, I trust you can find it yourself. Not every writer who ever put quill to scroll will be cited here. Some of my own favorite writers are missing, but I don't plan to be encyclopedic.

Furthermore, my conviction is that in good writing, *every sentence is good*, and point-of-view choices have been embedded in every phrase, every image. There is no "filler." I not only believe that you can tell a lot from a small sample of a piece of writing but that it's the best way to learn the craft. Working on that micro level forces you to really focus. You'll never mistake a sentence from Marcel Proust as a sentence from Stephen King. You should be able to take that sentence of Proust or King and extrapolate to the whole work, the way an archaeologist begins to reconstruct the skeleton of the brontosaurus from the one fossil, or the way the homicide detective takes the stray hair down to Forensics for the DNA.

Take this first line from an undergraduate short story that has stayed with me for decades:

The man ran through the misty forest.

Not only does the line make me want to teach a journalism class instead so we can discuss the five *W*'s necessary in a lede (Who? What? When? Where? Why?) but it also makes me think about how fiction is different from journalism. Mostly, it makes me think about point of view. What man? Who's watching? Is this a fairy tale? (For some reason I imagine the fellow in a fur loincloth.) And when, dear author, will you reveal what he's running *from*?

Come to think of it, that's kind of an intriguing first line. I might read to the second line. As you, I hope, will proceed to the second chapter, to discuss this very topic.

CHAPTER TWO

FIRST LINES AND FIRST PARAGRAPHS

"COME HERE OFTEN?"

In this chapter, we begin at the beginning, putting some first paragraphs under a microscope. We'll continue to look at short passages throughout, often from the beginnings of works. Such passages are the most efficient way to see the calculations by which point of view is established. My argument is that point of view in good fiction is embedded in every choice about tone, description, and diction, even about plot and pacing, and furthermore, it has to be established very quickly.

A truism of creative writing classes is that a reader must be hooked from the very first sentence of a story or novel. Editors, we're told, drowning in boatloads of submissions, are impatient, and will throw your work overboard based on a first paragraph, maybe even a first sentence. If getting someone to pay attention to your words is a kind of seduction, then the first sentence is the pickup line. The first line can be casual, familiar, addressing a reader as if he's having a drink at the bar after work, as in Raymond Carver's "Cathedral": "This blind man, an old friend of my wife's, he was on his way to spend the night." Or the first line can aim to disarm, disorient, like the opening of Kurt Vonnegut's *Slaughterhouse-Five*: "All this happened, more or less."

Both sentences efficiently codify a relationship between the author and the reader, set up as an almost lawyerly Memorandum of Agreement about what is to follow.

Bad fiction, like all bad writing—bad college application essays, bad term papers, even bad love letters—follows some half-understood formula and tries to give a stern, unyielding, arbitrary committee what it is supposed to want and expect, with maybe a kind of brave feint toward feisty confidence. An editor probably would not read past the first sentence of the following gem from an actual undergrad story submission:

> Amanda woke up face down in throw up with throw up all around her in the bed and on the floor.

Here the problems are deliciously obvious, including the writer's ignorance of a cardinal rule: Never start a tale with the character waking up unless that character is about to discover that he has been transformed into a gigantic insect. Creative writing teachers like to add that "all rules are made to be broken," and it's true that one can always rustle up some counterexamples; later I'll quote a fine wake-up novel beginning that doesn't involve a man-to-insect transformation. But maybe those broken rules by seasoned pros should come with the same warnings as car ads featuring wildly speeding vehicles on twisting roads in the snow: "Professional driver on closed track. Do not attempt."

I would argue that the central problem here is a point-of-view problem. The author has chosen to use an automatic, default third-person point of view. But who is telling us about Amanda? How does the author want us to feel about her? Why should we care? *How* should we care? Are we meant to chuckle knowingly at what a cheap drunk she is, or did something serious happen to her—was she raped? Was she drugged and robbed of a kidney?

Probably not. The name "Amanda" suggests that the story

is set in a realistic current America where a messy undergrad
hangover constitutes a critical hardship, and that we won't be
venturing into the territory of stolen black-market body parts.
But my point is—we know this from the first word. We know it
from the choice of the name Amanda rather than, say, Alberta
or Afsheen. I think we can further intuit that the writer herself
is a young woman, and that she has had a similar experience—
but, by presenting the character from outside, from a standard
third-person point of view, she is trying to *separate herself* from
Amanda, cloak herself in some authority. To be, ahem, *authorial*.
And we also suspect that she doesn't have the worldly wisdom,
distance, or insight to put Amanda's social travails in a context
that would deserve our time as readers.

First person would help. If Amanda told us her own story, the
reader might be intrigued by the possibility that Amanda could
offer an honest insider's view of the college party scene. Amanda
could become a character about whom we can smile with fond
recognition or censoriously shake our heads—or, hopefully, both.
There are a million places the writer could go in the next sentence to establish character and that character's issues. But the
point is, we should know what those issues are, and very quickly.

Look how the nineteen-year-old narrator of Martin Amis's
The Rachel Papers lets us know immediately who he is and how
he is talking to us:

> My name is Charles Highway, though you wouldn't think
> it to look at me.

Right away we are told that the novel will ask us to become
intimate with the narrator. And right away we know something
about him, something that engages us enough to continue. We
hear his directness. But we also feel confident that he's going
to complicate things—even presumably uncomplicated things,

like his name. "You wouldn't think it to look at me" seems like a simple enough statement until you realize that (1) you aren't looking at him, actually, since it's a book, not a movie; and (2) Who "looks like" a Charles Highway? The suspense here is just exactly enough to drive you to the next line:

> It's such a rangy, well-travelled, big-cocked name and, to look at, I am none of these.

The name is pointedly unrealistic, fictional, invented. And here, as in our vomit example, is Martin Amis, a young man writing about the experience of being a young man, but we trust the telling more. We hear the author's—and narrator's—wry intelligence. We trust the slanginess and immediacy of "big-cocked." We appreciate the self-deprecation: from these first lines, the narrator promises us that he will not merely, in the style of young men everywhere, celebrate himself and sing himself, which means that the character (and, by extension, the young narrator) is claiming to have enough distance for honest self-appraisal.

We further know that the drama of this novel will be *about* self-appraisal. Well, about Rachel too, obviously. But also about how the young man who is in love with Rachel sees himself, how the author sees him, how we see him. We are sternly warned in English classes that the narrator of a first-person account is not the author, that only the most unsophisticated reader conflates author and character—we'll speak much more about this issue in Chapter 5. But in fact, when a reader turns to a tale about a fact-checker at the *New Yorker* who writes about the travails of working as a fact-checker at the *New Yorker* (Jay McInerney, *Bright Lights, Big City*); or a drug-addled, alcoholic doctor in Africa who writes stories about drug-addled, alcoholic doctors in Africa (Thom Jones, *Cold Snap*), our feeling that author and character collude lends the work credibility, authenticity. But not always.

Not every novel with a first-person narrator is a roman à clef.
(See *Lolita*, below: Vladimir Nabokov was guilty of impaling
butterflies on sticks, but he was not a child molester.)

Forthright as Amis's opening seems—old-fashioned in the
spirit of "Call me Ishmael"—the first line of his novel is also
rather snazzily postmodern. We know that it will not just be
about the self-consciousness of coming-of-age but about the
conventions of the coming-of-age novel.

That may seem like a lot to get from a first sentence. But I contend that, indeed, good fiction *always* gives you that much right
from the beginning. Bedrock in each first line is a blueprint for
how we will approach the fiction, what we expect from it, and
how confident we are that the author can deliver. The pleasure of
the rest of the work is watching how the combinations that the
author has put into play, encoded as genes, will gestate.

How comfortable and cozy will we be asked to feel with the
characters—or, conversely, will we mistrust them? Does the
sense of being *told something we didn't know* about the human
condition make us feel enlightened, or condescended to? Does
our attitude toward the characters undergo a change as the plot
progresses? Is the change subtle, or radical? How much is the
author's own voice audible in the telling—does the author aim
for a spy's invisibility, or offer sportscaster blow-by-blows?

These are the central questions about point of view. In some
sense, understanding point of view allows the writer to control
the drama of the works, because good fiction always challenges
rather than merely ratifies our sympathies and assumptions.

Let's play with some famous first lines and see how efficiently
we can intuit point of view.

It is a truth universally acknowledged, that a single man
in possession of a good fortune, must be in want of a wife.

Who is talking to us in the first line of Jane Austen's *Pride and Prejudice*? Clearly, the author herself. She addresses us, introduces us to her cast. She bluntly tells us that this will be a novel about marriage and money. She expects us to know from the onset—partly from the playful passive construction, and partly from our own good sense—that the "universally acknowledged" truth may be not so reliable a truth after all. More than two centuries after the novel was published, the sly humor holds up; we hear it clearly, without footnotes. And since this is a novel about people's prejudices, about judging character from outside rather than inside, often with inadequate knowledge, she has efficiently signaled the novel's theme.

Within a couple of lines, she will move her focus from the "general and universal" to the drama of one particular family, the Bennets, and then further narrow her focus to marriage-aged Elizabeth; then she will get out of Lizzie's way, letting the young woman make her own mistakes (and letting her readers make mistakes, too—for we are surely part of the drama, missing clues, judging Lizzie's suitors wrongly, as Lizzie does). Austen is a guide, but a quiet, unobtrusive one. She exhorts us to observe, closely. She surprises us with our own misjudgments.

It's a third-person narrator, but surely one who speaks in a different voice than Charles Dickens':

It was the best of times, it was the worst of times, it was the age of wisdom, it was the age of foolishness, it was the epoch of belief, it was the epoch of incredulity, it was the season of Light, it was the season of Darkness, it was the spring of hope, it was the winter of despair, we had everything before us, we had nothing before us, we were all going direct to Heaven, we were all going direct the other way—in short, the period was so far like the present period, that some of its

noisiest authorities insisted on it being received, for good or
for evil, in the superlative degree of comparison only.

As quickly as Austen, Dickens sets up his themes in *A Tale
of Two Cities*—Paris and London, major metropolises experiencing major historical upheavals, opposites, or, as the SparkNotes
will tell you lest you failed to notice it from the prose or the
title, "The opposing pairs in this passage also initiate one of the
novel's most prominent motifs and structural figures—that of
doubles ..." Dickens also assures you that although the novel is
set in the past, you will surely discover that the past is relevant,
"like the present period."

Like Austen, Dickens flatters your intelligence. You are going
to see the patterns. But as a guide, Dickens is not insinuating himself subtly. He's on a platform. He proclaims. He's got
a megaphone. The tone is almost cheerfully circus barker-ish.
Yo, gather around, he says, step right up, hear my tale. It'll be a
substantial tale—hey, I'm being paid by the word—and I promise
I'll stay with you throughout, helping you to understand the Big
Picture.

In Dickens's case, the promise is grand. But it's also friendly.
He flatters his audience for standing apart from "the noisiest
authorities." It is, furthermore, a *group* of readers he addresses.
It's not just you and Charles under the glow of the gas lamp.

How very different from the narrator's voice in the famous
first line of Tolstoy's *Anna Karenina*:

All happy families resemble one another, but each unhappy
family is unhappy in its own way.

Like Dickens, Tolstoy promises a sweeping view. His tone is
serious, dry, declarative. He will speak for all of humanity. And,

if we're holding the novel in our hands (close to a thousand pages of small print), we already know that he has a lot to say. He is as authoritative, as philosophical, as another omniscient guy with a long white beard. But is Tolstoy's pronouncement really true about families? Sociologists, weigh in here: Aren't there patterns in dysfunction—alcoholism, adultery, spousal abuse—and doesn't joy, too, at least occasionally, take different forms? Is the chaotic joy of the family of eight really identical to the comfort of the long-married, childless octogenarians cataloguing their ailments?

You might as well just read on. Tolstoy will not be taking questions at this time.

Later in *Anna Karenina*, Tolstoy will draw you into the hearts and souls of a disparate cast of characters. But we will always be aware of him as the master of his domain. We'll talk in the next two chapters about third-person omniscience versus third-person–limited (also called third-person–close or –aligned) points of view. We'll talk about the evolution of the omniscient narrator and the move toward first person in fiction as a kind of anti-Tolstoy, achieving what in creative writing workshops is often called "immediacy," as in the beginning of J. D. Salinger's *The Catcher in the Rye*:

> If you really want to hear about it, the first thing you'll probably want to know is where I was born, and what my lousy childhood was like, and how my parents were occupied and all before they had me, and all that David Copperfield kind of crap, but I don't feel like going into it, if you want to know the truth.

On the most basic level, a narrative voice must establish who's talking and who's listening. Here Holden Caulfield lets us know right off the bat that he plans to cut out the middleman (the author) and tell the story directly to us. Voices like this are often called "raw" even though, as we investigate in the chapter on first person, the rawness is by default a trick: No matter how autobiographical a tale, an author is ventriloquizing. It's just a matter of whether we see the author's lips move as he makes the puppet's mouth move. Indeed, sometimes an author like Amis wants us to see him pulling puppet strings. But we know, from the first line of *The Catcher in the Rye*, that Holden promises his story will diverge from the rags-to-riches, Copperfieldesque narrative that novels have heretofore fed us—more contemporary, more real. It's a bold fictional declaration, delivered in a seductively slangy way.

Thomas Pynchon doesn't directly reference Dickens, but he similarly riffs on the history of the novel and our expectations for it in the opening sentence of *The Crying of Lot 49*:

> One summer afternoon Mrs Oedipa Maas came home from a Tupperware party whose hostess had put perhaps too much kirsch in the fondue to find that she, Oedipa, had been named executor, or she supposed executrix, of the estate of one Pierce Inverarity, a California real estate mogul who had once lost two million dollars in his spare time but still had assets numerous and tangled enough to make the job of sorting it all out more than honorary.

The sentence length, the circuitous and archly formal diction, suggest that you are about to enter an old-fashioned tale. At the same time, that suggestion is undercut and made ironic: by the absurd, unrealistic names Oedipa and Inverarity; by the references to Tupperware and fondue that set the action very much in the California swinging 1960s; indeed by the comically fairytale-ish vagueness of "one summer afternoon."

At first glance, this looks like a standard issue omniscient narrator. But the phrase "or she supposed executrix" shifts the intelligence to Oedipa herself—our searcher who will be trying to unskein a *very* tangled and/or perhaps merely paranoid conspiracy, often while under the influence of not only Kirsch but weed and LSD. The way that Pynchon segues between a magisterial omniscience and the heroine's own decidedly limited point of view, which is called *free indirect discourse*, will be discussed in detail in our next chapters. But you are confident that there will be some things for you to untangle as well, and that Pynchon assumes this is not your first rodeo, novel-reading-wise. The fun will be the vigorous and unpredictable ways that he tries to throw you from the horse.

A narrator you like and trust is the bedrock of a certain kind of storytelling—the kind that promises you "characters you like and care about." It is the bedrock point of view for all genre fiction. In a Western, the cowboy is going to be strong and smart. In romance fiction, the heroine is gorgeous and kind; she is mostly just in need of marriage and a good lay, in that order, preferably by someone with both stunning musculature and shitloads of money. It is amazing how seldom, in real life, that nerds who make billions on tech start-ups have ripped abs, but wish fulfillment and realism don't often skip off into the sunset together.

Note, though, that not *all* narrators you like, trust, and care about are limited to formula fiction. Alice Munro creates characters and worlds that are both realistic and deeply moving. When she puts a young girl on a train to go teach polio victims in the Canadian outback in "Amudsen"—then chronicles the girl's sad affair with the sanatorium's much-older doctor—we're riveted; by its end, the story haunts our memory as surely as it haunts the girl. When, in "To Reach Japan," another woman leaves her husband for a man she met only briefly, once, at a party, boarding another train with her young daughter and completely in the dark about whether the man will show up to greet her, or even (pre-e-mail) about whether he received her letter, we feel, almost as deeply as the character, "a shock, then a tumbling in Greta's insides, an immense settling." Certainly the fiction is feminist, in that it considers the lives of strong, smart, often independent women, but it's never didactic. Any points Munro wants to make about the world get made much more subtly.

Here, for another quick example of a sharp, likeable protagonist in a very different work, is the first line of William Gibson's *Pattern Recognition*:

> Five hours' New York jet lag and Cayce Pollard wakes in Camden Town to the dire and ever-circling wolves of disrupted circadian rhythm.

Like Pynchon (one of his literary heroes), Gibson has quickly established that he has access to, and is a reliable reporter of, his protagonist's innermost thoughts. Like Dickens, he takes for granted that his audience is intelligent—that we know where Camden Town is, that we know what circadian rhythm is, but mostly that we will understand, and appreciate, his linguistic suppleness and precision. The first chapter is called "The Website of Dreadful Night." That title, like Pynchon's opening, is a kind of gesture toward the big, old-fashioned novel, eliding old-fashioned diction (the Poe-etic "dreadful night") with something current ("website"), and Gibson therefore clues you in that his book will be *about* that new world, about its relationship to the old world, and that the relationship is a kind of jet lag, a metaphor he develops more fully in his next sentence:

> It is that flat and spectral non-hour, awash in limbic tides, brainstem stirring fitfully, flashing inappropriate reptilian

demands for sex, food, sedation, all of the above, and none really an option now.

Cayce may be jet-lagged and out of it. You are not. You and Gibson are sharp as tacks. You know what "limbic" means!

If a narrator you like and trust is the foundation of a certain kind of storytelling, we might posit Vladimir Nabokov's *Lolita* as the exemplar of unreliability:

Lolita, light of my life, fire of my loins.

Who's talking? Who knows? Who is he talking to? Lolita, evidently, as in a poetic apostrophe. He's not speaking to us. Who the hell is Lolita? Forge on, dear reader:

My sin, my soul. Lo-lee-ta: the tip of the tongue taking a trip of three steps down the palate to tap, at three, on the teeth. Lo. Lee. Ta.

What do you know at this point? Certainly that the novel will be about Lolita. Certainly that the narrator is a tad obsessed with the lady, and given to assonance. But, again, who is she? Read on:

She was Lo, plain Lo, in the morning, standing four foot ten in one sock. She was Lola in slacks. She was Dolly at school. She was Dolores on the dotted line. But in my arms she was always Lolita.

Say what, Vlad? Okay: her identity was fluid. Even her name is not fixed. Could you simply state for the record now, please, who you are, and what your relationship is to the subject?

Did she have a precursor? She did, indeed she did. In point of fact, there might have been no Lolita at all had I not loved, one summer, a certain initial girl-child. In a princedom by the sea. Oh when? About as many years before Lolita was born as my age was that summer. You can always count on a murderer for a fancy prose style.

Here the narrator just outright messes with our desire for clarity. He quotes Edgar Allan Poe, assuming you know the poem to which he refers, about Poe's love for his prepubescent cousin. His diction gets ludicrously fancy-schmantzy. And then he mocks his own mockery—revealing to us not who he is but that he is decidedly not to be trusted, before he delivers the last short paragraph of the novel's entire first short section, in a tone that confuses us yet again by *not* seeming explicitly comical:

Ladies and gentlemen of the jury, exhibit number one is what the seraphs, the misinformed, simple, noble-winged seraphs, envied. Look at this tangle of thorns.

So we end the introduction *still* not knowing who is telling the story, and why, and despite him addressing us as a jury (if he is indeed addressing us, and not someone else, as he addressed Lolita herself before), how he means for us to judge him.

The point of view here is a funhouse mirror. Some readers will be delighted to be included in the feint and Nabokov's cleverness. Many readers prefer a more straightforward identification with, and solicitude toward, character. The novel for these readers is not dead, needs no reinvention, can still engage us, and often those readers choose to go straight to a third-person-aligned point of view, like to be drawn in a straightforward way, no muss no fuss, right into the character's life and issues, as they are here in the first line of J. M. Coetzee's *Disgrace*:

> For a man of his age, fifty-two, divorced, he has, to his mind,
> solved the problem of sex rather well.

Critical there is the phrase "to his mind." When we are told, in the first paragraph, that the bedroom of the paid escort he visits at precisely 2 p.m. every Thursday afternoon is "pleasant-smelling and softly lit," we know that we are getting the protagonist's own impressions, not the stamp of approval of some Tolstoyean interior decorator-cum-narrator. We are aligned with Professor David Lurie—we will cleave closely to his thoughts— and yet the author stands by, as witness and interpreter. How different it would be if this novel were in first person:

> For a man of my age, fifty-two, divorced, I have, to my mind,
> solved the problem of sex rather well.

It doesn't work. You *hear* that it doesn't; it's so obvious it almost seems pointless to analyze why, but of course analyzing why is precisely why we're here. In first person, the narrator sounds quite pleased with himself, and also overly formal. We like him less in first person. Part of the problem is that he is then speaking directly to you, the reader, which makes him seem alarmingly exhibitionist, for drawing you into his sex life on the first page, whereas here a narrator is more discreetly parting a curtain.

About the escort Soraya's services, we are told, "He finds her entirely satisfactory." The important distinction here is that while it is clearly the character's feeling being expressed, it is the narrator's diction. If the character chose this formulation himself, he'd sound like he was Dr. Spock, or had Asperger's. So the narrator is still talking to you, translating, over the character's head as it were—but he is whispering to you, not yelling. He is voicing something that the character would never say, explicitly—or indeed, most critically, might not even know about himself.

Yet. We are confident, from the first page of *Disgrace*, that the professor's long-held beliefs are going to be seriously threatened. "That is his temperament. His temperament is not going to change, he is too old for that. His temperament is fixed, set." This is David's opinion, not ours. The author does not have to peer out from around David's back to intone a discreet eyebrow-wagging *"or so he believed."* And yet there's a crucial layering of judgment here provided by the third person.

A third-person–limited point of view of this kind can be elegantly reliable. We don't dispute that Coetzee knows David well. We also trust that the narrator will fill us in on salient information and scenes.

It's important to note that once you've decided on a point of view limited to a single character's perceptions, you can't tell us the thoughts in other characters' heads. Once you're in a first-person narration, you can't comment on the protagonist directly. Once you're in an omniscient viewpoint, you can't withhold essential information just because it's more convenient for you to unveil it later. Obvious exception: in a whodunit, the reader assumes you'll dole out the revelations at an appropriate pace, but that doesn't include a "gotcha" turn of events that was not prepared for in any way. We would be more than a little annoyed to discover, in the last chapter of *Disgrace*, that Soraya was a drag queen.

And now you might bring up *The Crying Game*, *The Sixth Sense*, *Psycho*, or any number of other movies where the shocking truth is revealed only at the end. Norman Bates's mother is not gazing out the window from her rocker, she's actually dead! Norman props up the mummified corpse and talks to it and he wears her clothes!

To this, I will point out that if you explicitly warn viewers that they're in for a shock, you're not exactly coming at them from behind with a knife. Expecting to be surprised is a very different kind of surprise. And movies aren't the same as books, for reasons we will discuss later. A movie that you attend for the explicit purpose of scaring you has already set up a different set of expectations for your satisfaction than a realistic novel like *Disgrace*.

Which is not to say that fiction can't offer surprises. It can and must. It's just that if, in *Pride and Prejudice*, Elizabeth Bennet decided to reject all suitors because she was a lesbian, or an uncle she never knew willed her ten thousand pounds so she could forgo marriage altogether and join Charles Darwin on the deck of the HMS *Beagle* (which she could in fact do, jumping continents and time, in a logic- and chronology-defying novel by David Mitchell), or she got eaten by a lion that somehow got loose in the streets of London, we would not be surprised. We would be annoyed.

In her essay "Engineering Impossible Architectures," Karen Russell, whose fiction involves vampires and girls sneaking into swamps to make love with ghosts, discusses the balance between realistic and more surreal or fantastical elements, which she calls the "Kansas: Oz shuffle." She argues that even in invented universes, certain things defy the rules of gravity in troublesome ways, and urges writers who work with such material to "follow your yellow brick road to a consistent, well-governed dream world":

> One lesson that I have to relearn continually is that writing fiction set in an alternate reality doesn't mean you get a free pass to do any crazy thing you want. If you're going to try a Kansas: Oz shuffle, a radical "rearrangement of nature," you have some additional responsibilities to the reader. Namely, that you don't get tripped out on your godlike power (or more likely just exhausted and forgetful) and violate the parameters of the world that you've created.

I hope the point is clear that the movement of a piece of fiction—its very plot—depends on how the reader is positioned in terms of the character and writer when the story begins, and where you want him to go. You know that he expects to go *somewhere*. He wants a map, too, or at least wants to trust that the author has consulted GPS, and isn't just randomly wandering around. (Unless, of course, the very point of the work is to be off the beaten track, and the author has made that clear. If you pick up Nicholson Baker's *The Mezzanine*, a novel the entire plot of which involves a guy who replaces a broken shoelace on his lunch break, you're not expecting a lot of action.) Furthermore, the choice of point of view locks us into our coordinates and makes certain turns later ill-advised, or even impossible.

If you ask lay readers what they know about point of view, it'll usually come down to this: Third person tells a character's story from outside. First-person characters tell the story themselves. Omniscient narrators know everything. And second person is—well, "you." Why? Dunno—to be different?

But as we'll see as we dive into the brush with our night-vision goggles and specimen kits, there's considerably more to establishing point of view than those rudimentary definitions, and quite a bit of skill required to keep the point of view clear, consistent, and yet paradoxically—yes—surprising.

CHAPTER THREE

ON OMNISCIENCE

A CENTURY PLUS OF MISERABLE MARRIAGES AND SEVERAL WARS

O mniscience should be the very easiest point of view to discuss. It's the one we all know instinctively, the classic "once upon a time," the default mode for narration. In omniscience, the author gets to be the most authorial. The author is the pilot, the architect, the chef in a tall white hat.

Like God, the omniscient narrator is separate from the characters and superior to them, sympathizing with them or judging them but definitely not trusting them to tell their stories "in their own words." He doesn't have to look at the characters from as great a distance as heaven, or as we see suburban backyards from a plane, the kids on their jungle gym bug-sized, the swimming pools mere fingernails. He can zoom in. Here's the mother, bored, drumming her fingernails on the book on her lap. The author can even know that, as her potbellied husband curses over his attempt to muster the upper body strength to start the lawnmower, she's daydreaming about her clandestine lover, the next-door neighbor. So the author has the option to enter what is called a third-person–limited point of view, where she cleaves to the thoughts and perceptions of a single character or a series of characters. (I also use the alternate terms "close" or "aligned" third person, which to me more accurately describe the purposeful choice to track a character's perceptions.)

We'll discuss third-person limited in more detail in our next chapter. There are still plenty of opportunities for a writer to speak directly to the reader—over the characters' heads, as it were—even if the narrator is not forcefully insinuating himself into the scene to interpret the action. For now, though, please be advised that the writer who is intimately familiar with the thoughts of even a single character is still humming a genetically modified omniscient tune. Only God can read minds (except in certain memorable episodes of *The Twilight Zone*).

As we'll see in this chapter, third person isn't a one-size-fits-all approach to point of view. There are multiple ways to shade a third-person narrative, and the biggest variable is how prominent the author makes her own voice in the telling. Scholars have argued that standard, old-fashioned omniscience—in which the author knows everything about everything—has fallen out of favor partly because contemporary readers are more trusting of subjective accounts. So instead of lecturing us, fiction writers employing omniscience will often present us with a series of third-person–limited sections or chapters, without nearly so much authorial commentary as novelists indulged in previously. We trust the limitations, the myopia of individual characters mired in separate realities. The author's skill resides in how many viewpoints he can penetrate, and how cleverly he interweaves them.

All of this is a matter of *voice*, of how the writer talks to the reader, as well as the assumptions the writer makes about the reader's beliefs and frame of reference. A writer's voice can be anywhere from lyrical to matter-of-fact, soulful or sarcastic, expansive or terse. Within the third-person omniscient point of view, we find a large range of narrative approaches to examining character and motive, and a large spectrum of options in how often or forcefully the writer's voice colors the telling.

Let's revisit the aforementioned famous first line of *Anna Karenina*:

> All happy families resemble one another, but each unhappy family is unhappy in its own way.

Here Leo Tolstoy is the setter of themes and the teller of truths. He knows more than Anna K herself, more than her ex-husband and lover, and more than Kitty and Levin, the other primary characters whose marriage will be examined in detail. Tolstoy does not shy away from proclamations. Even when he claims to be discussing a character's emotions, we see his hand in interpreting them:

> Levin had been married for three months. He was happy, but in quite a different way from what he had expected. At every step he met disillusionments in his old fancies and new and unexpected enchantments. He was happy, but having embarked on family life he saw with every step that it was not at all what he had anticipated. At every step he took he felt as a man would feel who, after admiring the smooth happy motion of a little boat upon the water, had himself got into the boat. He found that besides sitting quietly without rocking he had to keep a lookout, not for a moment forget where he was going, or that there was water under his feet, and that he had to row, although it hurt his unaccustomed hands; in short, that it only looked easy, but to do it, though very delightful, was very difficult.

We can't imagine Levin himself formulating this thought in this way, and even if we accept that Tolstoy is *translating* his character's emotions, the diction here—words like "enchantments," "disillusionments," and "unaccustomed," the artful repetitions of "he was happy" and "with every step," the length of the paragraph's final sentence—assures us that Tolstoy is the conductor of this symphony.

That's true not only on the level of how Tolstoy discusses a character's reactions but in how he stages the motion of the plot. Many scenes in *Anna Karenina* have parallel scenes for contrast or commentary. So, for instance, Levin, who has just proposed marriage to Kitty, walks the streets of Saint Petersburg at dawn while waiting to hear her answer, and is deliriously happy. He sees a bakery opening, children playing, a pigeon flying: "All these things were so unusually beautiful that Levin laughed and cried with joy." Much later in the novel, when a completely miserable Anna walks down the identical streets, needless to say, things don't look so rosy to her. The children she passes are scuzzy and annoying. The men driving carriages don't tip their hats as they pass in shared delight or chivalry—Levin was enchanted by even the city's carriage drivers—but are, to Anna, bald, boring, and venal. She thinks, "there is nothing amusing or merry. Everything is nasty."

With its scope and *gravitas*, Tolstoy's novel exemplifies what we mean when we reference conventional omniscience. To a contemporary reader, the way Tolstoy plants the thoughts in his characters' heads may seem a little starchy, or even unconvincing. But that's partly a matter of shifting styles. Fiction writers now have, for the most part, abandoned the phrase "she thought to herself" in favor of *free indirect discourse*, in which the author pivots quickly into a character's thoughts without planting a flag to mark the shift. Once more, this represents a respect for the reader's agility in making a quick transition, without heavy-handed guidance.

A quick example of free indirect discourse to show how a writer with the benefit of omniscience can take deep dives into a character's private thoughts. E. L. Doctorow's *Ragtime* weaves together a large crew of characters at the turn of the century. Historical figures like Sigmund Freud, J. P. Morgan, and Archduke Ferdinand intermingle with invented characters. The father of a fictional family joins Peary on his daring expedition to the North Pole, and here escape artist Houdini muses about that journey, the breathless news of the day:

> Houdini walked through the streets. His ears burned with humiliation. He wore a hat with the brim turned down. He wore a tight-fitting double-breasted linen jacket and he kept his hands in the pockets of the jacket. He wore tan trousers and brown and white shoes with pointed toes. It was a chilly autumn afternoon and most people wore coats. He moved swiftly through the crowded New York streets. He was incredibly lithe. There was a kind of act that used the real world for its stage. He couldn't touch it. For all his achievements he was a trickster, an illusionist, a mere magician. What was the sense of his life if people walked out of the theater and forgot him? The headlines on the newsstand said Peary had reached the Pole. The real-world act was what got into the history books.

Doctorow moves seamlessly into Houdini's thoughts. You know it has happened after the word "lithe," without the telltale marker of "he thought." Although the words are simple, the picture of Houdini is imagistically rich. We see him from the outside as he would be filmed: walking fast, lost in thought, parting the crowds. We can even stage the movement from his burning ears (How would a pedestrian or reader know why his ears were red, were it not for that omniscient narrator?) to the close-up of his stylish, period-accurate shoes. His hat covers his face and his hands are in his pockets, so he's hidden, closed off, yet he's also exposed—inadequately dressed for the cold. So all of that presumably flat description of his dress and appearance is not actually so flat after all. It helps to set up Houdini's fear of thwarted ambition, of being inadequately celebrated, lost in the crowd.

Of course, Doctorow's declarative style owes more to Hemingway than Tolstoy. Hemingway stated, "If I started to write elaborately...I found that I could cut that scrollwork or ornament away and throw it out and start with the first true simple declarative sentence I had written." But we have skipped over more than a century in the form's evolution to get to that style. So let's return to the nineteenth century, and another unhappy marriage.

In *Middlemarch*, the charming Dorothea Brooke eschews a virile, handsome, age-appropriate suitor in favor of a stiff, mean, sexless, much-older scholar. She figures out her mistake almost right away, but in 1871 England, as in 1877 Russia, no-fault divorce was not an option. Here's how George Eliot posits herself as commentator on Dorothea, who weeps alone in a Rome hotel room on her honeymoon while her husband, the dry and pompous Casaubon, abandons her for his so-called research, as she begins to realize that his scholarship is not so very brilliant after all:

> Not that this inward amazement of Dorothea's was anything very exceptional: many souls in their young nudity are tumbled out among incongruities and left to "find their feet" among them, while their elders go about their business. Nor can I suppose that when Mrs Casaubon is discovered in a

fit of weeping six weeks after her wedding, the situation will be regarded as tragic. Some discouragement, some faintness of heart at the new real future which replaces the imaginary, is not unusual, and we do not expect people to be deeply moved by what is not unusual. That element of tragedy which lies in the very fact of frequency, has not yet wrought itself into the coarse emotion of mankind; and perhaps our frames could hardly bear much of it. If we had a keen vision and feeling of all ordinary human life, it would be like hearing the grass grow and the squirrel's heart beat, and we should die of that roar which lies on the other side of silence. As it is, the quickest of us walk around well swaddled with stupidity.

Anna Karenina is 741 pages, *Middlemarch* 578. Plenty of room for asides in novels of that length. It goes without saying that there is less space for lectures on the human condition in a short story. What Eliot delivers above is something an omniscient narrator can do handily: speak to the reader directly, as if freeze-framing the film to hover over the character with a laser pointer. It is the equivalent of "Pay attention, reader! Show some sympathy for my young, unhappy bride!"

Watch Gustave Flaubert make a similar move about another unfortunate marriage in *Madame Bovary*. Emma Bovary's husband is a simple country doctor who does not in any way excite her lust or imagination. So she shops for much more couture and home décor than she can afford and takes a series of lovers. Here Gustave gives us intel on her first lover, Rodolphe, as Emma tries to sweet-talk him after sex:

> Because lascivious or venal lips had murmured the same words to him, he now had little belief in their sincerity when he heard them from Emma; they should be taken with a

grain of salt, he thought, because the most exaggerated speeches usually hid the weakest feelings—as though the fullness of the soul did not sometimes overflow into the emptiest phrases, since no one can ever express the exact measure of his needs, his conceptions, or his sorrows, and human speech is like a cracked pot on which we beat out rhythms for bears to dance to when we are striving to make music that will wring tears from the stars.

Another authorial set piece! Mind you, Flaubert indulges in these kinds of poetic flourishes much less frequently than Eliot. He proclaimed, "Nowhere in my book must the author express his emotions and opinions." Looks like he broke his own rule a bit. However, he also legendarily said, "Madame Bovary, c'est moi," as a way of noting his identification with his flighty heroine. When the novel was published in 1856, there was some outrage about the adulterous, superficial, spendthrift Emma Bovary as an "unsympathetic" character. We're now more willing to follow an unsavory protagonist. We understand—with some blind spots—that the protagonist is not the author, and there's something to be gained from examining the mind and motives of the less than saintly.

In *How Fiction Works*, James Wood argues that "Flaubert established, for good or ill, what most readers think of as modern realist narration." Wood's brilliant book explores how Flaubert lets the selected details do the work in a cinematic way, so that the reader can interpret the meaning of a scene without authorial commentary. So Flaubert sends Emma to rendezvous with her lovers in some locations that—even if Emma is too enamored to notice—make her trysts seem highly ridiculous. One background is an agricultural fair, with prize pigs and officials delivering boring small-town speeches; another is inside a church, where the votive candles begin to seem more like a sleazy porn shoot than a place of worship.

Irony in fiction almost always represents a direct communication between author and reader. The townspeople in Shirley Jackson's "The Lottery" don't marvel, "How could we even contemplate stoning a fellow citizen to death on such a 'clear and sunny summer day'?" But by the first line of the story, a savvy reader is alerted that less-than-sunny events will be coming. Similarly, Jane Austen's "It is a truth universally acknowledged, that a single man in possession of a good fortune, must be in want of a wife" trusts the reader to immediately question that assumption. *Foreshadowing* is another method by which an author can tip her hat at the reader and suggest "Pay attention!" without quite resorting to the use of a laser pointer. Our pleasure in deconstructing such hints once the plot unfolds represents a bond with the author. The clues in mysteries or thrillers want to be complex enough to keep the reader engaged—if we guess the identity of the murderer right away, there's little reason to keep reading, thus some red herrings are expected—but without so many feints of misdirection that we feel that the writer is just messing with us, or simply doesn't know where the plot is going. We might enjoy being in a maze, but we trust the designer of the maze to have cut out an exit.

It's worth noting that a writer can't manifest all qualities to all people at all times. With great solemnity like Tolstoy's, you rarely get lightheartedness or giddy humor (although he does enjoy mocking the foibles of some of his minor characters). A chatty author—one who is exuberant with lots of details and commentary—can't also be a strong, silent Hemingway type. (Check out "The Hemingway Project" for readers voicing contrarian complaints about Papa along the lines of "I don't like his descriptions. They're not flowery enough for me," or, more simply, "Screw short declarative sentences.") The very qualities that we identify as the reasons we like an author's voice may be the identical reasons why other readers dislike the voice. One reader finds the work *brilliant*, another *show-offy*. One reader's *philosophically deep* is another's *ponderous*. One reader's *funny* is another reader's *trivial*. Even a writer's lush imagery, her flights of poetry, may cause some readers to warn, "I don't care how dawn breaks on yonder sky. Get on with it!" In evaluating fiction, we don't want to ask whether it's what we want for dinner, but whether the food is properly prepared and presented— not whether we approve of the voice, but whether the writer has achieved the desired effect well and consistently.

Ralph Waldo Emerson said that "a foolish consistency is the hobgoblin of little minds." And Walt Whitman taunted, "Do I contradict myself? Very well then, I contradict myself. I am large, I contain multitudes." But I would contend that when it comes to point of view in fiction, consistency is critical. Many of the missteps in early drafts of writing come as a result of an unjustifiable instability in point of view. This is not to say that a work of fiction can't have modulations or crescendos. But such departures have to make sense and serve a purpose, not just be for the convenience of the writer at that particular moment in the storytelling.

Once Hemingway decides that he is going to call his protagonists "the American" and "the girl" rather than give them names in his story "Hills Like White Elephants," and thrusts his readers right into their disagreement over drinks about the abortion she's about to get quite against her objections; once he does not even allow either character to even use the word "abortion" but asks his readers to interpret their relationship and current dispute over the "operation" on the basis of their dialogue alone; then he absolutely cannot write the sentence "The girl dolefully remembers the day that they met." He simply cannot give us access to either of their thoughts or emotions, or even the facts that would allow us to judge the situation more fully (How much older is the man? Is he supporting her? Does she have parents?) except in how they report it through conversation.

In "The Country Husband," John Cheever takes a far more assertive role in examining the strained suburban marriage of unhappy Francis Weed. (What a source of material the unhappy couple has been for fiction writers!) Cheever speaks for Francis, whose powers of expression, if not feeling, are limited. It is the author, not Francis, who declares, "The Weeds' Dutch Colonial house was larger than it appeared to be from the driveway. The living room was spacious and divided like Gaul into three parts." It is the narrator, not Francis, who notes that when Francis's "pretty, intelligent" wife announces that dinner is ready and lights candles, she "strikes a match in this vale of tears." Cheever, not the character, makes analogies between ordinary suburban life and the cataclysmic world war that has just ended, as well as past wars from mythical days long gone, "where kings in golden suits ride elephants over the mountains." There's a doleful tone to the way Cheever compares the Weed family's problems to traumas of the past, present even in the title of the story: Weed lives in the suburbs, not the country, and "country" here also stands in for "America," its putatively comfortable denizens' state of trapped dissatisfaction. Cheever makes Francis Weed representative of all American Men, but in a cheeky, gently parodic way.

Though both are written in an omniscient point of view, the expansive Cheever voice and the tight-lipped Hemingway voice could not be more different. For a fun exercise in point of view, try leaving the plots and characters the same but reversing the styles and voices of the stories, even for a single paragraph.

Establishing expectations
with omniscient viewpoints

Indeed, as we discussed in the last chapter, the opening of a story or novel should set expectations for point of view in a decisive way. Often a writer will bring a protagonist to our attention with an omniscient overview, as Dorothy Parker does in "Big Blonde":

> Hazel Morse was a large, fair woman of the type that incites some men when they use the word "blonde" to click their tongues and wag their heads roguishly. She prided herself upon her small feet and suffered for her vanity, boxing them in snub-toed, high-heeled slippers of the shortest bearable size. The curious things about her were her hands, strange terminations to the flabby white arms splattered with pale tan spots—long, quivering hands with deep and convex nails. She should not have disfigured them with little jewels.
>
> She was not a woman given to recollections. At her middle thirties, her old days were a blurred and flickering sequence, an imperfect film, dealing with actions of strangers.

The omniscience here allows Parker to share not just Hazel's thoughts and dissatisfactions but her rather strong opinions on Hazel's sartorial choices and, later in the story, on the thoughts of her husband and procession of lovers, as well as those of the maid who discovers Hazel unconscious after a failed suicide attempt. The title, and the phrase "of the type" in the first sentence, alert you that Hazel will be representative of a certain kind of hard-partying, hard-drinking woman of the era. Like Cheever discussing Francis Weed, Parker doesn't credit Hazel with sufficient self-knowledge to talk about her own condition, so a purely aligned third person would not be adequate to the task.

It's quite common for a short story writer to introduce us to the protagonist with a quick, omniscient bio-sketch. At the beginning of "The Lady with the Lapdog," Anton Chekhov efficiently takes the measure of our cynical serial adulterer:

> He was not yet forty but had a twelve-year-old daughter and two sons in high school. He had been talked into marrying in his third year at college, and his wife now looked nearly twice as old as he did. She was a tall woman with dark eyebrows, erect, dignified, imposing, and, as she said of herself, a "thinker." She was a great reader, omitted the "hard sign" at the end of words in her letters, and called her husband "Dimitry" instead of Dmitry; and though he secretly considered her shallow, narrow-minded, and dowdy, he stood in awe of her, and disliked being at home. He had first begun deceiving her long ago and he was now constantly unfaithful to her, and this was no doubt why he spoke slightingly of women, to whom he referred as *the lower race.*

Readers get a clear picture of Dmitry Gurov's wife here even if they don't know Russian, and thus have no idea what omitting the hard sign at the end of letters means, or how pronouncing his name "Dimitry" rather than "Dmitry" makes her pretentious. But we can tell that she is pretentious, and how much her feints irritate her husband, which is how a good specific detail should work: it should scan for those "in the know" about the contemporary society being portrayed, but also be clear and meaningful from context. This is how a story about a life-changing seaside affair in 1899 can transcend its period and still speak to us. Notice

the subtle sarcasm of "a great reader," which lacks the quota-
tion marks Chekhov puts around "thinker" to clarify that this is
what *she said of herself,* but he has so quickly schooled us in his
method of observation that we know this is the wife's own judgment. Notice, too, the "secretly" and "no doubt," qualifiers that
give the narrator's opinion about his character's extra reliability.

Chekhov invites us to judge Gurov harshly. But the surprise
of the story is that this coldhearted man, who has lost interest
in past lovers so irrevocably that "their beauty aroused in him
nothing but repulsion, and the lace trimming on their under-
clothes reminded him of fish-scales," falls deeply in love. Chekhov doesn't deign to explain exactly what causes this ordinary
woman to become so essential to Gurov's happiness. The author
is neither therapist nor social scientist. Their powerful love
defies explanation.

Although she gets pride of place in the story's title, the object
of affection decidedly does *not* get equal airtime. In fact, we
only know about Anna's feelings through her dialogue, weeping,
trembling, or blushing. The story belongs entirely to the dude, as
much as Parker's story belongs to the boozy broad. Once Chekhov gives the omniscient overview, he cleaves to Gurov's feelings and observations.

But let's travel through time to a different seaside and a writer
who does bestow equal attention on both man and wife. The first
paragraph of Ian McEwan's *On Chesil Beach*:

> They were young, educated, and both virgins on this, their
> wedding night, and they lived in a time when a conversation
> about sexual difficulties was plainly impossible. But it
> is never easy. They had just sat down to supper in a tiny
> sitting room on the first floor of a Georgian inn. In the next
> room, visible through the open door, was a four-poster
> bed, rather narrow, whose bedcover was pure white and

stretched startlingly smooth, as though by no human hand. Edward did not mention that he had never stayed in a hotel before, whereas Florence, after many trips as a child with her father, was an old hand. Superficially, they were in fine spirits. Their wedding, at St. Mary's, Oxford, had gone well; the service was decorous, the reception jolly, the sendoff from school and college friends raucous and uplifting. Her parents had not condescended to his, as they had feared, and his mother had not significantly misbehaved, or completely forgotten the purpose of the occasion. The couple had driven away in a small car belonging to Florence's mother and arrived in the early evening at their hotel on the Dorset coast in weather that was not perfect for mid-July or the circumstances but was entirely adequate: it was not raining, but nor was it quite warm enough, according to Florence, to eat outside on the terrace as they had hoped. Edward thought it was, but, polite to a fault, he would not think of contradicting her on such an evening.

The first sentence asks the reader to understand that this was a different time, and to take the couple's sexual issues seriously. Notice the subtle glide from past to present tense in the first two sentences: these particular difficulties may belong to a more repressed era, but not exclusively to that era, in case you were inclined to dismiss this awful initiation into the ways of the flesh as an irrelevant anachronism. After that setup, the author refrains from commentary. Look how nimbly, and with how little fuss, McEwan establishes his access to both of his newlyweds' minds. The omniscience here is trustworthy, low-key, as if McEwan doesn't want to intrude too much on the honeymooners—though later, of course, he'll draw us quite close to them as they fumble with their (non)consummation. The one flourish, the description of that virginally white bedspread "stretched startlingly smooth, as though by no human hand," is clearly the author's language (down to the poetic alliteration of s's and h's), but expresses the characters' reaction: viewed with trepidation through the doorway, that narrow bed is forbidding enough for a hospital.

Another work that emphasizes landscape is Annie Proulx's "Brokeback Mountain." Her tale of two male ranch hands in love, in Montana in the early 1960s, in a time and place that decidedly rejected homosexuality, is not called "Jack and Ennis." Like Gurov and Anna in "The Lady with the Lapdog," the characters are introduced as both highly individual and also representative of a certain kind of man whose sexuality is secret, surprising, and shameful:

> They were raised on small, poor ranches in opposite corners of the state . . . both high school dropout country boys with no prospects, brought up to hard work and privation, both rough-mannered, rough-spoken, inured to the stoic life.

It's important that Proulx be able to sum up the men for us in this way, since their own understanding of their situation is clipped and inarticulate. She generally keeps her telling as straightforward as the men themselves, saving the rushes of lyricism for accounts of their time together alone on the mountain, and using the landscape to help create the mood of intense, joyous isolation:

> They never talked about the sex, let it happen, at first only in the tent at night, then in the full daylight with the hot sun striking down, and at evening in the fire glow, quick, rough, laughing and snorting, no lack of noises, but saying not a goddamn word except once Ennis said, "I'm not no queer," and Jack jumped in with "Me neither. A one-shot

thing. Nobody's business but ours." There were only the two of them on the mountain flying in the euphoric, bitter air, looking down on the hawk's back and the crawling lights of vehicles on the plain below, suspended above ordinary affairs and distant from tame ranch dogs barking in the dark hours. They believed themselves invisible, not knowing Joe Aguirre had watched them through his 10×42 binoculars for ten minutes one day, waiting until they'd buttoned up their jeans, waiting until Ennis rode back to the sheep. . . .

Without the omniscient narrator, we could not know that the characters' secret love is less secret than they think.

The detail about the binoculars is an example of how an omniscient narrator can make herself known in subtle ways. The specificity about the binocular size lets us know that Aguirre can zoom in on the lovers' pants as they button them, carrying on the metaphor of "looking down" and "the plain below" that the author built in the passage above. As well as helping to create the visual, it also rather forcefully changes the mood of the paragraph, from lyrical to starkly factual, which is pretty much what happens to the pair's love once society intrudes. Later, following Chekhov's famous dictum that if there's a gun on the wall in an early scene, it better go off by the end, Jack tells Ennis that when he next visited Aguirre "he says to me, he says, 'You boys found a way to make the time pass up there, didn't you,' and I gave him a look but when I went out I seen he had a big-ass pair a binoculars hangin off his rearview."

In a climactic scene, Jack and Ennis reunite after four years, and Jack's wife witnesses their passionate reunion kiss in a narrow hallway, a very different location than the sweep of Brokeback Mountain, although they carry the memory with them:

"He could smell Jack—the intensely familiar odor of cigarettes, musky sweat and a faint sweetness like grass, and with it the rushing cold of the mountain." Again, we see Proulx entering the men's thoughts from the overview of omniscience. Titles always belong to the author; it is Proulx, not the character, who stresses the mountain's metaphorical pride of place.

You can think about such omniscient descriptions of landscape, especially at the beginning of a piece of fiction, as the equivalent of establishing shots in a movie. *The Fugitive* starts with an overhead view of Chicago at night, ritzy and glittering, forbiddingly large, before we swoop into the bedroom where the dead woman's bloody body lies. On the simplest level, the establishing shot gives us an overview of the location; it also alerts us that it will be challenging to catch the murderer. Despite his small budget, Alfred Hitchcock used the expensive then-new technology of a crane shot in *Psycho*, to hover outside a hotel window, then zoom into the room where Marion meets her clandestine lover on her lunch break. So much for privacy. And that urban hotel is so different from the Bates Motel where, about a half-hour later, she'll be murdered.

But as we'll discuss later, a sentence isn't a camera. For our current purposes, it's worth establishing that a writer describing the landscape in detail, in third person, is usually using her authority to set a theme and mood. The beach in the McEwan novel is as cold and rocky as the marriage. The opening chapter of Colum McCann's *Let the Great World Spin* makes New York City itself the overarching character, and lets you know that, as the old TV show intoned, "There are eight million stories in the naked city. This has been one of them." As crowds gather everywhere to watch a tightrope walker cross between the tops of the two towers of the World Trade Center in 1974, the writer establishes himself as the master of all urban domains:

They found themselves in small groups together beside the traffic lights on the corner of Church and Dey; gathered under the awning of Sam's barbershop; in the doorway of Charlie's Audio; a tight little theater of men and women against the railings of St. Paul's Chapel; elbowing for space at the windows of the Woolworth Building. Lawyers. Elevator operators. Doctors. Cleaners. Prep chefs. Diamond merchants. Fish sellers. Sad-jeaned whores. All of them reassured by the presence of one another. Stenographers. Traders. Deliveryboys. Sandwichboard men. Cardsharks. Con Ed. Ma Bell. Wall Street. A locksmith in his van on the corner of Dey and Broadway. A bike messenger lounging against a lamppost on West. A red-faced rummy out looking for an early-morning pour.

The omniscience is fully Dickensian, delighting in its own jazzy rhythms and its breadth. McCann writes, "Every now and then the city shook its soul out. It assailed you with an image, or a day, or a crime, or a terror, or a beauty so difficult to wrap your mind around that you had to shake your head in disbelief." He wants us to come to the novel with the same sense of surprise and wonderment that the city dwellers give to the tightrope walker. As well as reaching for a persuasive overview of the city's multiplicity, McCann needs to connect the individual stories: he needs to assure his readers that they weren't plucked at random.

Generally, this style of omniscient narrator makes more sense for a story with a large cast than it does for the examination of a single person or relationship. Gabriel García Márquez covers a century and many generations of a family in the tiny village of Macondo in *One Hundred Years of Solitude*, but he keeps his style much more matter-of-fact than you'd expect given the bizarreness of many of the events he recounts. The style of magic realism descends from Franz Kafka and the notion that the stranger the truth, the less the narrator wants to wave his hands around and scream: Gregor Samsa wakes up to discover he has been transformed into a gigantic insect in "The Metamorphosis" and then tries to solve the problem of exactly how he's going to manage to get a train to work on time. Wonderful images in *One Hundred Years of Solitude* are presented simply: "the glass with his false teeth, where some aquatic plants with tiny yellow flowers had taken root."

Without grandstanding, García Márquez certainly establishes his authority, and the power of his binoculars, from the novel's first line:

> Many years later, as he faced the firing squad, Colonel Aureliano Buendía was to remember that distant afternoon when his father took him to discover ice.

Talk about a starting gun that explodes with a bang. Despite the journalistic style, that first sentence brings up *so* many questions that we really must keep reading. But we know that García Márquez knows.

In his opening, García Márquez shows his mastery of *temporal distance*. He knows the whole story, so he's moving through not just generations of the Buendía family (there is a handy chart for you in case you lose track) but the precise fate of each character. Temporal distance almost always increases our trust in the narrator. In creative writing workshops, we often talk about telling the story "in scene," so that we have a visceral view of the unfolding events. But it can be equally powerful, often more so, to remove us from the scene, to offer an overview.

García Márquez often starts chapters with time markers that demonstrate his full command of the story's scope: "Colonel Aureliano Buendía organized thirty-two armed uprisings and he lost them all"; "The war was over in May"; "The events that would deal Macondo its final blow were just showing themselves when they brought Meme Buendía's son home"; and "Aureliano did not leave Melquiades' room for a long time." In each case, García Márquez does not only move between characters as he starts a new chapter but between time registers. Since the author's goal is nothing less than a portrait of Latin America and its ongoing struggles, the scope is appropriate, and essential.

Expressing the unspeakable

Magic realism represents a new way for fiction to confront larger societal injustices, different from the social realism that Dickens used to expose and condemn poverty in Victorian Britain. With *The Orphan Master's Son*, his novel set in North Korea, Adam Johnson makes use of some of the techniques of magic realism. The novel follows Pak Jun Do, an orphan (talk about Dickensian), on his picaresque adventures, narrow escapes, and harrowing brushes with death in the brutal North Korean state. Little is known about the oppressive regime, but some of the plot points that seem most absurd—like that the regime kidnapped South Korean actresses to star in North Korean films—are actually true. So Johnson specifically wants his readers to be alert to the way that storytelling itself works to confirm or challenge our beliefs, the way narrative can be used to shape (or squelch) identity. One narrator is an interrogator, who collects detailed biographies of his soon-to-be-tortured victims the way an author would; many chapters (including the novel's first lines) start with a breathless, chipper announcement from the official state propaganda channel:

> Citizens, gather 'round your loudspeakers, for we bring important updates! In your kitchens, in your offices, on

your factory floors—wherever your loudspeaker is located,
turn up the volume!

We hear the author in the energy and exuberance of the imagination, even when, as above, the voice is not his own. He trusts
us to understand enough about both current geopolitical realities, and the history of the novel, to appreciate what he is doing
with the form—which elements are as time-honored as Dickens,
and which he has permuted to suit the story being told.

Another writer clearly influenced by García Márquez is Colson Whitehead, whose novel *The Underground Railroad* recon-
ceives the story of slavery to include a literal underground
railroad, a dreamlike, magical train to freedom. Once runaway
slaves Cora and Caesar escape and board that train, they learn
that, as the station agent foretells, "Every state is different. . . .
Each one a state of possibility, with its own customs and way
of doing things." And thus each section of the novel and stop
along the train's route exposes them to new depravities in the
Carolinas, Tennessee, and Indiana. Whitehead doesn't shy away
from recounting the accurate horrors of slavery. But the novel
also contains many wholly invented elements, like a "Museum
of Natural Wonders" where runaway slave Cora's job is to enact
"living" scenes of slavery behind glass, for the edification of
White museum-goers. On another part of her journey north, at
dawn, Cora is allowed to peek her head out of the wagon where
she's hiding to get a glimpse of a road lined with dead bodies,
gruesome as something from *Game of Thrones*:

> The corpses hung from trees as rotting ornaments. Some
> of them were naked, others partially clothed, the trousers
> black where their bowels emptied when their necks
> snapped. Gross wounds and injuries marked the flesh of
> those closest to her, the two caught by the station agent's

lantern. One had been castrated, an ugly mouth gaping where his manhood had been. The other was a woman. Her belly curved. Cora had never been good at knowing if a body was with a child. Their bulging eyes seemed to rebuke her stares, but what were the attentions of one girl, disturbing their rest, compared to how the world had scourged them since the day they were brought into it?

"They call this road the Freedom Trail now," Martin said as he covered the wagon again. "The bodies go all the way to town."

Whitehead starts with something real, the lynchings so common in the South, and ups the ante, creating a visual that is surreal in its ghastliness. Generally speaking, any work of fiction that introduces such invented elements will call attention to the author, to the power of his imagination (and, in Whitehead's case, his unflinching eye as witness to unimaginable violence). And although the novel follows Cora and Caesar most closely, Whitehead claims access to the thoughts and histories of other characters, including the brutal slave catcher chasing our protagonists and a surgeon turned grave robber.

This is classic omniscience, updated. Whitehead is in essence saying to the reader, "There's lots you can read to learn about slavery. Start with the slave narratives! But if I'm going to tell the story again, I've got to find a new, compelling way to do so." Whitehead isn't the first novelist to invent past the historical record; Toni Morrison gives voice to a baby ghost in *Beloved* who talks, albeit not in complete, orderly sentences. But Whitehead's take is undeniably original.

Of course, many historical novels still cleave more closely to the record, with as little as possible in the way of embellishment or distortion. The movie *The Bridge on the River Kwai* chronicled the horrific conditions in a Japanese POW camp during World

War II; an estimated thirteen thousand prisoners of war died doing forced labor to construct the Burma-Siam railway. But the movie was riddled with inaccuracies, and one of the goals of Richard Flanagan's novel *The Narrow Road to the Deep North* is to correct them. That author approaches us in a different posture than Whitehead's: Here, he says, is a story told in a classic manner—I don't need to reinvent the wheel—but on a subject and with a cast of characters that you have not encountered. The author will get you close enough to the protagonists' lived experience so that you can really feel their pain.

In most cases recounting harrowing events, a less emotive, more journalistic approach will be more effective. Sounds counterintuitive, but in fact the lack of wailing and gnashing of teeth inspires confidence in the reliability of the teller. Look at the flatness of affect in this passage from *The Narrow Road to the Deep North*:

> They found him late that night. He was floating head-down in the benjo, the long, deep trench of rain-churned shit that served as the communal toilet. Somehow he had dragged himself there from the hospital, where they had carried his broken body when the beating had finally ended. It was presumed that, on squatting, he had lost his balance and toppled in. With no strength to pull himself out, he had drowned.

By the end of that passage, Flanagan reports more passionately on the prisoners' sense of solidarity with the dead man: "For them, forever after, there could be no I or me, only we and us." But he leads you to that pitch slowly, without melodrama.

Similarly, Anthony Doerr describes the destruction of the French town of Saint-Malo by German bombs during World War II in *All the Light We Cannot See*:

Doors soar away from their frames. Bricks transmute into powder. Great distending clouds of chalk and earth and granite spout into the sky. All twelve bombers have already turned and climbed and realigned high above the Channel before roof slates blown into the air finish falling into the streets.

Flames scamper up walls. Parked automobiles catch fire, as do curtains and lampshades and sofas and mattresses and most of the twenty thousand volumes in the public library. The fires pool and strut; they flow up the sides of the ramparts like tides; they splash into alleys, over rooftops, through a carpark. Smoke chases dust; ash chases smoke. A newsstand floats, burning.

The passage serves as a kinetic visual of the destruction in the ways we discussed earlier. No one watches or filters the observations. It's an overview before Doerr moves into his characters' own experiences. The specificity of the twenty thousand volumes functions like the binoculars in the Proulx story: it inspires a feeling of documentary accuracy.

This description isn't *entirely* flat, of course, because Doerr's verbs—"soar," "spout," "scamper," "strut," "splash"—are active, and alliterative (thus clearly showing the author's hand in the construction). So is the sentence length and use of semicolons.

In "The Things They Carried," Tim O'Brien carries the omniscience further. He offers long lists of what soldiers in Vietnam had in their heavy knapsacks:

The things they carried were largely determined by necessity. Among the necessities or near necessities were P-38 can openers, pocket knives, heat tabs, wrist watches, dog tags, mosquito repellant, chewing gum, candy, cigarettes, salt tablets, packets of Kool-Aid, lighters, matches, sewing kits, Military Payment Certificates, C rations, and two or three canteens of water. Together, these items weighed between fifteen and twenty pounds, depending upon a man's habits or rates of metabolism.

The omniscience is aggressive: it denies the men, "called legs or grunts," their individuality, as the war did. O'Brien establishes that he is knowledgeable, and trustworthy, about the soldiers' travails. You don't really need to read his bio to suspect that he served, because he convincingly demonstrates that he is familiar with the lingo—"P-38," "C rations"—and as in our Chekhov example, you don't need footnotes to explain each item.

By the end, O'Brien extends the word "carried" to cover not just the items, the rations, and weapons, but the soldiers' emotional states: "For the most part they carried themselves with poise, a kind of dignity." The end of the story focuses on one lieutenant's emotions as a soldier in his platoon dies, and it's Lieutenant Cross who observes, "It was very sad, he thought. The things men carried inside. The things men did or felt they had to do." Although the thought is attributed to one man, the thematic overview, and the poetic slide from general soldiers to specific ones, belongs to the author. And by compressing so many fates into a short story—as opposed to an epic like *War and Peace* or an epic movie like *Saving Private Ryan*, where a series of characters from different walks of life take their turns in the spotlight—O'Brien emphasizes how little an individual life matters in a war. He wants to make you feel by suppressing feeling, as the soldiers themselves had to do, and as the lieutenant does as he knows he has to address his men "in a calm, impersonal tone of voice, an officer's voice, leaving no room for argument or discussion."

Themes almost always belong to the author, and allow the author to speak directly to the reader: Here are the issues you will consider. Here are why they matter. Even in the tight-lipped "Hills Like White Elephants," Hemingway gets out his thematic highlighting marker to let you know that the couple's pregnancy, like the items at a white elephant sale, is unwanted. Even if you have to google "white elephant," it's quite clear that a point is being made, because there it is, loud and proud, in the title.

James Salter has written eloquently about Hemingway, and you can see the influence on Salter's own spare, precise work. Here is how his story "Last Night" begins:

> Walter Such was a translator. He liked to write with a green fountain pen that he had a habit of raising in the air slightly after each sentence, almost as if his hand were a mechanical device.

Compared to the "overview" first sentences we looked at by Parker and Chekhov, this is bizarrely specific and small. Is this the thing most essential to know about Walter Such—his pen and ink color choices? Salter gives us a couple of equally puzzling statements about Such's translations before telling us blandly that the man's wife, Marit, is ill.

But with what? Something pretty serious, it appears, because the story chronicles the night of her assisted suicide. This particular story has an ending too shocking for even me, the Spoiler Queen, to give away. Plot twists, like themes, are authorial. No one is in charge of the plot of his own life and death. Well, maybe a suicide. The ritual disemboweler bravely committing seppuku with his long, gleaming sword in Yukio Mishima's "Patriotism." But suicides don't always go as planned, and it's the very issue of mortality, how much control we have over our own destinies, that Salter wants to consider in the story. He hints at this theme in the title's clever pun: "Last Night" means both the final night of one's life, and also the much more casual "night before this one."

Omniscience in literary versus "popular" fiction

So far, this chapter has exclusively considered examples from literary fiction. If you read a James Salter collection, or "Last Night" in the *New Yorker* where it originally appeared, you have probably long ago read the Guy du Maupassant story "The Necklace," so you have a history with and opinions about the tradition of Surprise Endings, and will be able to evaluate how well Salter achieves his goal.

Have you ever watched a TV commercial, felt put off or dumbfounded, and realized, "I guess I'm just not the target demographic for this ad"? That you don't want or need adult diapers, or a really tough truck? Fiction writers target their audiences in a not completely dissimilar way. Some readers have no intention of spending time devoted to the dull, workaday account of a failing marriage. "Why should I read that? I have my own boring life and my own boring wife." Other readers have very low tolerance for thrillers in which women are eaten or dismembered. When we talk in these pages about the nature of a reader and writer's relationship, such expectations form a kind of bedrock.

(For the record, because I know you're about to ask, I put Stephen King, with his almost one hundred [!!] books, in a category of his own, as one of the rare writers who can both appeal to a large audience and also produce solid, serious work. His book *On Writing: A Memoir of the Craft* is well worth your time.)

On the most literary end of our spectrum, we have a novelist like David Mitchell. His work represents the direction in which omniscience has gone in literary fiction. Mitchell writes novels where large casts of characters don't ever cross paths. *Ghostwritten* has nine primary characters whose stories are utterly disparate. The six primary characters in *Cloud Atlas* are in wildly different locations and also wildly different time periods, with the action spanning roughly a thousand years, from the mid-nineteenth century to far into the future. The nature of the storytelling (some sections in first person, some in diary form, some in heavy dialect) adds another complication. Clearly Mitchell's readers have to be up to the challenge of following the stories, no less deciphering them, and they would pride themselves on being able to appreciate the formal invention.

On the other end of the spectrum, we have Dan Brown.

Brown has been resoundingly mocked for the quality of the writing in *The Da Vinci Code*. You can google very funny blogs analyzing the spectacular badness of his prose, like the first lines of the best-selling novel:

> Renowned curator Jacques Saunière staggered through the vaulted archway of the museum's Grand Gallery. He lunged for the nearest painting he could see, a Caravaggio. Grabbing the gilded frame, the seventy-six-year-old man heaved the masterpiece toward himself until it tore from the wall and Saunière collapsed backward in a heap beneath the canvas.

Omniscience of this kind, with its focus on action and sportscaster-style "active" verbs, does not really purport to penetrate recesses of character, or to give deep insight, or to blind us with glittering imagery. It simply introduces the next character in the next scene, and many of those characters are baldly "types." Such thrillers translate handily to the screen, because the characters can so easily be summed up. The first two sentences of Michael Crichton's *Jurassic Park*:

The tropical rain fell in drenching sheets, hammering the corrugated roof of the clinic building, roaring down the metal gutters, splashing on the ground in a torrent. Roberta Carter sighed, and stared out the window.

I don't mean to deride the talent it takes to imagine a theme park with living dinosaurs replicated from the DNA in amber. It certainly qualifies as what Hollywood calls "high concept." As a visual of rain, or as a bio-sketch of Dr. Carter, this is far from scintillating, but it doesn't need to be: the question is who will be eaten next by what prehistoric beast. Like the park itself, the novel is an amusement ride. We know what we're in for, and we look forward to screaming. If we wait for the movie, we won't be missing much and in fact will get more in terms of special effect thrills and chills.

In fairness, both novels of this type and movies have gotten more self-conscious about their own devices, often greeting the reader, or viewer, with a wink and a nod. The author knows that you know that if a character is an extra, especially a callous or unappealing extra, that character is sure to meet an ugly fate. It's the principals who will hang on until the end, and they deserve to live because—they're the stars. (In actual life, as opposed to make-believe, people you care deeply about do indeed sometimes die prematurely, but this rarely happens in thrillers, just as the leads in a romantic comedy pretty reliably wind up together.) The author also knows that you know that if it's a disaster movie, a *lot* of people are going to die.

David Koepp, who wrote the screenplay for *Jurassic Park*, as well as other movies like *Spider-Man* and *The Mummy*, knows this formula intimately, and is able to have some fun with it. His debut novel, *Cold Storage*, is about a deadly, rapidly proliferating fungus that is about to cause the extinction of the entire universe, and as omniscient narrator, Koepp speaks for everyone including the fungus itself: "*Cordyceps novus* was driven. Over thirty-two years of isolation, it had changed very little, except to note that its growth environment was for shit." Koepp kills people early and often, and knows we know that more deaths are coming, so he can speak to us over the victims' heads, or in this case, from the angle of their feet:

> Teacake and Naomi had both stepped in smears of active fungal colonies when they were in the main hallway of sub-level 4. It would have been impossible not to, even if they had been aware that *Benzene-X* had the adaptive capability to eat through the thick rubber soles of the boots. The bottoms of all four of their boots were alive with that process even now, as they made their frantic way back up the tube ladder. They didn't know it, but they had less than a minute to get out of the suits before *Benzene-X* finished its work and the fungus would be able to pass through and make contact with their flesh.

Another critical difference between this kind of fiction and literary fiction is that we don't expect to be haunted by the deaths. We're not going to pause for a memorial service for each victim. Furthermore, we don't really expect to be surprised, or rather, we want to be surprised exactly the right amount. Being surprised too much in genre fiction is like ordering meatloaf and getting sushi. The very point of writing within a genre is that there *is* a formula, so the work can be formulaic. That doesn't mean that the writer doesn't have to provide some twists. But it does mean that a Western will be set in the West, a ghost story will have ghosts. Freddie from *Halloween* is not going to become a black belt, or learn to love through therapy.

Excellent literary fiction, on the other hand, can aim to offer nothing *but* surprises. I'd like to end this chapter with the first paragraph from the Joy Williams story "Taking Care." Notice the supple slides from the omniscience to the third-person-aligned point of view that we'll dive deeper into momentarily:

Jones, the preacher, has been in love all his life. He is baffled by this because as far as he can see, it has never helped anyone, even when they have acknowledged it, which is not often. Jones's love is much too apparent and arouses neglect. He is like an animal in a traveling show who, through some aberration, wears a vital organ outside the skin, awkward and unfortunate, something that shouldn't be seen, certainly something that shouldn't be watched working. Now he sits on a bed beside his wife in the self-care unit of a hospital fifteen miles from their home. She has been committed here for tests. She is so weak, so tired. There is something wrong with her blood. Her arms are covered with bruises where they have gone into the veins. Her hip, too, is blue and swollen where they have drawn out samples of bone marrow. All of this is frightening. The doctors are severe and wise, answering Jones's questions in a way that makes him feel hopelessly deaf. They have told him that there really is no such thing as a disease of the blood, for the blood is not a living tissue but a passive vehicle for the transportation of food, oxygen and waste. They have told him that abnormalities in the blood corpuscles, which his wife seems to have, must be regarded as symptoms of disease elsewhere in the body. They have shown him, upon request, slides and charts of normal and pathological blood cells which look to Jones like canapés. They speak (for he insists) of leukocytosis, myelocytes and megaloblasts. None of this takes into account the love he has for his wife! Jones sits beside her in this dim pleasant room, wearing a grey suit and his clerical collar, for when he leaves her he must visit other parishioners who are patients here. This part of the hospital is like a motel. One may wear one's regular clothes. The rooms have ice-buckets, rugs and colorful bedspreads. How he wishes they were traveling and staying overnight, this night, in a motel. A nurse comes in with a tiny paper cup full of pills. There are three pills, or rather, capsules, and they are not for his wife but for her blood. The cup is the smallest of its type that Jones has ever seen. All perspective, all sense of time and scale seem abandoned in this hospital. For example, when Jones turns to kiss his wife's hair, he nicks the air instead.

To start with the simple question we often ask in exploring point of view: Who do you "hear" in this passage? Is your primary relationship with Jones or with the story's writer? Obviously Williams wants you to feel for Jones as you keep him company in the hospital with its trippy, Alice in Wonderland distortions. Many of the observations are from Jones's own vantage point. The slides of blood look like hors d'ouevres to him; this part of the hospital is motel-like. The hospital is "fifteen miles from their home": definitely his observation, measured on his own odometer, because an author might take the opportunity to give us an overview of, say, in what state the couple lives.

But some of the observations and diction clearly belong to the author. The word "committed" for the hospital is the author's, as is the structure of the sentence that begins "They speak (for he insists)," or the idea that "one" may wear their regular clothes—most writers in that sentence would reach for a more casual "you," or "he." There's a kind of slightly mocking formality to the writing style, even in the weird first line, "Jones, the preacher, has been in love all his life." Why *the* preacher, as if the world has only one? Or is it that there are so many Joneses in the world, but this one is ours? Why is she calling him by his last rather than first name, doesn't that depersonalize him some? And while we're expecting some "establishing shot" to let us know that he's in a hospital with his ailing wife, we instead get puzzling, jarring, "has been in love all his life." With this wife, or with others? Didn't his mother love him?

So we've identified omniscient lines, and third-person–aligned lines, but there is yet another area here: some of the observations are simply hard to pinpoint. Is it the author, or Jones himself, who comes up with the startling image that he is "like an animal in a traveling show"? How about the sentence "None of this takes into account the love he has for his wife!" Is that meant to be the preacher's own declaration, in free indirect discourse? If so, isn't the diction awfully starchy from the man who also notes, "She is so weak, so tired" (for that is clearly free direct discourse)?

So many mysteries! And that's just in the first paragraph. Seeking clarity, finding answers, is part of what keeps us turning the pages, even though no T-Rexes are about to gobble up tourists.

For many of our analyses here, we've done close readings of first paragraphs or passages out of context, but it goes without saying that as you read, your understanding of the characters and the author's aims expands, or changes course. And it isn't just the wife's illness that's driving us here. In the very next paragraph, we learn that the couple's adult daughter has parked her infant with them while she runs off to find herself. The "taking care" in the title refers not only to Jones and the ailing wife, but to the baby girl. That baby might be able to be twice abandoned, so Jones will be left to care for her alone—as well as caring for his parishioners.

Without the entry into Jones's thoughts, this kind of realism, about the thorny problems in particular contemporary American lives, would risk becoming pretty dull or typical. Just another cancer patient, as anonymous as her blood cells on a slide. On the other hand, Williams wants us to know that she plans to serve as an interesting—one might even say idiosyncratic—tour guide into ordinary problems. She has points to make about life and death, maybe even about God and fate—after all, Jones is a man of faith, and his daughter is an astrology nut who, we learn, "is going to Mexico where soon, in the mountains, she will have a nervous breakdown. Jones does not know this, but his daughter has seen it in the stars and is going out to meet it." Williams has reserved the right to understand things that Jones doesn't. And those points (or, more accurately, areas for rumination) will be amplified as we go to other stories, with other characters.

In the next chapter, we'll discuss why the third-person–limited point of view has become so essential to contemporary writers, and also why it sometimes proves so challenging to achieve.

CHAPTER FOUR

THIRD-PERSON LIMITED

THE HOUSE OF FICTION'S MANY WINDOWS

Writers being interviewed about their process, when asked how they came up with the idea to have their protagonist murder her boss or dig up the rose bushes to look for the stolen jewels, will sometimes say, "Really, I just let her decide. It was *her* idea." As if, once the character is breathed into life, she has a will of her own and her own locomotion, like a Slinky pushed down the stairs. Once you're burrowed deep into a project, and have tasked yourself with fully imagining a scene, it can sometimes feel like your character is crooking a finger to intone "Follow me."

Having that sensation—that you as writer are breathless with anticipation about what will happen next—is the polar opposite of omniscience. You channel the character, séance-style. Unlike the writer who knows all and has the story plotted out on index cards, you are purposely limiting the scope of your knowledge to what the character can perceive. At least on a first draft, it's almost like a dream, the imagined events unfolding before you.

Why do this?

For starters, for realism. Life doesn't come with voice-overs. Unless you're a firm believer in horoscopes, your fate remains a mystery to you. You need to live each day without full knowledge about whether you'll fall madly in love or get hit by a bus. So contemporary writers tend to cleave to subjective accounts, often with far narrower time frames than in nineteenth-century fiction. Even though James Joyce named his epic novel after the Greek mythological figure in *Ulysses*, his protagonist does not circumnavigate the globe for decades attempting to return home, but lives through a single, uneventful day in his native Dublin. Everyone is the hero of his own story.

Modernists like Joyce, Virginia Woolf, and William Faulkner heavily emphasized subjectivity, often employing the technique called "stream of consciousness," in which a character's inner monologue is presented without mediation—thoughts that are pointedly disjointed, rambling, or enigmatic. Gone is the George Eliot-style translator we met in the previous chapter, bestowing shape and theme to a character's less-than-articulate musings. Instead we get language like this, from one of the fifteen characters who "speak" in Faulkner's *As I Lay Dying*:

> The first time me and Lafe picked on down the row. Pa dassent sweat because he will catch his death from the sickness so everybody that comes to help us. And Jewel dont care about anything he is not kin to us in caring, not care-kin.

This is different from free indirect discourse because the narrator steps back entirely. The thoughts are not smuggled into the narrative, as they would be in free indirect discourse; they *are* the narrative.

For those with an academic bent, there are many books, in fact entire disciplines of critical inquiry, that parse out the definitions and distinctions we'll cover in this chapter. In *Transparent Minds: Narrative Modes for Presenting Consciousness in*

Fiction, Dorrit Cohn maps out third-person points of view into five categories. From the most objective (omniscient), we proceed next to "psychonarration" (in which the narrator reports on a character's inner state), then "close third person" (quoted interior monologue; "she thought"), to free indirect discourse (interior monologue completely absorbed into the narration), and, finally, to the most subjective (stream of consciousness). For our purposes, I think it's useful to examine a writer's relationship to a character in third person as existing on a spectrum of closeness and distance from a character—a series of gradations with infinite possibilities. There are so many shades of identification and judgment that a writer can attain, and those shades are critical to determining how we react to the fiction.

What did she know, and when did she know it?

Subjectivity is by no means exclusively a twentieth-century invention, and plenty of earlier fiction writers have decided to directly report only what their protagonists can perceive. The heroine of Jane Austen's *Emma* is truly clueless about her own motives, no less other people's, and the reader's journey is to follow her until she comes to her senses. Austen can give us information through dialogue that we can "read" far better than Emma herself does: the kind of irony we discussed in the last chapter. Sometimes we have to snort, "Yeah, right," as we do when Emma avows that she has no intention of marrying, ever. But we do not get access to the consciousness of her eventual beloved, or her chief competitor, or the eligible bachelor about whom she's daydreaming. We have to wait for all to be revealed. A wonderful chapter in Wayne C. Booth's classic work of criticism, *The Rhetoric of Fiction*, discusses how Austen "controls the distance" of the authorial voice "to allow the reader to laugh

at the mistakes committed by the heroine and at her punish-
ment, without reducing the desire to see her reform and thus
earn happiness."

No one has ever chronicled the crossed and missed signals
of courtship better than Austen, and her plots move toward the
delicious moment when the woman learns that her longed-for
beloved returns her feelings. "She spoke then, upon being so
entreated.—What did she say?—Just what she ought, of course. A
lady always does," Austen tells us toward the end of the novel, in
one of her rare direct authorial intrusions. A saucy joke: her con-
temporaneous reader would know that a man and woman were
not even supposed to be alone together, unchaperoned, so when
she chides her readers to give them some privacy, she's also pok-
ing fun of current social mores, including what constitutes being
a "lady" (the very subject on which Emma has been so naïve and
wrongheaded). And to a contemporary reader, one not knowledgeable about Regency customs (as the makers of the movie
adaptations often are not—their lovers are always meeting barefoot, alone, in enticingly transparent night clothes, by moonlight), it's the gently ironic fade to black that old movies used to
do as the couple began to kiss. None of this could happen—there
is no plot—if we are given access to her suitor's thoughts.

Similarly, if a novel chronicles a spectacular betrayal, it simply will not do for the writer to show us the clandestine affair
in flagrante delicto. Henry James articulated why it was so
essential for him to cleave to the insights of his heroine:

> The house of fiction has in short not one window, but a
> million ... at each of them stands a figure with a pair of
> eyes, or at least with a field glass, which forms, again and
> again, for observation, a unique instrument, insuring to the
> person making use of it an impression distinct from every
> other. He and his neighbours are watching the same show,

but one seeing more where the other sees less, one seeing
black where the other sees white ...

So James, in *The Portrait of a Lady*, has to lead us slowly through
Isabel Archer's growing suspicions of her husband. Nothing so
gauche and definitive as how, in the movies, The Wife Finds the
Hotel Receipt in Her Husband's Suit Pocket When She Picks
Up His Dry Cleaning. The clues are smaller, shadowy. As she
returns from a walk, Isabel sees her husband standing with
Madame Merle—ostensibly her close friend!—in the drawing
room, and begins to suspect they know each other in a very different way than they have let on:

> Madame Merle was standing on the rug, a little way from
> the fire; Osmond was in a deep chair, leaning back and
> looking at her. Her head was erect, as usual, but her eyes
> were bent on his. What struck Isabel first was that he was
> sitting while Madame Merle stood; there was an anomaly
> in this that arrested her. Then she perceived that they had
> arrived at a desultory pause in their exchange of ideas and
> were musing, face to face, with the freedom of old friends
> who sometimes exchange ideas without uttering them.
> There was nothing to shock in this; they were old friends in
> fact. But the thing made an image, lasting only a moment,
> like a sudden flicker of light. Their relative positions, their
> absorbed mutual gaze, struck her as something detected.
> But it was all over by the time she had fairly seen it.

As with the Austen example, James cannot tell us, outright, that
Merle and Osmond are in cahoots. We can have suspicions, but
we can't know for sure until Isabel knows.

Critical to the third-person–limited point of view is that the
perceptions seem convincingly the character's. This may seem

obvious. If you're writing from the point of view of a blind girl surviving World War II in France, as Anthony Doerr does in *All the Light We Cannot See*, you'll want to figuratively blindfold yourself as a writer so you can be as exquisitely sensitive to sound and touch as your character.

So, if you're completely inhabiting the character, why not just write in first person?

Because you sometimes want the option of stepping back at key moments. That distance allows the reader to reflect, and to feel for the character in ways that would be less effective if the character were directly demanding the reader's sympathy. Also because, as we're about to see, there are protagonists so self-contained, and private, that having them chattily relating their own version of events directly to the reader, as a first-person account essentially requires, would not be convincing or would actually betray the character.

Inarticulate characters, speaking (mostly) for themselves

Marilynne Robinson's novel *Lila* highlights the benefits of working with a closely aligned third person. Robinson was fascinated enough with two families living in a small Iowa town to write four novels about them. Each novel inhabits one point of view. *Gilead* belongs to John Ames, one of the town's aging ministers. *Home* follows the other minister, Reverend Boughton, Ames's closest friend, as Boughton deals with grief about his wayward, alcoholic son, and *Jack* follows the son himself. The third in the series, *Lila*, concerns the eponymous Lila, a homeless woman who appears in the town, enters the church to get out of the rain, and, improbably, becomes widower Ames's second, much-younger wife.

We first meet Lila as a starving, sickly child of four or five. She doesn't even have a name, no less a birthday. She hides under a table, hoping for scraps. A hardened woman named Doll kidnaps her. Bonded as tightly as "a cow and her calf," the two struggle through the Depression until Doll is arrested for a murder she committed in self-defense and escapes, not to return. When Lila shows up in the town of Gilead, she's withdrawn, mistrustful, almost cataclysmically lonely. She had one year of school, so while she can read, she's an unlikely match for the bookish minister. But slowly, convincingly, they fall in love.

We don't learn about Lila's miserable past all at once but in jagged glimpses throughout, as the memories intrude on her days. There is absolutely no authoritative, Chekhov-like biosketch. Robinson keeps the focus as narrow, as targeted—as limited—as that of the unloved child peering out from under that table, or, later, hiding her money under a loose floorboard in the abandoned shack where she's squatting, shivering under a scrap of blanket.

But the author also makes a claim that Lila is the perfect conduit for a novel that meditates on religion: that her poverty, her suffering, her awareness of both life's hardships and its unexpected joys, make her thoughts about faith more profound than that of a minister merely reciting scripture. As Lila quizzes Ames on religion's conundrums, she becomes more articulate while also helping her husband to think about his faith in new ways. Observe the slide into free indirect discourse in this passage:

> She told the old man she'd been thinking about existence, that time she was out walking, and he didn't laugh. Could she have these thoughts if she had never learned the word? "The mystery of existence." From hearing him preach.... She wished she'd known about it sooner, or at least known

there was a name for it. She used to be afraid she was the
only one in the world who couldn't make sense of things.

If that passage doesn't move you, it may partly be blamed on
my habit of taking passages completely out of context, because
Robinson has a whole novel in which to build empathy for Lila's
way of thinking. Lila's observations have a heft and precision,
often based on a wonder of nature: "There is a way trees stir
before a rain, as if they already felt the heaviness." Her husband
on the pulpit "spoke with a tenderness he wasn't even aware of
anymore, that you could read if you knew how, like reading the
bottom of a river from its pools and flows." We—or at least I—
believe these perceptions as Lila's, with Robinson a steady and
unobtrusive translator. In his review of the novel, critic Ron
Charles says that "Robinson, for all her philosophical brilliance,
captures clearly and without a trace of condescension the mind
of an uneducated woman struggling to comprehend why things
happen, what our lives mean."

Yet there are naysayers. In the *New York Times*, critic Michiko
Kakutani isn't as convinced by the third-person–aligned point
of view, and says the novel

is hobbled, at times, by the author's curious decision to
tell the story in third person, robbing it of the emotional
immediacy of *Gilead* and resulting in occasional passages
that seem to condescend to Lila, an uneducated, almost feral
creature. Perhaps Ms. Robinson decided to tell the story in
the third person out of concern that such an unlettered girl
might not have the language for communicating her state of
mind, or perhaps it was difficult to find a voice for Lila that
could comfortably address the big existential questions of
life while remaining authentic and plain-spoken.

May I plead Robinson's case here? First of all, why would a character as stonily secretive as Lila narrate a story in first person? To whom would she be talking? She's too stoical to even talk to herself in large chunks. Kakutani doesn't note that the minister's book, "narrated in first person," is in fact a diary that the dying Ames is composing for his seven-year-old son. It's a written record—a very different thing than a first-person narrative. (See Chapter 7 for more discussion of epistolary techniques.)

Second of all, we *want* those flashes of distance. We are forced to perceive Lila as she fears others perceive her as she skulks in the back of the church: stupid, plain, filthy. We want to grow into our empathy, not just take it as a sentimental given. She isn't easy to get to know, so why should we have the chummy access to her that first person bestows?

We do hear Lila speak in the novel, in dialogue to her husband. It's in unadorned sentences far different from the complexity of her thoughts. Would we want to read a whole novel in which the character uttered lines like "Somebody like you got no reason at all to marry somebody like me"? The difference between the private and public Lila is essential to the book, to the very slow movement the couple makes toward trust and understanding, and toward Robinson's larger argument about the relationship of each lowly consciousness to God.

The third-person–aligned point of view lets Robinson have it both ways. She allows us intimacy with Lila's most secret self. But of course we're still aware that the author has shaped the narrative. It's the author who bestowed each of these three novels the one-word titles, with all of their implication of both narrow focus and thematic grandeur. It's the author who trusts we'll get the biblical implications of the title *Gilead*, who has the chutzpah to dedicate *Lila* "to Iowa"—to the whole blooming state. Lila may be small, but Robinson's goals for her are large. Robinson, like God, is both invisible, and everywhere, in each rustling tree, starving child, and hug between man and wife. Or more humbly, think of her as an excellent minister, interpreting the word of God, tenderly seeing to each lowly member of her flock.

I'll be quoting both positive and negative reviews as we continue, to remind that even Pulitzer Prize winners take occasional heat, and to make the point that, as fourteenth-century poet-monk John Lydgate said, "You can please some of the people all of the time, you can please all of the people some of the time, but you can't please all of the people all of the time." On top of being densely philosophical, *Lila* is not heavily plotted, and readers in search of a rollicking tale of adventure will be severely disappointed.

Such readers might prefer *My Absolute Darling*, which includes an action adventure film's worth of violence, danger, narrow escapes, and intense visuals (Raw scorpion for dinner, anyone?). Gabriel Tallent closely tracks the reactions of his fourteen-year-old protagonist, Julia "Turtle" Alveston, and, like Robinson, denies us access into anyone else's thoughts except through what they communicate in dialogue, or through what Turtle intuits. Tallent ends a chapter in *My Absolute Darling* that recounts a spectacularly cruel act of abuse by the girl's father with this paragraph about the naked, wounded, exhausted girl:

> She raises her head and ropes of muscle stand out from her mons pubis to her sternum like a bread loaf. She watches him and then she lays her head back down and she closes her eyes and she feels her soul to be a stalk of pig mint growing in the dark foundation, slithering toward a keyhole of light between the floorboards, greedy and sun-starved.

That Tallent has her look up from a prone position to inspect her own body, almost as if it doesn't belong to her, communi-

cates the dissociation that helps her cope. Note that once you
are in a closely aligned point of view, you can't comment on how
a character looks except in how she looks *to herself*: She has to
be studying herself in the mirror, or following the eyes of someone else looking at her. She also has to assume you know what
pig mint is. The author can't stop for footnotes. Otherwise it disrupts your close identification.

Obviously, the image of the stalk of pig mint is not something
that a fourteen-year-old would ever express herself, or even
think to herself in simpler diction: "Boy, inside, I kind of feel
like a weed growing under the house...." But Turtle, like Lila,
has lived in the wild, and Tallent has bestowed his heroine with
enough perceptiveness from her close study of nature to make
the metaphor apt. It is perfectly acceptable, and common, for
a writer to translate or amplify the feelings of a character. The
thoughts are the character's, the language (diction, sentence
structure, rhythms) the writer's.

But perhaps you object to "mons pubis" as a phrase that pulls
us too far outside the girl's point of view. I do, a bit, even given
the father's somewhat manic vocabulary lessons, especially
since at other times Turtle refers much more slangily (and also
disturbingly) to her "pussy." If the passage doesn't ring true for
you, it means that you think Tallent is intruding as author with
too heavy a hand, breaking the alignment's spell.

In a review of the novel on Goodreads, Roxane Gay complains, "I wanted more interiority from Turtle. The third-
person narration was a curious choice and I felt so much
distance from Turtle ... because we don't have the interiority
she deserves, the potential of her character is never realized."
Gay adds, "With respect, it felt like a man guessing at how a
young woman in her situation would feel. It was unbelievable
and not in a good way."

Autobiography, appropriation, and authenticity in third-person aligned

The complaint above gets us into questions about authenticity—about who is entitled to tell whose story, and about who is in position to tell the story well. The old adage "write about what you know" assumes that the prose will be stronger, richer, more accurate, and more compelling if the writer is deeply steeped in the subject through firsthand experience. And some readers insist on seeing evidence, in the author bio, that the writer shares experience with the book's character—that, for instance, Emma McLaughlin and Nicola Kraus, the writers of *The Nanny Diaries*, worked as nannies. There can be an enjoyable kind of salacious glee in a roman à clef, in which you either try to guess what "real person" the character is based on, or already know who is being skewered (Lauren Weisberger's takedown of *Vogue* magazine editor Anna Wintour in *The Devil Wears Prada*).

Like her heroine, Nigerian novelist Chimamanda Ngozi Adichie went to school in Philadelphia, held a fellowship at Princeton University, and lived in Baltimore. In *Americanah* she writes about neighborhoods as an insider, not as someone who cheated with Google Maps. Quite apart from the question of who is entitled to tell the story of an African American or an Iraqi refugee, a solid grounding in place and people, as Louise Erdrich demonstrates she has from her Cherokee heritage with *The Round House*, adds an imprimatur of believability and enriches the characterizations.

Part of the pleasure of a novel like Zadie Smith's *White Teeth* is how accurately, exuberantly, and affectionately she captures the thoughts and speech of her multiracial cast of characters, as you can see in these lines about a Jamaican person living in London:

"Clara! Come out of de cold."

It was the voice Hortense put on when she had company—an overcompensation of all the consonants—the voice she used for pastors and white women.

But even without the benefit of firsthand experience, there's always … research. And imagination. In combination, in the hands of a writer who can achieve a deep enough identification with his characters' experiences, they can be powerful tools. Jim Shepard is not a Polish Jew who survived World War II in Poland, but his *The Book of Aron* is an astonishing re-creation of the experience of the Warsaw Ghetto. Madison Smartt Bell has written a trilogy about the Haitian Revolution that began with a slave rebellion in 1791. He's white. Richard Price has tagged along with police and drug dealers to write novels like *Clockers*, and was adamant, in an interview, about his right to explore characters of color: "If you follow that reasoning, then I don't want to see any black guys writing about white people. I don't want to see any women writing about men. I don't want to see any Christians writing about Muslims. And nobody better write about what it was like to live in the 19th or the 20th century."

Flaubert's "Madame Bovary, c'est moi"—his declaration of solidarity with his female protagonist—may be a harder sell when a male writer chooses to explore the incestuous rape of a young girl. Because the third-person–limited point of view allows the writer to portray the girl from outside as well as from inside, the account risks having a kind of S&M-y, pornographic vibe. As a matter of taste, I personally do not enjoy narratives in which psychopaths torture women or bury them alive.

However, I've had female students boycott John Updike. They complain about his focus on male protagonists, and his dismissive, superficial portrayal of his female characters. It's certainly true that *Rabbit, Run*, his novel about high school basketball star

Harry "Rabbit" Angstrom's life in small-town Pennsylvania after his sports stardom ends, is strongly focused on one white male's disappointments. Although Updike does go for brief sections into other aligned points of view, Harry's longings are central. Here Rabbit observes his wife after the birth of their son, thinking about sex as he often does:

Those first days, full of rest and hospital health, she has more milk than the baby takes. Between feedings she leaks, the bodices of all her nighties bear two stiff stains. When he sees her naked, naked all but for the elastic belt that holds her Modess pad in place, her belly shaved and puffed and marked with the vertical brown line only mothers have, his whole stomach stirs at the fierce sight of her breasts, braced high by the tension of their milk, jutting from her slim body like glossy green-veined fruit with coarse purple tips. Top-heavy, bandaged, Janice moves gingerly, as if she might spill, jarred. Though with the baby her breasts are used without shame, tools like her hands, before his eyes she is still shy, and quick to cover herself if he watches too openly. But he feels a difference between now and when they first loved, lying side by side on the borrowed bed, his eyes closed, together making the filmy sideways descent into one another. Now, she is intermittently careless, walks out of the bathroom naked, lets her straps hang down while she burps the baby, seems to accept herself with casual gratitude as a machine, a white, pliant machine for fucking, hatching, feeding ...

The success of this passage—and the novel as a whole—depends upon the rift between what Rabbit himself feels and what the reader perceives. There's no way we can read this passage without feeling some disdain, or frustration. But we are also asked to "buy" the lyricism of his erotic impulses, his tenderness toward Janice, and accept Updike's contention that this imperfect Ordinary Man is worthy of our deep attention through the four novels that get him, by *Rabbit at Rest*, to be an old man with a Florida condo, grandchildren, and a heart condition.

Want a novel more from a female point of view about childbirth and motherhood? Try *The Lost Daughter* by Elena Ferrante. Or *Annie John* by Jamaica Kincaid. Or *After Birth* by Elisa Albert, a fiercely feminist account of new motherhood that serves as a useful tonic to Updike-like androcentrism. As opposed to a historical account like Shepard's or Bell's, which any writer, of any sex or race, would have to research, it's easy to see why a woman who has borne a child might be a good choice to discuss childbirth. Worth noting that all of these accounts are narrated in first person, subject of our next chapter: they are more directly related by the character ostensibly experiencing the events. If you want to hear about the joys and tribulations of caring for newborns, you wouldn't want Updike as your authority.

My own opinion is that following James's House of Fiction Has Many Windows theory, you can take the HGTV tour of both the Updike and Ferrante residences, given time enough and adequate bookshelf (or e-reader) space. Submerging us in one point of view is simply essential for telling certain stories. We can't adequately experience how trapped Rabbit feels in his marriage, or in his town, unless we join him there, just as we need Zadie Smith's intimacy with Londoners who aren't usually the heroes of novels to fully understand her characters' frustrations and aspirations.

If you accept my baseline contention that you can dislike and mistrust a character, but you must like and trust the author, your opinion about fiction is going to be different if you think, for example, that Updike is *celebrating* bad-boy behavior like married Rabbit having sex with an old flame, rather than believing that the author is quite aware of the ways in which Rabbit hurts others. There are also cases where the author's separation from his character simply seems unconvincing, incomplete, or self-serving. But it would be unfair to pin any of that on Updike. It's not easy empathy that is demanded of you. It is uncomfortable and nuanced.

An unsophisticated reader, similarly, will be offended by this passage in Flannery O'Connor's story "A Good Man Is Hard to Find," about a road trip with tragic consequences, in which the grandmother makes this observation from the back seat of the car where she is sandwiched in with her bratty grandchildren:

> "In my time," said the grandmother, folding her thin veined fingers, "children were more respectful of their native states and their parents and everything else. Oh look at the cute little pickaninny!" she said and she pointed to a Negro child standing in the door of a shack. "Wouldn't that make a picture, now?" she asked and they all turned and looked at the little Negro out of the back window. He waved.
>
> "He didn't have any britches on," June Star said.
>
> "He probably didn't have any," the grandmother explained. "Little niggers in the country don't have things like we do. If I could paint, I'd paint that picture," she said.
>
> The children exchanged comic books.

Many literature classes no longer include the story, because the outrage over the slur is so strong. But O'Connor, writing in 1950s Georgia, was condemning racism, not condoning it. She expects us to note the irony of the grandmother harkening back nostalgically to the genteel Olden Days of her youth, when children were respectful—but Blacks had only recently been freed from slavery. She expects us to notice the contrast between the almost naked child and the grandmother's hypocrisy: she has worn clean underwear on the trip so that "anyone sees her dead on the highway will know that she's a lady." She expects us to recognize, as the grandmother does not, that poverty is not at all picturesque or romantic. Last, she expects us to notice that however irredeemably and infuriatingly smug (and, yes, racist) the grandmother is, at least she's interested enough in the world to look out the window. The children can't be bothered.

That's a lot of layers to pack into a short passage in which the author pointedly doesn't comment or intervene. Some readers will miss all of that, become automatically indignant about the racism, and probably need the standard legal disclaimer: "The views, thoughts, and opinions expressed in the text belong solely to the characters, and not necessarily to the author."

Except, of course, they *do* belong partly to the author, who in her letters makes many baldly racist statements. In his *New Yorker* essay "Everything That Rises: How Racist Was Flannery O'Connor?," Paul Elie explores the conundrum. What are we to do with a writer whose fiction condemns racism, but who is personally guilty of so much of it? Should we follow the critical injunction against using a writer's biography as a tool for interpretation, limiting ourselves to what is on the page?

Please note that even if we do dismiss all extra-textual and biographical evidence, there certainly *are* situations in fiction where a racial slur would be offensive. Again, it would depend upon whether you sense the author's delight and complicity in hurling around the aspersion. Introducing us to a racist character is different from seeming to celebrate a character's racism. It would also depend on whether you think *any* white writer is justified in using the word. Is a white writer permitted to write about Native Americans? On the simplest level, should a reader of *Crazy Rich Asians* insist that the writer is himself Asian? There is a completely reasonable argument that women, or people of color, have been so underrepresented in fiction that their voices should be granted

primacy now. On the other hand, some cries of cultural appropriation can also be unnecessarily limiting to a writer's imagination.

In her essay "Who Gets to Write What?," Kaitlyn Greenidge
offers an excellent summary of both sides of this argument. She
approves of any writer approaching any subject, so long as they
can do it well, with insight and sensitivity. But she sees some
writers who decry narrow political correctness as guilty of being
overly broad and defensive:

> It's the wish not so much to be able to write a character
> of another race, but to do so without criticism. And at the
> heart of that rather ludicrous request is a question of power.
> There is the power of rendering another's perspective,
> which is not your own. There is the adage "Don't punch
> down," which sits like the shiny red lever of a fire alarm,
> irresistible for some writers who wish to pull it.

For an interesting test case of how such issues play out critically, see the reviews of *Girl*, in which Irish novelist Edna O'Brien
writes about Nigerian girls kidnapped by Boko Haram and forced
to endure all manner of cruelty. "It has been suggested to me,"
O'Brien says, "that as an outsider I am not eligible to write this
story. I do not subscribe to that devious form of censorship." In
the *New Yorker*, Ian Parker notes that many readers will see that
the girl's struggles make her "not much different from O'Brien's
young Irish heroines," and view the novelist taking on such a character as "a form of courage." Nevertheless, he says, readers might
still "react uneasily to a character from rural northeastern Nigeria
whose worldview includes egg cups, perambulators, and bottles of
vanilla essence, and whose inner life is conveyed by such expressions as 'an ungodly hour' and 'jolted hither and thither.'"

Similar critical debates played out about the novel *American
Dirt*, with Latinx writers decrying the fact that Jeanine Cum-

mins, a white American, got a seven-figure advance for a novel on the subject of Mexico, and not a Mexican writer. "There's no shortage of talented Latinx writers with all kinds of stories to tell. Let's make space for them," says critic Rose Cahalan, who provides a list of seventeen lesser known but excellent works of fiction as alternatives.

This is obviously a much larger subject, but I hope I've convinced you that questions of authenticity and appropriation are largely point-of-view questions. Who is telling a story about Mexico, to whom? Is the writer an insider, or an outsider? On the most basic level, these questions involve the reader's trust of and respect for the author. A reader can insist that the writer be "one of us"—from the same gender, race, or ethnicity as the character. But that is a political judgment, not a *literary* judgment, the way it would be, for example, if a reader objects that Edna O'Brien doesn't convincingly penetrate the consciousness of a kidnapped girl, gets many details about Nigeria wrong, or makes judgments that supersede identification with the character too forcefully.

Inhabiting a character— and stepping outside of one

Let's look in more detail at the mechanics of creating a successful third-person–aligned narrative, as well as when that point of view is useful and appropriate. We'll revisit a couple of stories and authors we examined in Chapter 2.

The plot of many a short story involves an oblivious or deluded character, with hints about the true nature of his journey being revealed to the reader little by little, until the end when all becomes clear. In essence, the reader is enclosed in the consciousness of the protagonist until the *aha!* moment of the ending.

In John Cheever's "The Swimmer," Neddy Merrill decides to return home by way of a series of suburban pools. It's eight miles, and since he is served a drink at many of the pools, he gets drunker and drunker, as well as more discouraged. Here he is after traversing the pool of some neighborhood nudists:

> Beyond the hedge he pulled on his trunks and fastened them. They were loose and he wondered if, during the space of an afternoon, he could have lost some weight. He was cold and he was tired and the naked Hallorans and their dark water had depressed him. The swim was too much for his strength but how could he have guessed this, sliding down the banister that morning and sitting in the Westerhazys' sun? His arms were lame. His legs felt rubbery and ached at the joints. The worst of it was the cold in his bones and the feeling that he might never be warm again. Leaves were falling down around him and he smelled wood smoke on the wind. Who would be burning wood at this time of year?

It's important for the story that we experience the events as Neddy himself experiences them, until the serially unfaithful alcoholic realizes at the story's end that he is divorced, that his wife and four children have left, that his house is empty and boarded up.

But again, in the closely aligned third person, Cheever is able to give us glimpses of Neddy from the outside: "Had you gone for a Sunday afternoon ride that day you might have seen him, close to naked, standing on the shoulders of Route 424, waiting for a chance to cross." It's essential that Cheever uses such switches from Neddy's own view of things carefully, and at key moments. They function almost in the same way as musical bridges.

In Alice Munro's "In Sight of the Lake," Nancy "has wondered whether her mind is slipping a bit," and travels to an appointment with a neurologist. She gets terribly lost trying to find the doctor's office. At the end, we discover that her increasingly fraught efforts to locate the physician were all in her head—that she did not drive to the small town at all and is, in fact, already living in a locked dementia ward. The "it was all a dream!" ending has fallen quite out of favor since *The Wizard of Oz*, but Munro's handling of the closely aligned point of view is so masterful that it helps us to see how the woman—in her former life plucky, observant—attempts to function and find joy despite her shattered memory.

There is simply no way at all to experience this looking at the character from outside. And unlike Cheever, Munro *never* intrudes to interpret or hint. She requires that her readers get lost along with Nancy.

Needless to say, a trick ending isn't required to make the choice to use a closely aligned third person. "The Shawl," Cynthia Ozick's story about a woman's march to a concentration camp with her two daughters, one an infant, would make no sense at all without the intense focus on the woman's own reactions, which are in turn very narrowly focused on the baby hidden at her breast.

> Rosa did not feel hunger; she felt light, not like someone walking but like someone in a faint, in trance, arrested in a fit, someone who is already a floating angel, alert and seeing everything, but in the air, not there, not touching the road. As if teetering on the tips of her fingernails. She looked into Magda's face through a gap in the shawl: a squirrel in a nest, safe, no one could reach her inside the little house of the shawl's windings. The face, very round, a pocket mirror of a face: but it was not Rosa's bleak complexion, dark like cholera, it was another kind of face altogether, eyes blue as air, smooth feathers of hair nearly

as yellow as the Star sewn in to Rosa's coat. You could think
she was one of *their* babies.

Ozick never interprets from outside. She does translate her
character's feelings: in a line about the infant like "Magda was
quiet, but her eyes were horribly alive, like blue tigers," we know
that the simile is Ozick's, but believe that the observation about
the intensity of the infant's gaze is Rosa's. Ozick demands that
we experience the brutality of the story's ending exactly as Rosa
does, without a larger overview of the concentration camp and
its atrocities. Rosa is focused solely only on her own survival,
and her baby's.

We feel Ozick's authorial presence in the soaring rhythms of
the prose, in the beauty of the metaphors, in the overall serious-
ness of purpose. All accomplished writers have signature methods and styles. It is not required that the author *vanish* inside the
character's point of view and, in fact, very few writers manage
to achieve that kind of invisibility. Even in cases where we're
deeply invested in the character, we're aware that a writer is
fashioning the tale, and have a sense of the writer's concerns:
that she cares about the lives of ordinary women living ordinary
lives, for example. Or we can hear the writer's sharp sense of
humor and engagement with the absurdities of contemporary
American culture, as we do with T. C. Boyle's short stories.

In "Sorry Fugu," in which chef Albert has a crisis about a
negative review that could tank his new restaurant, Boyle sticks
closely to the chef's perceptions:

> There are nights when it all comes together, when the
> monkfish is so fresh it flakes on the grill, when the pesto
> tastes like the winds through the pines and the party of
> eight gets their seven appetizers and six entrees in palettes
> of rising and delicate colors so perfect they might have

been a single diner sitting down to a single dish. This
night, however, was not such a night. This was a night when
everything went wrong.

It goes without saying that the writer can make himself heard in a
passage like this. Boyle, not Albert, skewers the fancy restaurant
scene; Boyle creates the larger metaphor about the making of art,
about how creative cuisine, like fiction itself or like any art form,
struggles to reach an appreciative audience. And there's a recognizable kind of Boyle-ean simile. Albert "shuddered and blanched
and felt his stomach drop like a croquette into a vat of hot grease"
both belongs to Albert and to Boyle; sure, it's a cooking metaphor,
but over the course of an entire collection a reader will notice
that Boyle favors metaphors that allude to extreme mortal danger. The dishwasher "lifted the supersprayer from its receptacle
as he might have drawn a rapier from its scabbard." Albert "was
watching her—Willa Frank—as transfixed as the tailor-bird that
dares look into a cobra's eye." Fugu itself is a Japanese blowfish
that, cooked incorrectly, can poison and kill. We know that Boyle
knows, and he knows that the reader knows, that getting a good
review is actually not life or death, and that he's having some fun
with the chef's do-or-die commitment to his craft.

   Lorrie Moore's story "Two Boys" is another example of a story
where the author's voice and the character's voice seem to merge
or overlap:

   For the first time in her life, Mary was seeing two boys at
   once. It involved extra laundry, an answering machine, and
   dark solo trips in taxicabs, which, in Cleveland, had to be
   summoned by phone, but she recommended it in postcards
   to friends. She bought the ones with photos of the flats, of
   James Garfield's grave, or an Annunciation from the art
   museum, one with a peacock-handsome angel holding up

fingers and whispering, *One boy, two boys.* On the back she wrote, *You feel so attended to! To think, we all thought just one might amuse, let alone fulfill. Unveil thyself! UnBlacken those teeth and minds! Get more boys in your life!*

She lived in a small room above a meat company—Alexander Hamilton Pork—and in front, daily, they wheeled in the pale, fatty carcasses, hooked and naked, uncut, unhooved. She tried not to let the refrigerated smell follow her in the door, up the stairs, the vague shame and hamburger death of it, though sometimes it did.

Unlike in some short story collections, where there's a pointed variety of characters to suggest the author's range—young and old, male and female, janitors and nuclear physicists—at least in her early work, Moore's characters were all smart, funny, creative, quirky young women who seem as if they could indeed be stand-ins for the writer herself. Some, like Moore, are academic transplants from Manhattan teaching in the Midwest.

So why not write in first person? Notably, Moore seldom does. Her third-person voices allow her to achieve a cool, appraising distance from her protagonists—to essentially separate herself from them. In this story, the character's wisecracking voice is decidedly *not* the author's voice. The character supplies her own irony with "two boys" (she's not in seventh grade) and her witty postcards, but this character would not note "the vague shame and hamburger death" of the meatpacking district. Moore isn't just serving as the translator of the character's feelings here; she's supplementing, assuring the reader that real sadness, and consequences, lurk behind the girl's defensively playful, buoyant manner. Mary just hurries upstairs. Moore implies that she's hurrying past something—ignoring something—with her dating, too. The suspense of the story becomes whether Mary will figure it out, and how.

Dueling points of view in third-person aligned

Another common technique is for the writer to have access to two primary characters' movements and minds, although the characters don't have access to each others'. The pleasure in such a narrative derives from how the two contrasting narratives diverge, and eventually converge. To create tension, the writer will often leave Character 1 at the end of a chapter or section in a fraught situation, and switch to the thoughts and actions of Character 2. The success of this approach depends on how well the switches are handled. A reader will enjoy having a plot point dangled suspensefully—unless (1) it feels like an obvious, cheap trick, the equivalent of "Meanwhile, back at the ranch"; and/or (2) the next character explored is not as compelling, and leaves the reader itching to get back to the previous tale.

Boyle uses this technique in his novel *The Tortilla Curtain*. The husband in a rich L.A. couple hits an illegal Mexican immigrant with his car. The Mexican's young wife is pregnant; they're camping out in a ravine, struggling to get enough money to eat, suffering unimaginable dangers and hardships, while the rich L.A. wife, a realtor, ponders weighty matters like this while touring a house:

> The interior was cool and quiet and it smelled faintly of almonds. That was a good smell for a house to have, a clean patrician smell, and Kyra realized it must have come from the furniture polish the maid used. Or could it have been an air freshener?

It's important that Boyle doesn't just mock the rich couple, and doesn't settle for making us feel simple pity for the poor immigrants. His penetration of character has to go deeper. By cleaving closely to these characters, he is trying to make a larger argument about wealth inequality, about the ways in which Americans misunderstand "the other."

Indeed, contrasting close third-person points of view may be one of the most effective ways to expose cultural rifts or shifts. In *Americanah*, Chimamanda Ngozi Adichie considers Ifemelu and Obinze, young lovers in Nigeria whose lives take radically different paths. Ifemelu gets an American education and becomes romantically involved with several American men. But she still harbors longings for Obinze, who immigrated illegally to London, suffered indignities there while trying to arrange a marriage that would earn him citizenship, then is deported. Back in Nigeria, he marries, becomes a father, and makes a fortune in real estate. When Ifemelu decides to return to Nigeria, the two reunite, their feelings for each other as intense as ever. Unlike Boyle, who alternates in short story sections and novel chapters between the characters, Adichie introduces the characters together, then devotes longer sections to each of her lovers as they occupy separate continents and quite different problems.

Many of the reviews consider the heroine as a "stand-in" for Adichie herself, and it's true their experiences as immigrants to the United States track closely. Adichie has much to say about the experiences of Black women, including much discussion of their hair. The novel begins with Ifemelu visiting an African hair braiding salon in Trenton, and includes details such as:

> Ifemelu had brought her own comb. She gently combed her hair, dense, soft, and tightly coiled, until it framed her head like a halo. "It's not hard to comb if you moisturize it properly," she said, slipping into the coaxing tone of the proselytizer that she used whenever she was trying to convince other black women about the merits of wearing their hair natural. Aisha snorted; she clearly could not

understand why anybody would choose to suffer through combing natural hair, instead of simply relaxing it.

Obviously, in terms of authenticity, better for Adichie to write about the challenges of Black hair than someone who has never had to warn a stylist that she was coiling too tightly.

A Nigerian reader will respond in one way to such specifics, an African American reader in another, but Adichie clearly addresses white readers as well, who may feel surprise rather than pleased recognition. She doesn't want to just "preach to the choir" of her Black African sisters. This is what we mean when we ask, "Who is the author addressing?": how you, as an individual reader, form a bond with the writer. In one scene, Ifemelu schools her white boyfriend, ostensibly totally woke, about the racism in women's magazines. As she states in a TED Talk called "The Danger of a Single Story," Adichie wants to highlight how different cultures evaluate things differently, and to explore the clashes that result. It's important that those evaluations happen on a daily level, not as big philosophical lectures, as here, where Obinze observes a rich London friend's antique desk:

> Obinze wondered if Emenike had so completely absorbed his own disguise that even when they were alone, he could talk about "good furniture," as though the idea of "good furniture" was not alien in their Nigerian world, where new things were supposed to look new.

In terms of proportion, Ifemelu does get a bit more space in the novel than Obinze. But unlike *Pride and Prejudice*, this courtship novel would not work if we only got access to Ifemelu's point of view, since it purports to be as much the man's story. Also, the world Adichie portrays is quite different from the narrow one of Austen's England. Despite the distance, the pair has sources of information about each other, ways to track each other, apart from letters and gossip: Facebook, fast-moving e-mail, even googling each other. Both characters' possibilities are broad, and in considering all of those possibilities, Adichie asks complex questions about belonging, class, and identity.

Since she argues that identity is fluid, that arriving at a "true" identity is a fraught process, she also includes many of Ifemelu's blog posts. What is the point of making Ifemelu a writer, but not of novels? There *is* a novelist in this novel, but she's hardly the stand-in for our author; in fact, she comes off as narrow and narcissistic. The blog posts, which sound so very different from the third person in which the rest of the novel is written, serve not to make the character and the author the same, but actually to separate them: this novel represents *my* writing, Adichie alerts you, and the blog posts my character's. Of course you're aware that Adichie herself is writing both, but the author goes to the trouble to make the tone and rhythms of her character's prose different from her own. Writing itself, Adichie says, is a kind of representation in which distortions can happen.

The choice to use a pair of aligned points of view is such a common method that we could spend much more time looking at examples of how the writers organize the material. Are the switch-offs quick and frequent, like the passing of a baton in a relay race? Or are the sections more marathons where we stay with one character for a while until we think we feel confident that we know the end of the story, only to get a completely new version when the point of view changes?

Two examples of this latter approach, just for fun.

There's *The Sheltering Sky*, by Paul Bowles, about an American couple's travels in North Africa after World War II. We pretty much track the husband, the adventuresome one who insisted on coming to Africa, until he dies of typhoid, at which point we switch to his grief-stricken wife. Bizarrely, she finds

herself as the newest addition to the harem of a Bedouin chief-
tain. (Warning, in terms of our discussion about authenticity,
the portrayal of the Africans in this novel has not dated very
well.) And, more recently, there's *Fates and Furies*, in which Lauren Groff tells his-and-hers stories of a marriage in completely
disparate halves of the novel. Although the sections are aligned
with the characters, Groff makes her authorial presence known
throughout, always putting authorial thoughts in brackets, most
very short, like this:

> Somehow, he's frittered his potential away. A sin...
> [Perhaps we love him more like this, humbled.]

> Did she burn to see what was behind those locked doors?
> She did. But she didn't pick the locks. [Already, a miracle of
> self-possession.]

> Fine, Chollie thought. You'll see how well I can wait. When
> you're least expecting it, I will explode your life. [Only fair;
> she had exploded his.]

Interestingly, in such cases, omniscient comments often serve
not to make the story more solidly reliable, as in many of the
examples in Chapter 3—"the author is telling me this, so it must
be true"—but to call your attention to storytelling itself as artifice, construction. Robert Coover's story *The Babysitter* offers a
series of clipped sections about an evening in the life of a suburban couple at a boozy dinner party, their babysitter at home with
their bratty kids, and the horny teenage boys who hope to crash
in on the babysitter while she's alone. Oh, and there's a potential
murderer loose in the neighborhood, or maybe that's just on a TV
show; as the sitter manically flips channels, and the author goes
from reality to the characters' fantasies, you're not entirely sure

what's real and what's not. Did the entire drunken dinner party really stumble into the bathroom to help Bitsy out of her girdle? Did the babysitter take a bath? Did the psycho killer find her there, and did the dad attempt to seduce her? "Babysitter" here refers both to the underpaid teenage employee, and the TV, its way of organizing the longings and fantasies so central to our lives.

About his novel *Tumbledown*, which considers the fates of a large cast of characters having therapy at the same outpatient center, the novelist Robert Boswell coined the term "unreliable omniscience." The reader is exhorted to think about the author not as the ultimate authority on the character's thoughts and actions but as an interpreter, with all of the foibles and limitations of any character. Boswell, who like one of his characters once worked as a mental health counselor, told an interviewer:

> I would see other counselors' clients for two or three weeks at a time. I'd give them a series of tests. . . . At the end of an evaluation, I'd write a report, recommending certain kinds of training, education, or employment, while putting the nix on other such endeavors. This report was enormously useful to a counselor trying to put together a rehabilitation program; however, I discovered that some counselors put too much faith in the test scores, as if they were infallible or omniscient. . . . Ultimately, I came to think of the reports as a form of unreliable omniscience, and at some point in the long writing process (I worked on the novel for ten years) I decided that the novel ought to be told in that point of view. Once I made that decision, I began noticing other examples of unreliable omniscience: the GPS system in my car, the nightly news, missiles with supposed pinpoint accuracy.

Keep in mind, just because GPS sometimes leads you astray, it doesn't mean it's always wrong, or that you shouldn't consult it on

a road trip. Healthy skepticism does not mean that there's no accuracy or truth, ever. This is what students often get wrong in workshop discussions: "That's just your opinion" assumes that there are
no facts upon which we can agree. Groff offers that little "perhaps"
in her authorial aside—she isn't quite sure. On the other hand, "she
had exploded his life" is presented as *not* open to debate. We're
always looking at a spectrum of reliability and believability in narration. In evaluating what to trust, that dance of confidence and
suspicion is an essential part of what keeps us turning pages.

By the way, in workshops, writers are often told to hold their
tongues while others discuss their work, because the fiction
must sink or swim without the writers' justifications. However,
I'll be quoting some writers on their goals, as I did for Boswell
above. We do want to keep in mind the critical idea of the *intentional fallacy*, which reminds us that a writer's goals can't be
used as final proof in evaluating the work—the writer may not
have achieved the goals, and furthermore the goals might be
misguided. Still, knowing a writer's intent can be enlightening,
especially in discussing a draft. If we know what the writer was
trying to achieve, we might be better able to address missteps.

The more, the merrier: multiple characters in third-person aligned

As we discussed in the last chapter, many novels now approach
a large cast of characters with defining third-person–aligned
approaches devoted to each. But by default, the more characters
are in play, the more the point of view begins to feel like conventional omniscience, with the author assembling a cast that represents all aspects of the subject under discussion. Also by default,
the more characters there are, the less space there is to develop
each one. Many of the players introduced in *War and Peace* are

basically walk-ons. Tolstoy identifies a certain Princess Bolkon-sky by noting that she has a rather hairy upper lip. A "barely visible black moustache": barely visible, but worth noting, on each entrance.

In *Empire Falls*, Richard Russo develops closely aligned third-person sections for many of the residents of a small, declining Maine town. The pleasure of a novel like this is witnessing all of the ornate ways the characters crisscross: wives, ex-wives, high schoolers and their teachers, priests, rich dowagers, aerobics instructors. Central to all of the action is quietly unhappy Miles, the proprietor of the local diner:

> The Empire Grill was long and low-slung, with windows that ran its entire length, and since the building next door, which had housed a Rexall drug store, had been condemned and razed, it was now possible to sit at the lunch counter and see straight down Empire Avenue all the way to the old textile mill and its adjacent shirt factory. Both had been abandoned now for the better part of two decades, though their dark, looming shapes at the foot of the avenue's gentle incline continued to draw the eye. Of course, nothing prevented a person from looking up Empire Avenue in the other direction, but Miles Roby, the proprietor of the restaurant—and its eventual owner, he hoped—had long noted that his customers rarely did.

Here the reader follows Miles's eye, and the writer modestly recedes. Of course in a novel with this many characters, even a long novel, some will be more developed and central than others, but Russo is careful to avoid the Tolstoyean Hairy Upper Lip Trap and tries to give even his extras souls and aspirations. For the most part, the characterizations are good-natured and tender. Russo also evinces a kind of authorial modesty because he

isn't claiming to reinvent the novel form: *Empire Falls* is squarely
and unapologetically in a realistic tradition, and in that way, too,
the author seems to be doing a kind of respectful, slightly self-
deprecating hat tip to his readers, welcoming them to the novel's
world, exhorting them to pay attention to ordinary lives.

Let's end with a radically different use of multiple third-
person–aligned points of view, in George Saunders's story "Victory Lap." Saunders presents sections from the points of view of a
girl home alone and about to be kidnapped; the neighbor boy with
Tourette syndrome and cruelly strict parents, also home alone,
who is going to save her; and, by the end of the story, the kidnapper himself. While Russo seems to embrace the character in question during each section, trying to capture their observations in a
realistic and unobtrusive way, Saunders sinks *so* deeply into their
thoughts, and their thoughts are so jarring, that it is, ironically,
the author himself we hear—especially since this is a story, not
a novel, and the shifts between characters are whiplash fast. His
identification with his characters and speedy segues into stream
of consciousness are playful, challenging. The story begins:

> Three days shy of her fifteenth birthday, Alison Pope
> paused at the top of the stairs.
>   Say the staircase was marble. Say she descended and
> all heads turned. Where was {special one}? Approaching
> now, bowing slightly, he exclaimed, How can so much
> grace be contained in one small package? Oops. Had he
> said *small package*? And just stood there? Broad princelike
> face totally bland of expression? Poor thing! Sorry, no way,
> down he went, he was definitely not {special one}.

The first phrase implies that this will be a Normal Story. From the
structure of the sentence and the specificity of the time stamp,
you expect the author to announce something consequential—

"Three days shy of her fifteenth birthday, Alison Pope's mother died"—but he doesn't. We take a sharp turn into her state of mind, her elaborate fantasy of the boy as prince, with no setup. Who on earth exactly is {special one}? *Is* the staircase marble, and who is saying it is? And who's providing the weird brackets? In the Groff example, we know the brackets are authorial intrusions. It is less clear here. They seem at first like free indirect discourse, but then again, do fifteen-year-old girls think in typographical elements?

Each character in the story has his own idiosyncratic language, from the boy's Tourettic style of cursing to the kidnapper's faux-military way of thinking about his plan for the crime:

> The following bullet points remained in the decision matrix: take to side van door, shove in, follow in, tape wrists/mouth, hook to chain, make speech. He had the speech down cold. Had practiced it both in his head and on the recorder: *Calm your heart, darling, I know you're scared because you don't know me yet and didn't expect this today but give me a chance and you will see we will fly high. See I am putting the knife right over here and I don't expect I'll have to use it, right?*

In an interview, Saunders said he writes in "this thing that I can third-person ventriloquist, which is a kind of a standard third-person voice at first. And then, as quickly as I can, I try to get into the person's thoughts but then with the extra kicker of trying to really use/restrict myself to his or her diction." He told another interviewer that the goal is to "try to create a representation of consciousness that's durable and truthful, i.e., that accounts, somewhat, for all the strange, tiny, hard-to-articulate, instantaneous, unwilled things that actually go on in our minds in the course of a given day, or even a given moment." All told, pretty close to the definition of stream of consciousness that began this chapter, although in its high-spirited humor it's a very different approach from the modernists' solemnity.

Saunders's voice is perhaps the polar opposite of Russo's. You are aware of Saunders in just about every line of every story. No matter how diverse the characters, the subject of each story is, finally, storytelling itself: the ways we use narrative to construct our realities, even in our own most private thoughts. Paradoxically, although almost all of the observations are aligned with character, the author never vanishes inside the character. It would not suit Saunders's aim to do so, since one of his projects is to attempt to recast, or at least expand, the short story form.

And yet, just because Saunders makes his presence known does not mean that he's preening, unappealing, or dismissive of his characters. There's real tenderness in his work—the same kind of good-natured appreciation of ordinary people that we see in Russo. Look at how this section both has some fun with the girl's diction and frame of reference, while still taking her affection for people in her world, and thoughts about morality, no matter how half-baked, seriously:

> But as far as that rainbow idea? She believed that. People were amazing. Mom was awesome, Dad was awesome, her teachers worked so hard and had kids of their own, and some were even getting divorced, such as Mrs. Dees, but still always took time for their students. What she found especially inspiring about Mrs. Dees was that, even though Mr. Dees was cheating on Mrs. Dees with the lady who ran the bowling alley, Mrs. Dees was still teaching the best course ever in Ethics, posing such questions as: Can goodness win? Or do good people always get shafted, evil being more reckless? That last bit seemed to be Mrs. Dees taking a shot at the bowling-alley gal. But seriously! Is life

fun or scary? Are people good or bad? On the one hand, that clip of those gauntish pale bodies being steamrolled while fat German ladies looked on chomping gum. On the other hand, sometimes rural folks, even if their particular farms were on hills, stayed up late filling sandbags.

The passage is so delicious, it's hard not to keep quoting. Saunders basically states the theme of his story, *in the character's own diction.* He knows that you know that's what he's doing. Like the Salter passage we looked at in the last chapter, he's counting on your sophistication about the short story form.

The goal of the playful passage above is not to submerge you into the character's viewpoint, or at least not only that. The goal is not to let you forget for a moment that you're reading fiction, not experiencing "real life." Actually, I'm not even sure that Saunders believes in Real Life, as conventionally constituted. And yet—teenage girls do get kidnapped. The Holocaust was real, rural flooding is real. Can we feel for people and their situations, while still maintaining a posture of ebullient ironic detachment? Saunders hopes we can.

For all of their differences, all of the passages we've discussed in this chapter function by pulling the reader closer to the character to varying degrees—then calculatedly pulling back to make points or change direction. In the next chapter, we'll explore why that kind of distance is so difficult to achieve in first person, and why sometimes a writer might want to eliminate the distance—or at least appear to be eliminating it: in first person, different kinds of modulations are possible.

CHAPTER FIVE

FIRST PERSON

OBJECTS IN MIRRORS MAY BE CLOSER THAN THEY APPEAR

To a contemporary ear, narratives in first person feel more authentic and natural. You dispense with the starchy artifice of a mediating storyteller and hear the tale "straight from the horse's mouth"—the phrase hails from the track, meaning that as you place your bets, you're so near to the race that you're getting your tips from even better than the trainer, or the jockey. Who better to tell a story than the subject of the story?

But as is the case with every point of view we're examining, it's complicated, because the character is not, in fact, telling the story—the author is still the author—and because first-person accounts, no matter how straightforward and chatty, are rarely completely trustworthy.

Think of a first-person account as a selfie. A person taking her own photo can only get an arm's length (or selfie stick) away, so her image is by default too close for accuracy. There are going to be distortions and enhancements. There's how we want to be seen by others, and how we really are. In a first-person account, that schism—the distance between the character's self-image and the truth—becomes central to the drama.

When a third-person narrator calls attention to a character, it is an act of empathy or provocation: Join me in examining the life of this depressed housewife, self-made millionaire, war hero, or serial killer. When a first-person narrator addresses the reader himself, without an intermediary, a different calculus occurs. Since the address feels so confidential, the reader may feel comfortable and trusting, only to have the character's untrustworthiness sneak up as the tale progresses. Conversely, if the character is stridently unappealing, as so many first-person narrators are, the reader must immediately ask, Why are you telling me this? Why should I spend valuable time listening to you?—and then grow into empathy.

It's as if the character has written his own bio for a dating site. We know to be suspicious of people's professed height, weight, or age in dating profiles. A first-person narrator can't declare "I am very funny"; he has to simply *be* funny. A first-person narrator can't promise "I am brilliant and erudite," because he will merely sound stuffy and show-offy. Furthermore, a first-person narrator can't counteract the problem of seeming like a braggart by imploring, "If I may take just a moment of your time," because it's going to come off as false modesty, a humble brag.

Most irksomely, all first-person narrations confront the Too-Much-Information Problem. A third-person narrator who brings you through many more details than you need about his character's day, from first yawn through bedtime rituals, may be instructed by an exasperated reader, "Cut to the chase." But a first-person narrator guilty of TMI comes off as narcissistic. It's like being forced to march through someone else's vacation itinerary, look at close-ups of every creative cocktail and appetizer clotting someone else's Instagram feed.

These thorny issues of self-presentation become even more complex if the fiction is autobiographical, if the reader perceives the character as a stand-in for the author. A young male writer whose protagonist is a serial seducer, marching you through blow-by-blows of each conquest, is going to seem like he's engaging in some not-so-subtle wish fulfillment. So the author has to find a sneaky way to communicate some irony or psychological depth about his coxswain's adventures. A reader might also wonder, if the tale is in fact true, why the writer doesn't simply write nonfiction and present the facts directly, rather than fabricating a false distance. Is the author changing some names and facts to protect the innocent? Or changing them to skew the truth?

So a first-person narration is not, in fact, simple, direct, and authentic, but requires as many machinations and manipulations as a third-person account. A reader always looks behind the curtain of the narrator's declarations, and the reader's relationship to the writer is less sure-footed. This very instability is at the heart of the drama of first-person accounts.

There is one huge advantage of an eyewitness account, however, and that even if the reporting of some details is suspect or imperfect, the "I" saw the events unfold firsthand. As Walt Whitman declared, "I was the man, I suffered, I was there." In writing about a war, or a childhood in a dysfunctional family, the people who know the most details will be the most compelling. Julia Alvarez grew up under a dictatorship in the Dominican Republic, and her series of first-person accounts in *In the Time of the Butterflies* conjure the textures of the place with the force of someone who lived there:

> The four of us had to ask permission for everything: to walk to the fields to see the tobacco filling out; to go to the lagoon and dip our feet on a hot day; to stand in front of the store and pet the horses while the men loaded up their wagons with supplies.

We'll try this technique for examining point of view in more detail in Chapter 9, but one way to tell how appropriate first person is for an account is to try changing it in third person. Look how different even the short passage above becomes, and it's a passage with hardly any pronouns:

> The four of them had to ask permission for everything: to walk to the fields to see the tobacco filling out; to go to the lagoon to dip their feet on a hot day; to stand in front of the store and pet the horses while the men loaded up their wagons with supplies.

In third person, we sense the narrator's pride in vividly conjuring the setting. Look, the narrator seems to be alerting you, there's only one store! The DR was such an outback that even into the 1960s they didn't have cars or trucks! But the first-person narrator takes those facts as a given of her childhood. The long sentence full of semicolons seems rather formal in third person; in first person, we sense someone cramming in a series of quick, rich memories without making too big a deal of them.

It is worth noting that the *most* reliable first-person accounts are the ones in which the narrator is not the primary protagonist. Hamlet's claim that his father's ghost paid him a visit would make him delusional except that others saw the ghost, too, according to Hamlet's longtime consigliere, Horatio. Horatio is as sane, straightlaced, and reliable a witness as they come—he's a soldier. (That used to make one trustworthy.) Josef Conrad's *Heart of Darkness* is not narrated by Kurtz driven half-mad by the atrocities of colonialism he witnessed in the Congo but by a sailor who hears Marlow tell Kurtz's story. F. Scott Fitzgerald doesn't have Jay Gatsby tell his own rags-to-riches story or profess his love for Daisy Buchanan. The narrator of *The Great Gatsby* is neighbor Nick Carraway:

I'm inclined to reserve all judgments, a habit that has opened up many curious natures to me and also made me a victim of not a few veteran bores.... Most of the confidences were unsought—frequently I have feigned sleep, preoccupation, or a hostile levity when I realized by some unmistakable sign that an intimate revelation was quivering on the horizon; for the intimate revelations of young men, or at least the terms in which they express them, are usually plagiaristic and marred by obvious suppressions. Reserving judgment is a matter of infinite hope.

Notice how Carraway characterizes himself as listener in this passage. Reader, he says, I share your concern that this story will not be worthy of your time—but let me assure you, as someone who has endured a lot of stories, this is a good one.

The enormous, silent Indian who narrates Ken Kesey's *One Flew over the Cuckoo's Nest* is a patient at the mental institution with a mop, pretending to be a deaf mute. As a fly on the wall, he stays as far away as possible from Big Nurse, the cruel autocrat who rules the floor:

I let the mop push me back to the wall and smile and try to foul her equipment up as much as possible by not letting her see my eyes—they can't tell so much about you if you got your eyes closed.

He alerts us from the novel's first page about Big Nurse's cruelty. He's there when McMurphy is admitted and confesses that he's intrigued by how the new man will adjust:

One of these days I'll quit straining and let myself go completely, lose myself in the fog the way some of the other

Chronics have, but for the time being I'm interested in this new man—I want to see how he takes to the Group Meeting coming up.

Although first-person account can feel more contemporary—because the character can address us in a slangy, colloquial voice—it is by no means a new device. Nor is it a recent invention to demand that the reader take the narrator's words with a grain of salt. You know something right away about Tristram Shandy as the narrator of eighteenth-century novelist Laurence Sterne's *The Life and Opinions of Tristram Shandy: Gentleman* because Tristram starts the first chapter of his purported autobiography not with his birth but with his conception—if his mother hadn't interruptus'd the coitus to remind his father to wind the clock, Tristram believes he would have been a far better person:

> I tremble to think what a foundation had been laid for a thousand weaknesses both of body and mind, which no skill of the physician or the philosopher could ever afterwards have set thoroughly to rights.

Our narrator establishes himself as a kind of lovable buffoon. See, also, *The Adventures of Huckleberry Finn*:

> You don't know about me without you have read a book by the name of *The Adventures of Tom Sawyer*, but that ain't no matter. That book was made by Mr. Mark Twain, and he told the truth, mainly. There was things that he stretched, but mainly he told the truth.

What you have before you, Huckleberry declares, isn't a novel; it's the unadorned truth, and you know it's the truth because my grammar isn't fancy. Except you know that this is also in fact a novel, and Twain is writing this novel, too. The voice is saucy double-talk. Its use, in Twain, is mainly to establish a tone of playfulness toward the swashbuckling adventure. In most contemporary novels, the instability of voice becomes more fundamental to how the revelations unfold.

On unreliability in first person

Ford Madox Ford's *The Good Soldier: A Tale of Passion* is often used as the textbook example of unreliable narration. We looked at a series of marital infidelities in Chapter 3, but this one is narrated by the passive, cuckolded husband. Nine years before, he discovered that his wife had been carrying on for years with the gentleman half of their best double-dating couple friends, and our narrator was the only one who didn't know—even the Good Soldier's wife was fully in on it. He must now wonder whether his cluelessness about the affair (or, rather, affairs), and the suicide and madness that befall the secondary characters, amounts to a kind of collusion, or at least a spectacular failure. Except he won't really wonder that—he's too clueless. Here's novelist Julian Barnes discussing the novel's legendary first line:

> "This is the saddest story I have ever heard." What could
> be more simple and declaratory, a statement of such high
> plangency and enormous claim that the reader assumes it
> must be not just an impression, or even a powerful opinion,
> but a "fact"? Yet it is one of the most misleading first
> sentences in all fiction. This isn't—it cannot be—apparent at
> first reading, though if you were to go back and reread that
> line after finishing the first chapter, you would instantly
> see the falsity, instantly feel the floorboard creak beneath

your foot on that "heard." The narrator, an American called Dowell (he forgets to tell us his Christian name until nearly the end of the novel) has not "heard" the story at all. It's a story in which he has actively—and passively—participated, been in up to his ears, eyes, neck, heart and guts.... And if the second verb of the first sentence cannot be trusted, we must be prepared to treat every sentence with the same care and suspicion. We must prowl soft-footed through this text, alive for every board's moan and plaint.

We looked at how Henry James followed Isabel Archer as she made her grisly discovery about her husband's motives in *The Portrait of a Lady*. But Isabel is smart, sensitive, exquisitely sympathetic. Dowell is a bit of a dolt. So why choose him to narrate? Well, obviously, so we can see how a person in a marriage can badly miss the clues, and rationalize his own inadequacies. Dowell is the opposite of the pathologically jealous Othello. Listen to him justifying his own narrative method:

I have, I am aware, told this story in a very rambling way so that it may be difficult for anyone to find his path through what may be a sort of maze. I cannot help it. I have stuck to my idea of being in a country cottage with a silent listener, hearing between the gusts of the wind and amidst the noises of the distant sea the story as it comes. And, when one discusses an affair—a long, sad affair—one goes back, one goes forward. One remembers points that one has forgotten and one explains them all the more minutely since one recognizes that one has forgotten to mention them in their proper places and that one may have given, by omitting them, a false impression. I console myself with thinking that this is a real story and

that, after all, real stories are probably told best in the way
a person telling a story would tell them. They will then
seem most real.

Of course, we know that Ford, not Dowell, is actually composing
this novel, that this is no more a "real" story than Huckleberry's.
And yet the author himself seems to retreat, to let the *ars poetica* above actually belong to his storytelling character—at least
on a reader's first trip through the maze. It is essential to understanding both the events and the narrator that we believe in his
laconic befuddlement.

Such verisimilitude can be a goal of first-person narration,
but it is not always the goal. Case in point is the outrageously
named Humbert Humbert, the narrator of *Lolita*. From the
first page, Vladimir Nabokov enjoins us to wildly mistrust the
account, ostensibly written from prison, of his child molester
and murderer—page one actually being a fake "foreword" from
a "PhD" who provides some details "For the benefit of old-
fashioned readers who wish to follow the destinies of the 'real'
people behind the 'true' story." Humbert is not only a child
molester but snarky and supercilious: "You can always count on
a murderer for a fancy prose style," he taunts us "ladies and gentlemen of the jury." Nabokov's presence—his sense of linguistic
play, his rejection of traditional methods of literary interpretation, all that stuff about Theme and Motive we learned in high
school—is all over *Lolita*. Listen to Humbert relating his sojourn
in an institution after a breakdown:

> The reader will regret to learn that soon after my return
> to civilization I had another bout with insanity. . . . I owe
> my complete restoration to a discovery I made while being
> treated at that particular very expensive sanatorium. I

discovered there was an endless source of robust enjoyment in trifling with psychiatrists: cunningly leading them on; never letting them see that you know all the tricks of the trade; inventing for them elaborate dreams, pure classics in style (which make *them*, the dream-extortionists, dream and wake up shrieking); teasing them with fake "primal scenes"; and never allowing them the slightest glimpse of one's real sexual predicament. By bribing a nurse I won access to some files and discovered, with glee, cards calling me "potentially homosexual" and "totally impotent." The sport was so excellent, its results—in *my* case—so ruddy that I stayed on for a whole month after I was quite well (sleeping admirably and eating like a schoolgirl). And then I added another week just for the pleasure of taking on a powerful newcomer, a displaced (and, surely, deranged) celebrity, known for his knack of making patients believe they had witnessed their own conception.

Actually, Humbert's modus operandi as a child molester cleaves pretty closely to what we know about how such deviants operate, including his methods for grooming his victim. But for that kind of story, Nabokov insists, we could attend an academic lecture by the author of the deadly dull foreword. The surprise of *Lolita* is that, as we continue reading, confident that we know how to position ourselves in relation to our dastardly protagonist, we grow surprised by his genuine affection for Lolita and more drawn in by his obsession with her, no matter how regularly he undercuts sentiment with sarcasm. The novel bears her name, not Humbert's. So in a way, unappealing as Humbert is, he partially redeems himself by his genuine focus on another. Or at least keeps us from one-dimensional condemnation.

Such are the complexities of reading a work with an unreliable narrator. We've grown comfortable being addressed by an antihero like the one Fyodor Dostoevsky gives us in *Notes from Underground*, who begins by admitting:

> I am a sick man.... I am a spiteful man. I am an unattractive man. I think my liver is diseased. Then again, I don't know a thing about my illness; I'm not even sure what hurts....
>
> I used to be in the civil service. But no more. I was a nasty official. I was rude and took pleasure in it. After all, since I didn't accept bribes, at least I had to reward myself in some way. (That's a poor joke, but I won't cross it out. I wrote it thinking it would be very witty; but now, having realized that I merely wanted to show off disgracefully, I'll make a point of not crossing it out!)

The directness of the address is essential. The protagonist admits his flaws and biases, and invites the reader to judge him—then hopefully forgive him—as Junot Díaz does in "This Is How You Lose Her":

> I'm not a bad guy. I know how that sounds—defensive, unscrupulous—but it's true. I'm like everybody else: weak, full of mistakes, but basically good. Magda disagrees though. She considers me a typical Dominican male: a sucio, an asshole.

The narrator takes a tone of supplication with the reader similar to how he addresses the girlfriend whom he has alienated with his serial infidelities. The "you" in the title is instructive: he and the reader are in this together. "You know how it is," he cajoles, in the first paragraph.

But a reader can also delight in the confrontational "tell it like it is" nastiness of a character not afraid to offend, like the narrator of Claire Messud's *The Woman Upstairs*:

> How angry am I? You don't want to know. Nobody wants to know about *that*.
>
> I'm a good girl, I'm a nice girl. I'm a straight-A, strait-laced, good daughter, good career girl, and I never stole anybody's boyfriend and I never ran out on a girlfriend, and I put up with my parents' shit and my brother's shit, and I'm not a girl anyhow, I'm over forty fucking years old, and I'm good at my job and I'm great with kids and I held my mother's hand when she died, after four years of holding her hand while she was dying, and I speak to my father every day on the telephone—every day, mind you, and what kind of weather do you have on your side of the river, because here it's pretty gray and a bit muggy too? It was supposed to say "Great Artist" on my tombstone, but if I died right now it would say "such a good teacher/daughter/friend" instead; and what I really want to shout, and want in big letters on that grave, too, is FUCK YOU ALL.

The "you" here refers to the reader as surely as Díaz's address does. Nora Eldridge condemns us as part of those who have underestimated her, taken advantage of her. She double dares the reader to doubt or diss her. As slangy as the narration seems, you're aware that the writer has modeled the length and intensity of the sentences. But Messud alerts you that she's going to let Nora "own" the self-righteousness. The narrator gains sympathy by being in-your-face—by refusing to bend over backward to ingratiate.

This kind of apologia is a common device in first person. It's related to the voice-over in a movie, when Ferris Bueller in *Ferris*

Bueller's Day Off or Cher in *Clueless* or Henry Hill in *Goodfellas* turns to face the camera and pleads his case directly to the audience. Often these set-pieces are played for comedy, almost like stand-up routines. Here's part of the "cool girl" riff from Gillian Flynn's *Gone Girl*:

> Men always say that as *the* defining compliment, don't they? *She's a cool girl.* Being the Cool Girl means I am a hot, brilliant, funny woman who adores football, poker, dirty jokes, and burping, who plays video games, drinks cheap beer, loves threesomes and anal sex, and jams hot dogs and hamburgers into her mouth like she's hosting the world's biggest culinary gang bang while somehow maintaining a size 2, because Cool Girls are above all hot. Hot and understanding. Cool Girls never get angry; they only smile in a chagrined, loving manner and let their men do whatever they want. Go ahead, shit on me, I don't mind, I'm the Cool Girl. ....

Flynn gets her readers (at least her female readers) nodding in gleeful recognition, even though Amy Dunne will do some truly evil things over the course of *Gone Girl*. Amy is an antihero in the classic Humbert Humbert vein, euphorically unapologetic.

Flynn lets Nick Dunne, the husband, present his side of the story in first person as well, so Flynn offers dueling versions of the narrative of Amy's disappearance. And Nick makes similar plays for (male) sympathy: "One of us was always angry. Amy, usually." Why does Flynn choose to use competing first-person accounts rather than alternating third-person–aligned points of view, of the kind we discussed in our last chapter? Because this is a mystery, after all, a missing person case to be solved, and Flynn asks her readers to be the detectives, evaluating the evidence, the statements of the persons of interest, as a detective would. We do trust Flynn to be present in the unspooling of the clues, but we don't want her imposing her interpretation too heavily.

Reliable (or at least likeable) first-person narrators

A scan of the 2,256,909 (at current count) Goodreads reviews of *Gone Girl* shows that some readers are disgruntled about the characters being "unlikeable," and demand protagonists they can "root for." It's easy to mock such readers for their lack of sophistication, given the prevalence of villainous first-person narrators in contemporary literary fiction. But a first-person narrator in literary fiction can also be likeable and sympathetic. She can be witty, clever, modest, earnest, intense, frank, endearing, insightful, brave, inventive. She can confide in the reader, exhorting him to "pull up a chair." She can tell the reader an "inside story."

Margaret Atwood makes sure that we feel for Offred, the "handmaiden" in her dystopian *The Handmaid's Tale*. Offred is the woman, she suffers, she is there as all reproductively viable young women are commandeered as slaves to the ruling class in an oppressive, futuristic society, kept as prisoners, given the names of their captors, and forced to bear infertile rich women's babies:

> A chair, a table, a lamp. Above, on the white ceiling, a relief ornament in the shape of a wreath, and in the center of it a blank space, plastered over, like the place in a face where the eye has been taken out. There must have been a chandelier once. They've removed anything you could tie a rope to.
>
> On the wall above the chair, a picture, framed but with no glass: a print of flowers, blue irises, watercolor.

Flowers are still allowed. Does each of us have the same
print, the same chair, the same white curtains, I wonder?
Government issue?

The coolly observant tone, the stoical lack of self-pity, as Offred
presents the equivalent of an establishing shot, make her a wonderful narrator. She grounds the bizarre action, makes it believable. "I try not to think too much," she tells us. "Like other things
now, thought must be rationed. There's a lot that doesn't bear
thinking about. Thinking can hurt your chances, and I intend to
last." We want her to last, too.

Obviously Offred is not actually writing *The Handmaid's
Tale*. The dazzling breadth of imagination, the transposition
of current political realities to the future, belong to Atwood, as
we're reminded in the coda, which switches to an academic conference in an even more futuristic society, in which a scholar
talks about the laborious process by which he transcribed the
cassette tapes on which Offred told her story. But for the bulk
of the novel, Offred herself holds court in present tense. We
need to feel for her, one particular woman in that sea of identical
women dressed in red gowns and white hats.

The "I was there/it happened to me" approach is particularly
useful for futuristic or fantastical accounts. "My name is Kathy
H. I'm thirty-one years old, and I've been a carer now for over
eleven years." Those are the first two lines of *Never Let Me Go*,
Kazuo Ishiguro's novel about human clones raised and farmed
to be harvested for their organs until they "complete"—that is,
die—in some grim British future that looks pretty recogniz-
ably like the current country, with its rigid class systems. "That
sounds long enough, I know, but actually they want me to go
on another eight months," Kathy continues, and before you figure out what a carer is, or a "donor," you know that the clock is
ticking for poor Kathy. Her measured modesty, her affection for

her "classmates" at the famous clone school where she grew up, make her immensely appealing.

Similarly, you don't want anything bad to befall the innocent young narrator of Rachel Kushner's *The Flamethrowers* when she moves from Nevada to New York in the 1980s and falls into a decadent art scene. "There were tacit rules with these people, and all the people like them I later met: You weren't supposed to ask basic questions.... You pretended you knew, or didn't need to know." By admitting her naïveté, her outsider status, she establishes herself as trustworthy.

Which doesn't mean she knows everything. She can have blind spots—places where the reader sees a red flag that she doesn't. I was in an audience listening to Kushner read from *The Flamethrowers*, and when she got to this line, in which the character piles into the backseat of a car late at night with a bunch of people she met in a bar, and sits on the lap of a man who thus addresses her, everyone in the audience laughed:

"You do have a kind of tomboy allure, I might call it. Yeah."
Okay, I told myself. Something is starting to happen.

Kushner paused and said, mystified, "I don't know why people always laugh at that." An example of the kind of authorial "channeling" of character we discussed in the last chapter happening in first person: Kushner has invested in her character's good-natured naïveté—gone so all in that she doesn't even think to provide the obvious judgment. She can't, in first person. But the reader is able to see it.

A similar kind of sympathy—and ironic distance—happens in John Updike's story "A&P":

In walks these three girls in nothing but bathing suits.

A classic "pull-up-a-chair" first person: You can imagine the narrator, Sammy, casually relating this story to a bunch of other men. Another way of creating intimacy in first person is to imply that the narrator and the reader are part of the same group, share the same assumptions and values. High-schooler Sammy knows the objectifying way in which men are supposed to talk about women, and that's how he begins his story about the three girls in bathing suits coming into the small-town grocery store where he works. But Sammy is more "trying on" a male gaze than truly owning it. Look at this section, in which Sammy describes the ringleader of the three girls—and the reader learns things about Sammy that he isn't telling us directly:

> You never know how a girl's mind works (do you really think it's a mind in there or just a little buzz like a bee in a glass jar?) but you got the idea that she'd talked the other two into coming in here with her, and now she was showing them how to do it, walk slow and hold yourself straight.
>
> She had on a kind of dirty-pink—beige maybe, I don't know—bathing suit with a little nubble all over it and, what got me, the straps were down. They were off her shoulders looped loose around the cool tops of her arms, and I guess as a result the suit had slipped a little on her, so all around the top of the cloth there was this shining rim. If it hadn't been there you wouldn't have known there could have been anything whiter than those shoulders. With the straps pushed off, there was nothing between the top of the suit and the top of her head except just *her*, this clear bare plane of the top of her chest down from the shoulder bones like a dented sheet of metal tilted in the light. I mean, it was more than pretty.

That first line is how Sammy feels he should discuss women—
that leering, dismissive "locker-room talk"—and the rest of
the description how he really feels. It's a perceptive and poetic
description. There's more to Sammy than what he presents—
more even than he knows at this point in his young life.

(And if you don't buy it, if you don't believe that Sammy would
come up with the image of "a dented sheet of metal tilted in
the light" to describe the woman's shoulders, you are accusing
Updike of inserting himself into the narration too forcefully. A
writer who does that risks breaking the spell of first-person narration. I do accept that this creative young man could observe a
woman in this kind of detail, and I further believe that the business of learning *how* to observe is the business of his maturation
and the story. But to some of my feminist students, even the lyrical description would count as objectification.)

One of the best ways for a first-person narrator to establish
himself as likeable is to focus on people and things *other* than
himself—to seem to be open to the larger world, as Sammy is
in "A&P" about the girls and their subtle semaphores of social
class. Observations that seem kind and generous reflect well on
the teller. The narrator of Tillie Olsen's story "I Stand Here Ironing" starts with this declaration:

> I stand here ironing, and what you asked me moves
> tormented back and forth with the iron.
>
> I wish you could manage the time to come in and
> talk with me about your daughter. I'm sure you can help
> me understand her. She's a youngster who needs help and
> whom I'm deeply interested in helping.

Is the story about the troubled daughter, or the exhausted
mother at her ironing board, talking to the teacher or social

worker? Ultimately, it's about the mother—but we learn about her through how she discusses her daughter, with warmth, wonder, and affection:

> She was a beautiful baby. She blew shining bubbles of sound. She loved motion, loved light, loved color and music and textures. . . . She was a miracle to me, but when she was eight months old I had to leave her daytimes with the woman downstairs to whom she was no miracle at all, for I worked or looked for work and for Emily's father, who "could no longer endure" (he wrote in his good-bye note) "sharing want with us."

Here's a narrator with a very different voice—strident and confrontational—where Olson's is gentle and tentative. Hope Diamond, the narrator of Iris Owens's *Hope Diamond Refuses*, gains sympathy with her clever condemnation of her married lover:

> I could hardly wait for Leo Hermann to arrive in order to get rid of him. I was finished with the piker, and though I had no desire to see him, there were a couple of statements I preferred to make in person. I'd been refining and rehearsing my farewell address since he'd called from Kennedy to jubilantly announce his return, safe and sound, from a three-week safari in darkest Africa, of all places to convey his agoraphobic wife. In all fairness, it was Madame Hermann who insisted on the expedition, as she was compensating for twelve long years of being locked behind the guarded doors of their Central Park West fortress, which really, despite all the hand wringing, suited Leo like nobody's business. To have Mama confined to the house, eagerly awaiting her darling's reports on the state

of the world? It was perfect! And just when everyone in the Hermann family—Leo, the Crazy, and their twelve-year-old offspring, Cynthia, whose belated birth marked the onset of her mother's phobia—had adjusted to the situation, along came a new-style therapy, and in no time flat Muriel had confronted her fears and was out on the homicidal streets, hankering for wild beasts, guns, and a jungle or two to conquer.

It is immediately obvious that the narrator is by no means done with Leo. Despite the dismissive mockery, she's in deep, fascinated by how the Hermann family interacts. That fascination, and her buoyantly sharp humor, acts as a kind of tonic to her barking bitterness.

Humor is perhaps the most essential weapon in the first-person narrator's arsenal. It's a bulwark against the aforementioned trap of self-pity. Nora Ephron establishes her heroine's ability to laugh at herself from the first paragraph of *Heartburn*:

The first day I did not think it was funny. I didn't think it was funny the third day either, but I managed to make a little joke about it. "The most unfair thing about this whole business," I said, "is that I can't even date." Well, you had to be there, as they say, because when I put it down on paper it doesn't sound funny. But what made it funny (trust me) is the word "date," which when you say it out loud at the end of a sentence has a wonderful teenage quality, and since I'm not a teenager (okay, I'm thirty-eight), and since the reason I was hardly in a position to date on learning that my second husband had taken a lover was that I was seven months pregnant, I got a laugh on it, though for all I know my group was only laughing because they were trying to cheer me up. I needed cheering up.

Most readers diving into *Heartburn* would know that the work is semiautobiographical, based on Ephron's own contentious and very public divorce. Guessing which details of this roman à clef are real, and which are invented—separating Ephron from her protagonist—becomes part of the fun. Essential to the enjoyment is the knowledge that despite the elision of character and author, the obvious delight in the revenge of skewering the ex and his paramour with a bestseller, Ephron has enough distance, and self-awareness, not to get lost in her dismay. In both her fiction and her personal essays, Ephron assures her readers that, as critic Ariel Levy puts it, "humor always trumped loss." She is a master of the parenthetical aside: look how the ones above preempt any objections or doubts a reader might have. "Trust me," she says.

Temporal distance in first person

A first-person narrator can also establish trust by stating what he *doesn't* know, admitting to some flaws in his account or holes in his memory. "This was all a long time ago so I might have some of it wrong," Kathy H. admits, in talking about her childhood as a young British clone. And here is Patrick Modiano, in *Suspended Sentences*:

> I met Francis Jansen when I was nineteen, in the spring of 1964, and today I want to relate the little I know about him.

Look at the simplicity of the approach, the lack of grandstanding. I don't know *everything* about Jansen, the narrator admits, which paradoxically makes his account more believable, not less so. "Years have passed," the narrator says. "Rather than clouding the image of Capa and Jansen, they've had the opposite effect: the picture is much sharper in my memory now than it was that Spring."

This is *temporal distance*, and it's another important tool that a writer can use to establish reliability in a first-person narration. The tale is not being told in the heat of the moment, but with the benefit and cooling effect of hindsight. Here's novelist Josef Škvorecký in *The Bass Saxophone*, who, like his protagonist, lived through a series of invasions and occupations in his native Czechoslovakia:

> In the days when everything in life was fresh—because we were sixteen, seventeen—I used to blow tenor sax. Very poorly. Our band was called Red Music, which in fact was a misnomer, since the name had no political connotations: there was a band in Prague that called itself Blue Music and we, living in the Nazi Protectorate of Bohemia and Moravia, had no idea that in jazz blue is not a color, so we called ours Red. But if the name itself had no political connotations, our sweet, wild music did; for jazz was a sharp thorn in the sides of the power-hungry men, from Hitler to Brezhnev, who successively ruled in my native land.

Both Modiano and Škvorecký approach the reader unadorned, without any special supplication. There's wisdom in the simplicity. Both writers admit from the onset that there may be missing information or inaccuracies in the report—"what little I know," "the name was a misnomer"—which has the paradoxical effect of making the witness more reliable. Škvorecký is not "blowing his own horn," either—he admits he was no Miles Davis.

Temporal distance can result in trust for the writer as well as for the character. Not only has the writer bestowed the protagonist with the chance to speak for himself, showing some generosity and lack of hubris. But by default, temporal distance means that the writer knows the whole story, has plotted things out. In creative writing workshops, people often praise the "immediacy" of a piece of fiction—how well it places the reader "in scene"—but there's often an equal use for what Wordsworth called "emotion recollected in tranquility."

In writing four novels about two lifelong friends from Naples, Elena Ferrante employs many of the devices we've discussed here to gain sympathy for her first-person narrator, including temporal distance. Linu is in awe of her "dazzling" friend Lila, believes her courageous and whip smart, as you know from the title of the first novel, *My Brilliant Friend*. "I believed everything she told me," Linu says, characterizing herself as a trusting, generous person who is willing to play second fiddle. "Certainly I trained myself to accept readily Lila's superiority in everything," she says—while also implying that she will grow out of that trust over time as the competition between the two girls intensifies. Since the narrator is now an adult, we trust that she knows the whole arc of the story, thus can look back on those early days with more objectivity:

> I feel no nostalgia for our childhood: it was full of violence. Every sort of thing happened, at home and outside, every day, but I don't recall having ever thought that the life we had there was particularly bad. Life was like that, that's all.

It goes without saying that if you need to write four novels about two girls, with that level of detail about their lunch menus, Latin lessons, and crushes, you're presenting the friendship as mythic, full of tragedy and betrayal—think *Godfather*-movie epic. (Maybe it's an Italian thing.) It also goes without saying that, unlike with a narrator like Carraway in *The Great Gatsby*, the story has to involve the fate of the narrator as well as that of the brilliant friend. But the temporal distance is essential, otherwise we would less readily read page upon page about kids playing with dolls or competing for higher scores on a math test.

Temporal distance can be as important to a short story as it is to a novel. In her very short story "No One's a Mystery," Elizabeth Tallent's first-person narrator recounts an affair she had at age eighteen with a much older, married man. The entire story comprises a single conversation during a car ride, in which the couple banters about their future together. Except that they have no future. Although the narrator utters not a single phrase to tell us when and how the affair ended, we feel confident that it will, partly because we have some ideas about how the affairs of eighteen-year-olds with older, married men tend to go. ("No one's a mystery.") It's also clear that the young woman harbors little bitterness toward her lover—that she may, in fact, think about him and that brief affair in the arc of her life with a kind of fondness, or at least acceptance. All of this is achieved through the use of a simple, declarative past tense that assures us our narrator is no longer stuck in that car, shoved under the steering wheel to avoid detection and hiding with her head in Jack's lap as they pass his wife in her car, driving in the other direction. Think about how these details in the first paragraph—one of only two very brief sections in the brief story in exposition rather than dialogue—reveal a lot with a little:

> We'd been drinking tequila and the bottle was between his legs, resting up against his crotch, where the seam of his Levi's was bleached linen-white, though the Levi's were nearly new. I don't know why his Levi's always bleached like that, along the seams and at the knees. In a curve of cloth his zipper glinted, gold.

The description is evocatively sexual—almost comically so, that tequila bottle like an erection. It also does the double duty of calling attention to the cleverness of the story's construction: just as the narrator is crammed into a small space, the writer conjures the tale of the affair from an intentionally tiny, myopic vantage point. Like the Ozick story "The Shawl," Tallent self-consciously comments on the short story form as a vehicle to capture a whole life. This is a case where a reader is aware of both the writer and the narrator simultaneously; in fact, the two seem to bleed together seamlessly.

In her short fiction, Alice Munro is a master at deploying temporal distance to show how significant events shape a life, remaining with us but permuting in memory. "I barely remember that life," one first-person narrator tells us. "That is, I remember some parts of it clearly, but without the links you need to form a proper picture." Another narrator, recounting a major event in her family history, wonders:

> What could that dinner have been? I want to say curry, but maybe that's because my father didn't like curry, though he didn't make a fuss about it. . . . It occurs to me now that something might have gone wrong at the hospital that day, that somebody might have died who wasn't supposed to— perhaps the problem wasn't with the food at all.

Again, note the use of uncertainty as a way of establishing like-ability and reliability. But in Munro's stories, temporal distance is more than that. Time itself, the nature of memory, become central subjects. Each story is shaped so you believe you have gotten an account of an entire complex life, through a series of fractured but brilliant glimpses.

Not all grown-ups telling us about their pasts are older and wiser. Some are a bit, or more than a bit, befuddled. Here are some examples of fiction in which the retrospect fails to produce the expected wisdom and reliability.

Scott Spencer tells you right away that his narrator has never fully recovered from the events he recounts in *Endless Love*:

> When I was seventeen and in full obedience to my heart's most urgent commands, I stepped far from the pathway of normal life and in a moment's time ruined everything I loved—I loved so deeply, and when the love was interrupted, when the incorporeal body of love shrank back in terror and my own body was locked away, it was hard for others to believe that a life so new could suffer so irrevocably. But now, years have passed and the night of August 12, 1967, still divides my life.

Spencer tells the reader outright that the story will not be workaday. The narrator will go to prison. While the narrator is older now, and we assume somewhat different from his teenage self (no longer "in full obedience" to his emotions), he's still passionate about the events that he'll relate. Using temporal distance as a frame in this way has become a common method for establishing the tale's stakes.

In "The Cask of Amontillado," Edgar Allan Poe recounts the horrifying story of how a man buries his enemy alive. The diabolical murderer tells the tale himself. He leads the reader through the process by which he tricks the drunk Fortunato, who is decked out as a jester for a costume party, into following him deep into a catacomb, where cries for help cannot be heard. In the first paragraph, the narrator uses the phrase "You, who know so well the nature of my soul." To whom is the narrator speaking? A "you" always addresses the reader, at least in part, but in fact we do not know the nature of his soul—it's the first paragraph. An old friend? A priest? Is this a confession? Here's the last paragraph of the story (which I've already spoiled—Fortunato is bricked into his own tomb and buried alive):

No answer still. I thrust a torch through the remaining aperture and let it fall within. There came forth only a jingling of the bells. My heart grew sick; it was the dampness of the catacombs that made it so. I hasted to make an end of my labour. I forced the last stone into its position; I plastered it up. Against the new masonry I re-erected the old rampart of bones. For the half of a century no mortal has disturbed them. *In pace requiescat!*

Certainly this murderer is an unreliable narrator, and a deeply repulsive one. The story has the tone of letting us in on a secret, a device Poe used often in his first-person stories: see "The Fall of the House of Usher," in which our narrator recounts his visit to a doomed mansion and its half-mad inhabitants; or "The Purloined Letter," in which our narrator, pipe in hand, hears a rip-roaring story about the sneaky method by which his friend Dupin entrapped a blackmailer.

In the last example, however, the narrator is a safe distance from the action, with the attendant reliability. The fire roars; there is time for contemplation. In "The Cask of Amontillado," the narrator is the murderer himself. How are we to feel about his revelation? True, no one has discovered the crime, but the "rest in peace" that ends the story is surely ironic: not only would it have been far from a peaceful death for Fortunato, but the narrator seems haunted by his deed, as he is still vividly remembering all of the sights and sounds—or is he savoring the memory? Is this the narrator's own deathbed confession, is he asking for his own peaceful end? And how does the unnamed "you" react to hearing it? All of that information Poe intentionally omits, which gives the story a queasy, unfinished feeling, as if poor Fortunato were still weakly rattling his bells in that bricked-up tomb.

Self-conscious narrators

We've spoken at length about how first-person narratives can take advantage of directness to draw readers into a tale. But there's another strategy for first-person points of view in metafiction—fiction that calls attention to the artifice of its own construction. Some of these accounts don't give you a clear, believable, straightforward narrator at all, but instead make sure you know that the narrator is a creation, a distortion.

Nine of the novels by Philip Roth are narrated by a novelist, Nathan Zuckerman, often discussed as an alter-ego or doppelgänger for Roth himself. In some ways, Roth follows the formula we've outlined. His narrator focuses on someone *other than* himself, is intensely interested enough in that person to tell the other's entire story, which lends the narrative a sheen of truth and the narrator the good will of his sincere interest in others. In *The Human Stain*, Zuckerman, lonely in the Berkshires, befriends the charming, erudite, enigmatic Coleman Silk, and follows the retired dean's troubles at his college (involving accusations of racism) and troubled love affair with Faunia, a campus cleaning woman. Zuckerman admires Silk and bemoans the way Silk has been treated: fair enough. As someone whose prostate surgery has rendered him impotent, Zuckerman is understandably fascinated by Silk's erotic life: fair enough. However, whole long (very long) passages in *The Human Stain* report on incidents from Silk's past that Zuckerman simply could not have gotten, in that level of detail, from Silk himself. In fact, they sound exactly like third-person omniscient accounts. Then, to further complicate the narrative, Zuckerman also has access to the actions and thoughts of an array of other characters: Silk's girlfriend, the illiterate cleaning woman; that girlfriend's dangerous Vietnam vet ex-husband; the French professor who is

Silk's big adversary at Athena College. Furthermore, Zuckerman is the "fly on the wall" for whole long exchanges of dialogue
that he could not possibly have heard, either deep in Silk's past
or deep in his bedroom.

Far from making the report more reliable, as it would at first
appear, by inserting Zuckerman into the novel as interpreter and
reporter, Roth reminds you at almost every turn that the account
is *un*reliable. And that's important for this tale in which gossip,
slander, and misinformation about Silk abound, and which concerns an explosive secret about his identity that Silk has main-
tained throughout his life, and that Zuckerman learns very late.
Who tells the story, to whom—the central question of this book—
is also the central question of *The Human Stain*.

You can disagree about how convincingly Roth captures the
thoughts of this large cast of characters in free indirect discourse. You can also like or dislike the voice: Roth writes long,
ornate sentences and paragraphs, no doubt overly florid to
some. Certainly in creating characters from a large socioeconomic swath, Roth offers a portrait of not just these particular
people but of the whole American tapestry. The novel's ambition, its scope, belong not to Zuckerman but to Roth himself.
Roth knows you know that, and encourages you to remember
that proviso, no matter how fully he has brought the characters
to life:

> Only some three months later, when I learned the secret
> and began this book—the book he had asked me to write
> in the first place, but written not necessarily as he wanted
> it—did I understand the underpinnings of the pact between
> them: he had told her his whole story. Faunia alone knew
> how Coleman Silk had come about being himself. How do I
> know she knew? I don't. I couldn't know that either. I can't

know. Now that they're dead, nobody can know. For better or worse, I can only do what everyone does who thinks they know. I imagine. I am forced to imagine. It happens to be what I do for a living. It is my job. It's now all I do.

Needless to say, this kind of self-consciousness does not belong exclusively to Roth. We've discussed Nabokov. We should also acknowledge Jorge Luis Borges, whose mazes and puzzles are a model for much of the experimentation with form of writers to follow him—stories like "The Garden of Forking Paths," which discusses a labyrinth and is itself, in form, a labyrinth, in a collection of stories called *Labyrinths*. You don't read Borges to find out how people fall in and out of love, or anything daily about their lives—their jobs, what they had for breakfast. Fiction, Borges tells us, has a more essential goal, which is to force us to think epistemologically about the way we construct reality, to accept that *all* reality is a construction.

An important warning when making metafiction part of your own method: Nabokov, Borges, Roth, and many others got there first. The persona of Nathan Zuckerman, novelist, resonates partly because of the persona Roth built for himself as a novelist and memoirist over a career consisting of twenty-nine books. Doesn't mean you *can't* do it, but it means that the simple fact of doing it doesn't automatically make you a genius. You need to do it particularly well, or with a new slant, or for some interesting purpose.

Anyone who has taught freshman Composition knows how likely it is to get at least one paper a semester from a student coming up with the brilliant, original idea to make the topic of his paper how he can't think of a topic for his paper. Metafiction, badly executed, can feel a little like that. A reader may simply grumble "Been there, done that."

The talkers (who talk and talk)

On the spectrum of trustworthiness we've examined in this chapter, the most common in current fiction is the wantonly, exuberantly unreliable first-person narrator who goes on and on. It is no longer an oddity for the reader to discover, as a story progresses, that the narrator is stark raving mad, as we do when the wife confined to an attic bedroom to recover from "a temporary nervous depression" in Charlotte Perkins Gilman's "The Yellow Wallpaper" finally manages to claw off all of the wallpaper in the bedroom, to free the woman she believes is crouched and trapped behind the pattern. Often the speaker is both mad and bad. In first person, we witness such characters' voices and self-rationalizations, and like Humbert, the miscreants tend to be very chatty. So, we see less of the affectless existential languor that Albert Camus bestowed on his murderer in *The Stranger*, with its notorious opening—

> Mother died today. Or yesterday maybe, I don't know. I got a telegram from the home: "Mother deceased. Funeral tomorrow. Faithfully yours." That doesn't mean anything. Maybe it was yesterday.

—and more of the manic run-ons of a David Foster Wallace, supplemented by manic run-ons in footnotes.

Nabokov's influence cannot be overstated in the verbal play and the challenge for the reader to inhabit a less-than-orderly mind. If not homicidal, many contemporary first-person narrators are maimed in one way or another. The nameless narrator to whom Denis Johnson introduces us in his story "Car Crash While Hitchhiking" (addressed only as "Fuckhead") is so drug-addled that he stumbles away from the scene of an accident, handing off a baby:

A salesman who shared his liquor and steered while sleeping.... A Cherokee filled with bourbon.... A VW no more than a bubble of hashish fumes, captained by a college student...

And a family from Marshalltown who head-onned and killed forever a man driving west out of Bethany, Missouri...

I rose up sopping wet from sleeping under the pouring rain, and something less than conscious, thanks to the first three of the people I've already named—the salesman and the Indian and the student—all of whom had given me drugs. At the head of the entrance ramp I waited without hope of a ride. What was the point, even, of rolling up my sleeping bag when I was too wet to be let into anybody's car? I draped it around me like a cape. The downpour raked the asphalt and gurgled in the ruts. My thoughts zoomed pitifully. The traveling salesman had fed me pills that made the linings of my veins feel scraped-out. My jaw ached. I knew every raindrop by its name. I sensed everything before it happened. I knew a certain Oldsmobile would stop for me even before it slowed, and by the sweet voices of the family inside of it I knew we'd have an accident in the storm.

I didn't care. They said they'd take me all the way.

Although the story is told in the past tense, Johnson offers us no safety in the retrospect. Toward the end of the story, we're alerted that the narrator will later spend time in rehab, but we're not assured that it worked. There's no summing up or reconsideration of the Humbertian stance he takes in the hospital as he begins to hallucinate violently: "It's always been my tendency to lie to doctors, as if good health consisted only of the ability to fool them."

We should note that an author can employ a stream-of-consciousness technique in first person as well as in third person. For wildly meandering run-ons, it's hard to top the bravado of the fifty-odd-page, single-paragraph, single-sentence of first-person Molly Bloom cogitation that ends James Joyce's *Ulysses*. However, first-person narrators tend to be not so much trapped in their heads, as presenting themselves to an imaginary audience. Pleading their own cases directly to a listener or reader, as it were—as the narrator does in the story "Cold Snap" by Thom Jones. I won't quote the whole logorrhean first paragraph because it goes on for many pages, but here's part of the opening monologue:

> I just got back from Africa, where I was playing doctor to the natives, got hammered with a nasty case of malaria, and lost thirty pounds, but it was a manic episode I had that caused Global Aid to send me home. It was my worst attack to date, and on lithium I get such a bad case of psoriasis that I look like alligator man. You can take Tegretol for mania but it once wiped out my white count and almost killed me, so what I like to do when I get all revved up is skin-pop some morphine, which I had with me by the gallon over there and which will keep you calm—and, unlike booze, it's something I can keep under control. Although I must confess I lost my medical license in the States for substance abuse and ended up with Global Aid when the dust settled over that one . . .

Like Johnson, Jones had his own history with addiction. You certainly suspect that the author knows whereof he speaks about the cocktails used to treat depression. But are Jones and the narrator autobiographically joined at the hip? Even though the narrator speaks for himself, the author is very much visible in the plot and shape of the story: how Jones has a sister with even worse mental health problems becomes focal (thus making the narrator more sympathetic, in his solicitude for her); the way the "cold snap" of the weather is used as an extended metaphor for the character's mental states. In other words, you can simultaneously hear both the character and the writer breathing him into life. You are not completely trapped in the character's brain.

Same goes for Lionel, a young orphan with Tourette syndrome in Jonathan Lethem's *Motherless Brooklyn*:

> Context is everything. Dress me up and see. I'm a carnival barker, an auctioneer, a downtown performance artist, a speaker in tongues, a senator drunk on filibuster. *I've got Tourette's.* My mouth won't quit, though mostly I whisper or subvocalize like I'm reading aloud, my Adam's apple bobbing, jaw muscle beating like a miniature heart under my cheek, the noise suppressed, the words escaping silently, mere ghosts of themselves, husks empty of breath and tone. (If I were a Dick Tracy villain, I'd have to be Mumbles.) In this diminished form the words rush out of the cornucopia of my brain to course over the surface of the world, tickling reality like fingers on piano keys. Caressing, nudging.... Only— here's the rub—when they find too much perfection, when the surface is already buffed smooth ... then my little army rebels, breaks into stores.... That's when it comes, the urge to shout in the church, the nursery, the crowded movie house. It's an itch at first. Inconsequential. But that itch is soon a torrent behind a straining dam. Noah's flood. That itch is my whole life. Here it comes now. Cover your ears. Build an ark.
>
> "Eat me!" I scream.

Readers don't really believe for a second that the boy himself is crafting this tableau. The sentence rhythms and metaphors are jubilantly authorial. That's fine. We admire Lethem's words-manship. He is the king of his novel's domain. However, try the paragraph above in third person and it becomes irksome in its insistence on its own style. The first person buys the author more cover to show off his impressive authorial chops.

Some readers may find the passage too showboaty even in first person. You can shrug them off as dullards, but it is also true that if you choose to show off, you need to really impress. David Foster Wallace began using frenetic footnotes and end-notes decades ago, instead of the more routine parenthetical, so if a writer appears to be asking for praise for using them now, he doesn't seem cleverly postmodern. He seems derivative. And that is true even if the author insists that he has never read *Infinite Jest*. DFW is so famous that his initials alone are enough to identify him, as if he's an airport. Once you're that influential as a writer, your tones and trends are just in the air, like the flu.

If someone drafts a story he considers flat-out magnificent about a guy who eats an Oreo by carefully pulling it apart to expose the cream center and as he scrapes the cream off with his teeth he's plunged back into remembering his childhood, some-one is going to need to tell him about Proust's legendary mad-eleine. Doesn't matter if the writer himself has read Proust. The work is going to be derivative whether he knows the source or not. It's one of the many, many reasons why reading widely is so essential to a writer.

CHAPTER SIX

CHILDHOOD AND ANIMAL POINTS OF VIEW

OUT OF THE MOUTHS OF BABES (ALSO, DOGS AND CHIMPS)

It hurts to see a child get hurt. Children—innocent, defenseless—come with a baseline of built-in sympathy. Orphan them, give them violent drunks for fathers, send them out to fly kites in a war zone, and you're pretty much guaranteed that readers will fervently hope for their safety.

Furthermore, child narrators are less likely to provide the obvious judgments. A child narrator assures that we'll experience the blunt force of hardship firsthand, in visceral detail, rather than being lectured to. We also trust a child to see the unadorned truth, and to not be afraid to say so, unfiltered. It's a kid in the crowd who finally notes that the emperor has no clothes. As Atticus Finch asserts in *To Kill a Mockingbird*, to a child appalled at an all-White Southern jury's injustice and racism, "If you had been on that jury, son, and eleven other boys like you, Tom would be a free man."

Many of these accounts are written in first person. We can see the importance of temporal distance—whether or not the story is related from a point in the future, when the narrator is older and wiser—in how the writers approach the voices. We can also look at how details and tone can reinforce, or unproductively disrupt, the chosen viewpoint.

The classic way of telling a story about childhood is to set up the narrator as grown up, reminiscing. This is the structure of Harper Lee's *To Kill a Mockingbird* and Khaled Hosseini's *The Kite Runner*. With phrases like "when we were children" (Hosseini) or "when enough years had gone by to enable us to look back on them" (Lee), the temporal distance establishes trust in the narrators.

As significantly, the narrator telling a story of childhood in retrospect has the full arsenal of an adult vocabulary. We've discussed the ways that a writer can seem to merge or diverge from his protagonist. In the case of a child narrator in first person, we *know* a five- or ten- or even fourteen-year-old is not crafting the account. A writer creating a young child's point of view risks what is called faux-naif—when a writer is too obviously mimicking a child's voice, and has gone overboard by making the kid rather too adorably winsome and unsophisticated. That can be grating, and ring false. So in *To Kill a Mockingbird*, Scout recalls the trial that captivated her as a child many years later. Here, Scout watches her father question a witness:

> Atticus was proceeding amiably, as if he were involved in a title dispute. With his infinite capacity for calming turbulent seas, he could make a rape case as dry as a sermon. Gone was the terror in my mind of stale whiskey and barnyard smells, of sleepy-eyed sullen men, of a husky voice calling in the night, "Mr. Finch? They gone?" Our nightmare had gone with the daylight, everything would come out all right.

This is both adult *diction* ("amiably," "infinite capacity," "sullen") and adult *perception*. Scout may have felt calmer when her father began to question the witness, but she wouldn't have the arsenal of insight to note how fully he served as a bulwark against fear for her during the trial (and her childhood). The faux-naif formulation might sound something like this:

> Daddy stood up. I felt better already! He acted all calm and the guy before talked about all this scary stuff but Daddy didn't. . . .

On the other hand, a narrator looking back can express a childhood *perception* with an adult's *diction*. In "Gryphon," Charles Baxter sends a bizarre, tarot card-reading substitute teacher into a fourth-grade class. The first-person narrator is definitely remembering the event from an adult vantage point, since a fourth grader would never say "Since Five Oaks was a rural community, and in Michigan, the supply of substitute teachers was limited to the town's unemployed community college graduates, a pool of about four mothers." But while Baxter adds a note of an adult voice with that line, he also gives primacy to what the kid knows and feels, as he does here as well:

> Her fine, light hair had been done up in what I would learn years later was called a chignon, and she wore gold-rimmed glasses whose lenses seemed to have the slightest blue tint. Harold Knardahl, who sat across from me, whispered "Mars," and I nodded slowly, savoring the imminent weirdness of the day.

A fourth grader would notice the teacher's hairstyle, not the norm among the Michigan moms. But "what I would learn years later was called a chignon" saves Baxter from the faux-naif formulation of "her hair was all pulled back into this kind of weird knot on the back of her head." We also believe that the kid would be eager for a day that shatters the usual school routine. But he would not express it as "savoring the imminent weirdness of the day." And we don't want to hear him say "Boy, I thought, this will be weird!"

Not every tale requires a retrospective point of view. In "My Hard Bargain," Walter Kirn cleaves to both a boy's language and his perceptions as a family moves across the country:

> The whole way down to Phoenix in the car, my job was to tranquilize the dog. I hated the feeling. First I had to pack the pill in a crumbly wet lump of dog food, the way you'd hide a stone in a snowball. To get the pill in tight so it wouldn't fall out or show, I'd squeeze the lump in my fist for a second and sticky warm food juice would seep out between my knuckles. Then I had to climb over the seat and get my knees around Polly's neck, all without dropping the food. I had to grab her bottom jaw and push back the gums and tongue to work the lump in. She didn't like this a bit, and I had to be ready in case she snapped. I had to clamp my hands around her mouth and stay like that while she scratched the vinyl and tried her hardest to keep her throat shut. . . .

The diction here is decidedly the boy's own. So is the drama about the responsibility of his important, difficult job. Notice how Kirn keeps the words simple and short—"wet," "lump," "seep," "grab," "push"—without falling into cutesy. The delightful image of the stone in a snowball absolutely belongs to the boy. As we've discussed before, the image gains its power by relying on senses other than sight. We've got hard and soft, cold and warm, plus the sound of dog nails on car vinyl. Kirn never condescends to the boy's perceptions, even when they're wrong, as when the narrator tells his little brother "about attention spans, and how he hadn't developed one yet, which was fine if you lived in a town in Wisconsin where everyone knew your family and forgave you, but wouldn't be fine in an Arizona city."

Try the quote from "My Hard Bargain" above in present tense. Doesn't "The whole way down to Phoenix in the car, my job is . . ." sound mannered? You know that the writer is trying to achieve the fabled immediacy we seek from fiction, but our attention shifts distractingly to the writer, not the character—the kid isn't scribing during the ride. The very fact of a simple past tense bestows unstrained believability, and allows our identification to rest easily with the protagonist.

So, you might ask, what's wrong with a writer calling attention to his own voice while writing from the point of view of a child? The answer partly depends on your appreciation of self-consciousness in fiction. The fifteen-year-old narrator-turned-detective in Mark Haddon's *The Curious Incident of the Dog in the Night-Time* is autistic, brilliant, and prone to declarations like this:

My name is Christopher John Francis Boone. I know all the countries in the world and their capital cities and every prime number up to 7,057.

But also this:

But then everything was OK because Mother got a job on the till in a garden center and the doctor gave her pills to take every morning to stop her from feeling sad, except that sometimes they made her dizzy and she fell over if she stood up too fast. So we moved into a room in a big house that was made of red bricks. And the bed was in

> the same room as the kitchen and I didn't like it because
> it was small and the corridor was painted brown and there
> was a toilet and a bathroom that other people used and
> Mother had to clean it before I used it or I wouldn't use it
> and sometimes I wet myself because other people were in
> the bathroom. And the corridor outside the room smelled
> like gravy and the bleach they use to clean the toilets at
> school. And inside the room it smelled like socks and pine
> air freshener.

Children's accounts often use sentences with a pile of "and's" to indicate a child's breathless free association. It's true that children often talk like that in Real Life, but on the page, it can look annoyingly artificial; a little of it goes a long way. My threshold of tolerance for stagey run-ons is perhaps overly low. I also balk at the idea that a brilliant fifteen-year-old, even an autistic one, could not learn the terms "depression," "studio apartment," and "shared bath," and deploy them correctly in a sentence. To me this passage skirts dangerously close to faux-naif.

But of course Haddon aims to call attention to himself as author, rather than crafting a fully believable character. Haddon expects you to appreciate that he has created an unusual detective, as Jonathan Lethem did with the kid with Tourette's in *Motherless Brooklyn*. Generally characters of this sort will turn their handicap into a surprising advantage.

Another example of this more self-conscious approach is *Extremely Loud and Incredibly Close*, in which Jonathan Safran Foer takes on the first-person voice of a nine-year-old boy whose father has died in New York on 9/11, as the child sets out on a quest to find the lock that matches a key his father had hidden. Again, Oskar is exceptionally clever and creative, but it is also the cleverness and creativity of the author that we celebrate: we know that the point here is to discuss the grief and loss of 9/11 in an unusual way. From the first paragraph, we don't exactly believe that the boy is narrating:

> What about a teakettle? What if the spout opened and closed when the steam came out, so it would become a mouth, and it could whistle pretty melodies, or do Shakespeare, or just crack up with me? I could invent a teakettle that reads in Dad's voice, so I could fall asleep, or maybe a set of kettles that sings the chorus of "Yellow Submarine," which is a song by the Beatles, who I love, because entomology is one of my *raisons d'etre,* which is a French expression that I know. Another good thing is that I could train my anus to talk when I farted. If I wanted to be extremely hilarious, I'd train it to say, "Wasn't me!" every time I made an incredibly bad fart. And if I ever made an incredibly bad fart in the Hall of Mirrors, which is in Versailles, which is outside of Paris, which is in France, obviously, my anus would say, *"Ce n'etais pas moi!"*

Foer thrusts you right into the boy's oil-and-water mix of child-ishness and sophistication. He alerts you that misdirection will be the chosen direction as the child travels all over New York, looking for the lock his key opens. As we discussed in the last chapter, not all first-person narrations are strictly realistic. Part of Foer's *ars poetica* would be that conventional narrative is not adequate to cover the tragedy of 9/11, the way it fractured both families and reality.

In a way, Oskar's effort to place himself in not only the bor-oughs of New York but the world, within the range of those out-of-the blue mentions of France, is similar to this famous passage from *A Portrait of the Artist as a Young Man,* but look how different it is in third-person aligned, with James Joyce translating six-year-old Stephen Daedalus's thoughts:

> He opened the geography to study the lesson; but he could not learn the names of places in America. Still they were all different places that had different names. They were all in different countries and the countries were in continents and the continents were in the world and the world was in the universe.
>
> He turned to the flyleaf of the geography and read what he had written there: himself, his name and where he was.

Stephen Daedalus
Class of Elements
Clongowes Wood College
Sallins
County Kildare
Ireland
Europe
The World
The Universe

Try the same passage in first person. "I turned to the flyleaf of the geography and read what I had written there: myself, my name, and where I was." In first person, you get the sense that the boy is asking for praise for his cleverness, except you know that the author is actually asking for praise for his as well. Joyce credits his protagonist for the thought. The point both Joyce and Foer make is that it's an intimidatingly wide world out there, and our vantage points on that world are narrow. In both cases, the writers talk to the reader over their boys' heads.

Louise Erdrich could lecture you about the prevalence of rape on Indian reservations, but in *The Round House* she enmeshes you in seeing how rape embroils the community by filtering the story through the point of view of a thirteen-year-old boy whose mother becomes practically catatonic from the trauma—and he doesn't even really understand what rape is. He and his friends set out to find the perpetrator. On some level, you admire what a mesmerizing plot Erdrich has created. Her afterword cites Amnesty International statistics, but a novel is not, should not be, a political tract. She assures us that the first-person narrator is now an adult, with the power of retrospect:

> Much later, after I had gone into law and gone back and examined every document, every statement, relived every moment of that day and the days that followed. . . .

But most of the time, she cleaves to the events as they unfolded, helping you to sink deeply into the boy's helpless fear and confusion, and your eagerness for the mother to get well, for the rapist to get caught, for the boy to be out of danger, too.

Kids amid the rubble the bombs made

We've all seen photos of barefoot children setting up impromptu soccer games in the most desolate and dangerous settings. No matter how bad things get, they seem to find a way to play. Their stalwart insistence on remaining children in the worst circumstances keeps self-pity at bay. The impoverished, neglected toddler in Marilynne Robinson's *Lila* cherishes a doll fashioned from "a horse chestnut with a bit of cloth over it, tied with a string." That makes children an engaging choice of narrative center for tragic events. Often it's their very cheerfulness and resourcefulness that makes the account unexpected, and all the more poignant.

When we begin Imre Kertész's autobiographical novel, *Fatelessness*, we know from the flap copy that a Hungarian boy will be sent to Auschwitz. His beloved father had already been deported. But Kertész provides no foreboding tone as we approach the boy's arrival at the concentration camp. In fact, he volunteers to go, and Kertész takes the story step-by-step from the fourteen-year-old's curious, optimistic point of view, telling every detail of that period at a leisurely pace (including how the Jews had to scramble to acquire their yellow stars, "given that now there was a big shortage of yellow fabric"). The narrator's reactions are mostly clueless or wrong, as here, as he imagines what the labor camp will be like:

> What I could look forward to from working, though, was above all orderliness, employment, new impressions, and a bit of fun—all in all, a more sensible lifestyle more to my liking than the one here in Hungary, just as was being promised and as we boys, quite naturally, pictured it when we talked among ourselves, though alongside that it crossed my mind that this might also be a way to get to see a little bit of the world.

We're so used to the drama of the crowded boxcars being unloaded at Auschwitz among the shouting Germans and the barking shepherds that we're disarmed to learn that our narrator was able to take a little nap before arriving. We're so used to seeing the prisoners in their striped clothing that we're surprised at our narrator's reaction to them:

> It was quite a shock, for after all, this was the first time in my life that I had seen, up close at any rate, real convicts, in the striped duds of criminals, and with shaven skulls

in round caps. Naturally enough, I recoiled from them a little bit.

Here, the decision to *withhold* retrospect is essential to the novel's power. The narrator is mortally ill and feverishly hallucinating as the liberation of the camps approaches, but he doesn't know that he has to cling to life just a little longer. Unlike the boy, we suspect the liberating troops are close at hand; the rift between our knowledge, and the boy's, becomes part of the suspense.

Similarly, in *Room*, Emma Donoghue tells the story of a woman abducted and held prisoner as a sex slave from the point of view of a son, Jack, who was conceived in captivity and has grown up totally imprisoned there. The story is told in present tense and there is no retrospect whatsoever. Donoghue wants you to see how the five-year-old boy and his mother spend their days behind the steel door in the windowless, soundproofed eleven-by-eleven garden shed, as the mother strives to make a whole world for her child, protecting him from her rape visits by the man they call Old Nick (the kid hides in a wardrobe). Jack calls every object—Spoon, Thermostat, Chair, Skylight—in the shed that is his whole world by name, and voices sentiments like these:

> I jump onto Rocker to look at Watch, he says 07:14. I can skateboard on Rocker without holding onto her, and I *whee* back onto Duvet and I'm snowboarding instead.
>
> I choose Meltedy Spoon with the white all blobby on his handle where he leaned on the pan of boiling pasta by accident. Ma doesn't like Meltedy Spoon but he's my favorite because he's not the same.
>
> Silly Penis is always standing up in the morning, I push him down.

In her *New York Times* review of the novel, Aimee Bender says that "Jack's voice is one of the pure triumphs of the novel: in him, she has invented a child narrator who is one of the most engaging in years.... Donoghue rearranges language to evoke the sweetness of a child's learning without making him coy or overly darling." As with Foer, it isn't *just* an exercise in voice, because there's a page turner of a suspense story here: the mother plots a way for the child to escape, and when both of them are rescued, Jack confronts all of the things he has never seen. That's when faux-naif, at least for this reader, does inject a note of coyness. Here is Jack in the hospital:

> The floor's all shiny hard not like Floor, the walls are blue and more of them, it's too loud. There's persons everywhere not friends of mine. A thing like a spaceship all lit up with things inside all in their little squares like bags of chips and chocolate bars, I go look and try to touch but they're locked up in the glass.
>
> The woman is crying too, there's all black drips under her eyes, I wonder why her tears come out black. Her mouth is all blood color like women in TV. She has yellowy hair short but not all short and big gold knobs stuck in her ears above the hole.

With the benefit of retrospect, obviously, a narrator could know about vending machines, mascara, and earrings. But not in present tense. Once Donoghue decides to lock us into the child's consciousness with no temporal distance, she's stuck with these kinds of formulations, and there are other things she can't do as well. She can't tell us how the mother is feeling, except by having the child observe her, or having her (or doctors, or psychologists) quoted in dialogue. And that can produce some awkwardness, where we more hear the author communicating necessary information than we believe the kid has recorded, or even correctly heard, dialogue like this:

> [The doctor] and Ma talk about stuff like why she can't get to sleep, *tachycardia* and *re-experiencing*. "Try these, just one before bed," he says, writing something on his pad. "And anti-inflammatories might work better for your toothache. . . ."

On some level, any author who makes this unusual a choice in narrative perspective is, by default, calling attention to the choice, and thus to herself. Paradoxically, though, *Room* asks for our sympathies and attentions to rest solidly with the brave little boy. The story of the abducted woman, Donoghue might argue, has been told often enough, including by the real-life victims themselves.

Kids in third person

So far, this chapter has discussed only first-person points of view. Of course, there are still third-person tales of childhood. They tend to be in third-person limited, though, rather than third-person omniscient. Contemporary readers may be less willing to automatically bestow their pity on a character like Charles Dickens's sweet little crippled Tiny Tim Cratchit, WHO WILL DIE in *A Christmas Carol* and maybe not even get his Christmas goose unless Scrooge undergoes his change of heart. So third-person–aligned accounts of childhood in current fiction tend to be more hard-nosed and matter-of-fact, obviating any charge of sentimentality.

He's a little out of our age range for this chapter, but "the Kid" in Russell Banks's *Lost Memory of Skin* is a young man forced to live under a bridge with his pet iguana, wearing an ankle monitor as a registered sex offender, even though his "crime" was minor, he was entrapped, and he is still a virgin. Banks tracks the Kid's way of thinking pretty closely in free indirect discourse—

> It isn't like the Kid is locally famous for doing a good thing or a bad thing and even if people knew his real name it wouldn't change how they treat him unless they looked it up online which is not something he wants to encourage.

—but, as we've seen in countless examples, gets enough distance from the character to coax sympathy for the character, rather than take it as a given. Whatever your preconceptions about sex offenders, as Helen Schulman states in one review, this young man is "so lost and lonely and deprived it would take a heart of stone not to feel for him even at his most repulsive."

Banks also introduces contrasting older characters, deeply repulsive sex offenders. And of course we don't get the account of The Incident that landed our protagonist in this predicament in the first chapter. Discovering the exact nature of the young man's crime is one thing that keeps us turning the pages. The novel is not composed chronologically, and the childhood is not the whole story.

Same for *A Little Life*. One of the four men whose fates Hanya Yanagihara examines in her not-so-little novel (720 pages), the limping Jude with the mysterious past, grew up as an orphan raised by—and repeatedly tortured, raped, and pimped out by—pedophile monks in a monastery. We are given flashes of this fantastically ugly childhood as the novel progresses. We understand that Jude is trying to bury the trauma, so it makes sense that the memories of the atrocities would come to us as they surface for him, not in an orderly, chronological way.

But does the reader skip past the quite detailed accounts of law school, art openings, and dinner party chatter with the other three characters to get to the gritty center of Jude's trauma, the abuse that caused that limp, the things that made him bang his head against walls as a child, and now make him cut himself? There are interesting critical arguments about when such accounts bravely confront horrors, and when they become a kind of torture porn. Some readers, alas, will race to those parts. Other readers will recoil. Again we arrive at the slippery intentional fallacy: "Of course you recoil. You're meant to recoil. Rape and sex slavery are not nice things, and it's not my job to protect you from my protagonist's pain, in fact the opposite...." Again, I would contend that such critical disagreements always involve a discussion of point of view: about how close we are to the protagonist's experience, and whether we trust the author's accounts of those experiences to be empathetic rather than prurient.

Lions and tigers and bears, oh my (actually, mostly dogs and chimps)

When Bambi, Simba, Tramp, or Stuart Little prance into a story for children, the animals basically *are* children. They're winsomely innocent. They're spunky. They speak in squeaky voices. Such stories are almost always baldly allegorical, with heroes and villains and the triumph of good over evil, yay.

There are still adult readers left to cotton to the kind of unapologetic anthropomorphism of a *Watership Down*, Richard Adams's novel in which darling rabbits finally find a warren to call home. Orwell may have mocked that kind of plot when he wrote his satire *Animal Farm* in 1945, with its dictatorial pig named Napoleon, but sentimentality about animals is hardy and dependable. In the world of touching made-for-TV movies, dogs remain loyal to their boys—mostly boys and not girls—and the dogs are mostly golden retrievers or Labs (much to my dismay as a female and a greyhound person. *Represent*, greyhound bitches!).

In the world of contemporary literary fiction, however, authors with animal protagonists usually engage in some provocative play with point of view. None of that "Sure, I'm a day-old rabbit, but I already speak grammatical English." The voice in which the story is told becomes a major element.

When Paul Auster narrates his novel *Timbuktu* in a third-person point of view aligned with a dog, Mr. Bones, he has some fun with how wantonly the writing (well, any writing) *can't* be a dog's, even if the ideation mostly claims to be. Here Mr. Bones contemplates the health of his homeless owner:

> What was a poor dog to do? Mr. Bones had been with Willy since his earliest days as a pup, and by now it was next to impossible for him to imagine a world that did not have his master in it . . . it was more than just love or devotion that caused Mr. Bones to dread what was coming. It was pure ontological terror.

With whom are we aligned in this passage, Auster or Mr. Bones? Auster asks us to simultaneously hear both the dog (unlikely to use the term "ontological," well, *ruff!*, unlikely to use any term at all) and his dog whisperer. Not all readers will take the bait. In a review, Adam Begley complains that "Auster's doggy voice (and the whole manner of the implied author) is faux-naif. . . . Auster can't quite dodge the silliness inherent in transcribing canine cogitation."

As if aware of this pitfall, in *The Evolution of Bruno Little-more*, Benjamin Hale doesn't pretend to translate for his chimpanzee, but goes all in on the chimp as impossible teller of his own story:

> My name is Bruno Littlemore: Bruno I was given, Littlemore I gave myself, and with some prodding I have finally decided to give this undeserving and spiritually diseased world the generous gift of my memoirs. I give this gift with the aim and hope that they will enlighten, enchant, forewarn, instruct, and perchance even entertain.

"Perchance?" The first-person voice here is comically, self-consciously old-fashioned, in the tone of, say, Jean-Jacques Rousseau's *Confessions*. It definitely doesn't belong to a chimp, and assumes the reader knows as much from the onset. Hale has done his research, and the novel provides enlightenment on the subject of what we talk about when we talk about simian cognition. But Hale gives his chimp a rip-roaring, old-fashioned adventure story as well as an old-fashioned voice, including a hot-and-heavy love affair with his handler—one of my two favorite fictional interspecies romances (along with Ted Mooney's *Easy Travel to Other Planets*, about an affair between a woman and a very sexy dolphin).

The tone of Hale's novel is dauntlessly high-spirited. What if you're after a more somber philosophical consideration of animal cognition, and especially about the ethical issues involved in our treatment of animals?

In *A Beautiful Truth*, Colin McAdam introduces us to Looee, a chimp lovingly raised by a childless couple, who later surrender him to a primate center for biomedical experiments. McAdam uses a series of third-person aligned points of view for both the humans and the chimps, and he attempts to accurately represent how a chimp taught sign language might think and express himself. So there are free indirect sections like this, as Looee is trained to understand words:

> Dave taught them colours, and colours were the way you could describe the pictures that can't be pictured.
> Mama liked red.
> Dave would talk through the machine and hold up the fire truck.
> ? Mama what colour-of fire-truck.
> Red color-of that.
> ? Mama what colour-of lipstick.
> Red.

But a whole novel full of that kind of passage would grate (even as the chimps get smarter as the novel progresses—the change in their cognition and ability to express themselves is one thing McAdam tracks), so he also does some translation of his chimp's thoughts (Judy and Walt are his human "parents"):

> It was Looee's first summer that he could take to the next summer—his first real season of memory. He could look down at Judy from his tree and choose not to run to her, knowing now that he could do so later. And later he could sit on the porch and clean Walt, suck the salt out of his jean cuffs and think back to being in the tree. Memories were blue and yellow sheets hanging from the line (don't pull those down please Looee): fixed but restless colours blowing softly across his face. Memories made him pound on the porch, wanting to make more. He wanted to roll through all those flowers.

As in writing from childhood points of view, the senses become sharper, more primary—taste, texture. Later, McAdam captures the horrors of the caged primates from their points of view. Be forewarned, this is a much more painful look at animal cruelty than *Planet of the Apes*. It's enough to turn the stomach of one of the novel's research scientists, who realizes that "The remoteness of the researchers allowed them to think of the chimpanzees as a crop of data, numbered bodies to be harvested for information. Dr. Meijer had to know them by name as well as number."

Is there as much authorial *hubris* in this series of closely aligned points of view as in the Auster and Hale examples? I'd argue not. I'd argue that any convincing closely aligned point of view encourages us to focus more intently on the characters, rather than their creator (emphasis on *convincing*). Here, the primary protagonist happens to be a primate. Sure, on some level the writer wants you to admire the depth of his empathy and imagination. But the goal of the writer in a closely aligned point of view is intense identification.

Karen Joy Fowler, too, clearly researched primate centers to write *We Are All Completely Beside Ourselves*, and her setup bears similarities to the McAdams's: a chimp, lovingly raised in a family, must later endure the horrors of medical experimentation. But Fowler tells the story from the point of view of the chimp's human "sister"—or at least that's how the novel's narrator, Rosemary Cooke, thought of her beloved hairy older sibling Fern, once the chimp is gone:

> I felt her loss in a powerfully physical way. I missed her smell and the sticky wet of her breath on my neck. I missed her fingers scratching through my hair. We sat next to each other, lay across from each other, pushed, pulled, stroked, and struck each other a hundred times a day and I suffered the deprivation of this. It was an ache, a hunger on the surface of my skin.

Fowler declines to speak for the chimp. Her fierce love of Fern makes Rosemary likeable and trustworthy as a character. Like many of the accounts of childhood we've discussed in this chapter, the narrator is honest that the tale is a later (re)construction, with holes, blind spots, and embellishments:

> My father would surely want me to point out that, at five, I was still in Jean Piaget's preoperational phase with regard to cognitive thinking and emotional development. He would want you to understand that I am undoubtedly, from my more mature perspective, imposing a logical framework on my understanding of events that didn't exist at the time. Emotions in the preoperational stage are dichotomous and extreme.
>
> Consider it said.

The voice here is wry and casual. Fowler doesn't plunge us into haunting heartbreak all at once. She allows the full condemnation of the experimentation to sneak up on the reader. The reader, like Rosemary, can only bear to look directly for so long.

There are some daring moves in terms of construction in *All of Us Are Completely Beside Ourselves*: the narrative toggles in time, and the narrator is quite forthright about the fact that she's shaping the story ("The impulse to write a book appears to run like a fever through those of us who've lived with apes"). Fowler actually manages to let us forget for large swaths of time that she, not Rosemary, is penning this tale. So, remarkably, it's a self-conscious work of fiction that does not loudly present itself as self-conscious. And while Fern's fate is central to the book, Rosemary's fate is of equal, parallel importance. Without lecturing us, Fowler leads us to see that "in the phrase *human being*, the word *being* is much more important than the word *human*."

None of the three primates we've examined is childish or winsome or twee. They grow older and wiser. They manifest a full, distinctly nonanthropomorphic complement of insights and social interactions. So despite the differences in approach, the authors are all decidedly non-Disney in their respect for animal cognition.

We have not discussed the hyperarticulate bear of Yoko Tawada's *Memoirs of a Polar Bear*; or the sensitive, tortured elephants in Sara Gruen's *Water for Elephants*; or the many cats in the work of Haruki Murakami. Or the mouse (at age three, mother to more than three hundred offspring) in *Strangers and Cousins*, whose perceptions Leah Hager Cohen translates ("her whiskers touched moonlight"). But I hope we've covered a spectrum of approaches to representing animal consciousness, from anthropomorphism to—well, zoomorphism. In choosing an animal protagonist, a writer asks us to pay particular attention to the point of view as a central element of the tale. And that's true for every unusual point of view we'll consider in the next chapter as well.

CHAPTER SEVEN

NARRATIVE INVENTIONS

"YOU," "WE," EPISTOLARY, AND OTHER HIGH JINKS

We have repeatedly asked in these pages whether your primary relationship as a reader is with the writer or the protagonist. And we've discussed a strong authorial presence as the more blatantly egocentric choice—the author declaring "Yoo hoo! Love me, not that character over yonder!" But if we grant that all writing is *a priori* attention seeking, there's another way to look at writers with strong individual voices, and that is to grant that once writers deign to occupy your time, they want to make sure they've earned the right. These writers are like chefs who say, "If you're going out for dinner, you want to be served something you can't cook at home. My dishes are so unique you won't even know what all the ingredients are, and would never think to put them together the way I do." The writers' originality, their earnest desire to surprise and delight, can thus be seen as acts of generosity. They're working hard, but for no other reason than to keep your boredom at bay, facilitate your profound enjoyment.

Of course, there are nights on which you just want mac and cheese. On such nights, these points of view are not for you, and perhaps you would like to remark that a great red sauce, or a perfectly grilled fish, also take skill. It's not easy to create the illusion of simplicity. Everything must be done just right—no tricks, no frills to distract from mistakes or weaknesses. Nevertheless, in this chapter we'll look at a compendium of unusual choices that call attention to the authors' chance taking. Let's label them the anticomfort food, the *nouvelle cuisine*, of POVs.

Second person

Using "you" is not new. You know second person and have seen it in fiction before. You either like it, or you don't, kind of like foie gras, or wheat germ, or—maybe you'd better knock it off with the cooking metaphors. (Or maybe I should.)

The ostensible goal of second person is to forcefully shove your feet into the protagonist's shoes, creating a fierce identification. The beginning of Jay McInerney's *Bright Lights, Big City*:

> You are not the kind of guy who would be at a place like this at this time of the morning. But here you are, and you cannot say that the terrain is entirely unfamiliar, although the details are fuzzy. You are at a nightclub talking to a girl with a shaved head. The club is either Heartbreak or the Lizard Lounge. All might come clear if you could just slip into the bathroom and do a little more Bolivian Marching Powder. Then again, it might not . . .

Second person is like playing a video game. You insert yourself into the action and are filmed from behind as you plunge onto the court, or into battle, or, in the case above, right into the protagonist's bleary, drugged state of mind.

In workshops, second person is often said to produce "immediacy." It's surely true that McInerney's opening thrusts the reader right into the club. However, by forcing the reader to *be* the protagonist, second person is also paradoxically alienating and distancing. I am certainly *not* the kind of guy who would be at a place like the one above, for starters because I am not a guy. So, later, if our fella is going to bed a woman he picks up at that club, I'm going to feel decidedly strange.

Second person actually works best when it demands that you engage in an activity that is off-putting, even criminal, that takes you far outside of your comfort zone. It is not, in fact, identification that's asked from you, but an uncomfortable disassociation.

In his story "Shopgirls," Frederick Barthelme makes "you" into a creepy stalker who likes to go to the department store at his local mall and spy on the hot female staff. He does this surreptitiously, but alas, the women have noticed, and call him on it:

> "I don't know Jenny," you say. But when the girl tugs at your arm and points over the tops of the displays toward the shoe section, you don't need to look. You know the girl she's talking about, the tall girl with the very short hair who works in Shoes. You trailed her around the store and around the mall for a few weeks, watching her shop, watching her eat, watching her sit by the garishly painted fountain in the center of the mall—you trailed her until you got worried. Then you stayed out of the mall for nearly two weeks, and when you returned you carefully avoided Shoes. That's not entirely true. Once you spent half the morning going up and down the escalator so that you could see her over the thickly forested juniors' casual wear.

In the movie *Peeping Tom*, a killer likes to film his victims while he murders them, so he has a record of their terror as they die (by a spike attached to his camera, which sometimes, ghoulishly, punctures their eyes). Because we see the footage unspool during the murders, we're forced to identify with the murderer. The killer isn't the only Peeping Tom. We're complicit. Though the deed isn't as horrific, the second person in "Shopgirls" works in a similar way. When a group of girls corner the stalker above and take him to lunch, they quiz him about his motives—"The others think you're crazy," one salesgirl tells him. "I said you were just lonely"—the "you" in the story is alarmed to find himself permuted from the watcher into the watched.

In fact, this self-consciousness about watching is often central to second-person narratives. In *The Diver's Clothes Lie Empty*, Vendela Vida sends her "you" to Casablanca. "Your" backpack is stolen while you're checking into your hotel. Without cash, passport, or credit card in a country where you don't speak the language, you'd be out of luck—despite the police blithely giving you a backpack and credit cards that aren't yours, but certainly those cards will be canceled—until you're commissioned to work as the stand-in for a famous actress on a film set. In her wig, you do look a little like the star. Stand-in turns out to be not the strangest alternate identity you've taken on in your life. You've also served as a surrogate to have your twin sister's baby. In Casablanca, you give the baby's name as your own.

Try the plot summary above in third person ("Her backpack is stolen while she's checking into her hotel") or first ("My backpack is stolen..."). In one sense, much easier to follow—but takes away much of the sense of queasy uncertainty upon which the novel depends. Vida urges the reader to plunge into the indeterminacy:

> You arrived in Casablanca on the same flight over a week ago. Or maybe you didn't.... You have not been yourself lately.

The novel is an unsettling, often funny meditation on the hollowness and malleability of identity. Second person is ideally suited for the theme.

One thing that writers employing second person need to be careful about is too many subject-verb constructions. In a way, it's inevitable—"You watch," Vida writes, "You rewind," "You hear," "You turn back around"—but a close reading of her paragraphs reveals how carefully she varies sentence structure and also sentence length to avoid a glut of simple short sentences starting with "you" and then "verb." This is good advice for *all* writing, actually, except if you're entering the annual International Imitation Hemingway competition. But it's particularly important in second person, which can wind up feeling artificial in a silly, simplistic Dick-run-go-Jane-go kind of way. We see the same thing in the paragraph from Barthelme above: only two of the seven sentences start with "you." Second person is so artificial to begin with that you don't want to risk overkill. It's actually easier to compose a short story than a whole novel in second person for this reason.

"We" and communal points of view

A narrator positing himself as part of a group claims to speak on behalf of that group. All for one and one for all. In first-person plural, as this point of view is called, the "I" is like a union member on the factory floor, one of the gang—thus gains the same kind of good will and reliability we discussed in our chapter on first person, but more so. The best-known example of first-person plural is William Faulkner's story "A Rose for Emily," in which the narrator relates a Southern town's reaction to the death of its richest citizen. Gossip and conjecture about the old lady abound: What happened to her beau? Did she kill herself?

Almost always, the plot of a work in first-person plural involves the eventual differentiation of the speaker from the mass of others. And almost always, thematically, the fiction will consider questions of individual versus group identity. Little by little, the resolution of the plot involves the primary protagonist separating from the others in his "pack."

In Karen Russell's story "St. Lucy's Home for Girls Raised by Wolves," it's a literal pack: fifteen half-wolf, half-human girls, offspring of werewolves. "Our parents wanted something better for us; they wanted us to get braces, use towels, be fully bilingual. When the nuns showed up, our parents couldn't refuse their offer. The nuns, they said, would make us naturalized citizens of human society." Needless to say, some of the pack are more successful at becoming "purebred girls" than others. The narrator, one of the alpha wolves, tracks how the group treats Mirabella, the sister having the hardest time adjusting to human life.

Three brothers in *We the Animals*, by Justin Torres, grow up poor in Brooklyn, with an abusive father and an unstable mother. They almost never have adult supervision, and often don't have food. The narrator, the youngest boy, feels a great tribal loyalty to his family, erratic and dangerous as it often is. Torres's opening paragraph:

> We wanted more. We knocked the butt ends of our forks against the table, tapped our spoons against our empty bowls; we were hungry. We wanted more volume, more riots. We turned up the knob on the TV until our ears ached with the shouts of angry men. We wanted more music on the radio; we wanted beats; we wanted rock. We wanted muscles on our skinny arms. We had bird bones, hollow and light, and we wanted more density, more weight. We were six snatching hands, six stomping feet; we were brothers, boys, three little kings locked in a feud for more.

"When we were brothers, we were Musketeers," Torres says. But much as they cherish the moments when their parents are getting along, when their household is functioning—the rare times when "My brothers and I were clean and fed and not afraid of growing up"—they begin to pull apart, to respond to the hardship of their childhood in different ways.

Then We Came to the End, by Joshua Ferris, uses the collective point of view to examine workplace culture. The "we" are employees of a Chicago ad agency, amusing themselves with gossip and practical jokes in between generating billable hours—and then the layoffs begin. Characters so numerous that we can't believe we can remember all of their names and quirks send paranoid e-mails and meet in the employee lounge (sometimes there are bagels!) to trade the latest news until, one by one, they are forced to leave the building with the box of sad items from their cubicles. This mostly satirical look at white-collar jobs asks how much the workplace squashes individual identity:

> Good thing we never invited Joe Pope to join the agency softball team. Didn't like groups—well, what did he think he was doing working at an advertising agency? We had news for him. He was one of us whether he liked it or not. He came in at the same time every morning, he was expected at the same meetings, he had the same deadlines as the rest of us. And what an odd profession for him, advertising, where the whole point was to seduce a better portion of the people into buying your product, wearing your brand, driving your car, joining your group. Talk about a guy who just didn't get it.

It's tricky to maintain a whole novel in this kind of voice. The joke risks wearing thin. Ferris varies the first-person plural to avoid repetition, by allowing individual characters to deliver long set pieces of dialogue in first person, so he can get a range of voices. He also has characters telling *other* characters' stories, so that the reliability, or lack thereof, becomes a central question. ("But perhaps that paints too one-sided a portrait of Martin.")

Part of the suspense, of course, is whether our narrator will keep his job. It's a tongue-in-cheek mystery of the Agatha Christie's *And Then There Were None* or survival show ilk, in which each chapter knocks another character off the island. Ferris knows that you know this kind of plot, and knows that you know he's using it in an ironic way, updating it to tell a more substantive story in a different setting.

Jeffrey Eugenides adopts first-person plural to tell the mysterious story of the five Lisbon sisters in *The Virgin Suicides*. Over one year in the suburbs, all five sisters will commit suicide. But why? That question haunts a group of neighborhood boys in "our town," one of whom narrates the novel. "Everyone had a theory as to why [Cecilia] tried to kill herself," he tells us. The boys move in a barely differentiated adolescent mass as they analyze the evidence:

> Cecilia's diary begins a year and a half before her suicide. Many people felt the illuminated pages constituted a hieroglyphics of unreadable despair, though the pictures looked cheerful for the most part. The diary had a lock, but David Barker, who got it from Skip Ortega, the plumber's assistant, told us that Skip had found the diary next to the toilet in the master bathroom, its lock already jimmied as though Mr. and Mrs. Lisbon had been reading it themselves. Tim Winer, the brain, insisted on examining the diary ...

Why choose the group identity as the narrative stance? Eugenides stresses that the boys are typical teenage boys, and the

Lisbon sisters are typical teenage girls—until they aren't. The "evidence" marshaled to try to penetrate the girls' state of mind includes not just spying on them with binoculars but notes from a psychiatrist from "many articles he hoped to publish," torn-out pages from yearbooks identified as "Exhibit #4," and even lists of groceries from a Lisbon family delivery. We'll talk about the use of such "documents" shortly. Obviously Eugenides uses the evidence the boys are able to obtain not to make a convincing legal case or psychiatric case study but pretty much the opposite:

> We'd like to tell you with authority what it was like inside the Lisbon house, or what the girls felt like being imprisoned in it. Sometimes, drained by this investigation, we long for some shred of evidence, some Rosetta stone that would explain the girls at last. But even though that winter was certainly not a happy one, little more can be averred.

This is a case where the unusual choice of the first-person plural assures the novel's originality in considering adolescence, and adolescent groupthink. The more expected choice would be to narrate from the point of view of one of the sisters—one of the last ones to kill herself, for the obvious reasons. Or you could narrate from the point of view of one boy who loved one sister. Such a boy is indeed present here, just not as a primary protagonist. Novels, Eugenides suggests, can't solve all mysteries about human experience. All tales are merely "pieces of the puzzle," not the key to the lock.

Whiplashing points of view

We've already discussed omniscient points of view that present a series of sections from different characters' third-person–aligned perspectives. The more varied the characters, and the larger the tableaux, the clearer justification there is for the author to challenge the reader by engaging in this kind of variation. In *Station Eleven*, Emily St. John Mandel includes sections in third-person omniscient and third-person aligned from a host of characters, as well as found documents, letters, ephemera, lists, and even transcripts of interviews. Given that *Station Eleven* concerns an apocalyptic pandemic that has wiped out most of the world's population, these kinds of frantic, uninflected transitions make sense, and Mandel keeps her commentary to a minimum as she surveys a world where familiar pleasures have vanished along with electricity:

> No more diving into pools of chlorinated water lit green from below. No more ball games played out under floodlights. No more porch lights with moths fluttering on summer nights. No more trains running under the surface of cities on the dazzling power of the electric third rail. No more cities. No more films, except rarely, except with a generator drowning out half the dialogue, and only then for the first little while until the fuel for the generators ran out, because automobile gas goes stale after two or three years. Aviation gas lasts longer, but it was difficult to come by.

On the simplest level, we've become so much more supple with lightning-quick transitions—in fact we won't quite sit still for a long period of setting up and breaking down between acts. So this style of wide-ranging omniscience seems more camera ready and suits a Twitter-speed mood better. And of course Mandell expects her readers to notice the ironic contrast between her access to all of her disparate characters, when they no longer have phones, email, or snail mail to communicate with each other.

In many cases, sections can switch between third and first person. This used to be considered absolutely unacceptable, a line in the sand that a fiction writer could not cross, but the rules have considerably loosened. In *Fleishman Is in Trouble*, Taffy Brodesser-Akner alternates sections considering the fate of newly single Toby Fleishman (in third-person aligned), whose wife has suddenly vanished and left him with their two small children, as well as an array of hot new sex partners; and Libby, an old female friend of Toby's (in first person), reporting on him, but also having her own marital problems; then Libby reports on the missing wife Rachel, her motives and motions, but maybe it's Libby writing Toby's sections as well? The novel owes a great deal to the metafictional play of Philip Roth, especially since Libby, as narrator, is given almost identically Brodesser-Akner's own journalistic career.

In a *New Yorker* review, Katy Waldman argues that these shifts in perspective are justifiable as a way to revamp the novel about marriage to represent more than a single (usually male) perspective. "Brodesser-Akner prods the form of the marriage novel as though it were a sleeping lump on the other side of the bed," Waldman writes. "What if there were a third character? What if the talent chafing at domesticity were female, and the forlorn and long-suffering soul, the good parent, were male?" Readers will admire the novel, or not, depending on whether they enjoy the multiplicity of perspectives Brodesser-Akner offers, and whether they find brooding Libby as interesting as our befuddled, deserted dad with his sudden bounty of women.

Here are two other examples where the writer justifies a switch in point of view as essential to the fiction's meaning.

In *Less*, Andrew Sean Greer introduces us to Arthur Less, a doleful, middle-aged gay writer, terrified of growing old alone, who embarks on an international book tour as a way of avoiding the wedding of his ex-lover, the loss of whom still haunts him. The narrator seems at first glance to be an old-fashioned third-person author. Tongue in cheek, he refers to Arthur as "our hero" and knows everything about the contents of Arthur's (often lost) luggage as well as his worries and regrets about both his love life and his literary career. However, our narrator actually knows our protagonist intimately. As the book goes on, he reveals himself more directly. It's not that the narrator ever exactly *hides* his identity—"I remember Arthur Less in his youth," he tells us early on. "I was twelve or so and very bored at an adult party." And sometimes the narrator's knowledge of Arthur startles: "A truth must now be told: Arthur Less is no champion in bed. . . ." But by the satisfying ending, the reporter comes out of the shadows, as it were, as he and Arthur reunite.

At first glance, this is a first-person account in the vein of a Nick Carraway in *The Great Gatsby*, stepping back to discuss another—but with a twist. The narrator turns out to be a major protagonist as well.

Narratives with these kinds of twists usually want to challenge the reliability of any single viewpoint. Susan Choi, in *Trust Exercise*, tells the story of a cataclysmic year in the life of some high school drama students. The point of view is a putatively trustworthy third person. But midway through the novel, the voice switches to first person. One of the "real-life" students to whom the events "really" occurred—a mere extra in the novel's first part, now a central character—reveals that what we've been reading until this point is a novel, and that the representation of her in said novel is willfully, perversely wrong:

> "Karen" stood outside the Skylight bookstore in Los Angeles, waiting for her old friend, the author. Her old high school classmate, the author. Was it assuming too much, to say "friend"? Was it accepting too much, to say "Karen"? "Karen" is not "Karen's" name, but "Karen" knew, when she read the name "Karen," that it was she who was meant. Does it matter to anyone, apart from "Karen," what "Karen's" real name is?

In the universe of this novel, even a character's name doesn't constitute a stable, reliable truth.

A similar surprise turn in point of view occurs in the Lorrie Moore story "People Like That Are the Only People Here: Canonical Babbling in Peed Onk," where the characters don't even *have* names. A couple referred to only as The Mother and The Husband learn that The Baby has cancer. The story chronicles their baby's treatment in the hospital's pediatric oncology ward, where the fearful, grief-stricken parents await news and meet other parents of afflicted children. The Mother is clearly Lorrie Moore herself, since a doctor presents her with a copy of her last novel to sign. "Take notes," The Husband exhorts her. "We're going to need the money." The Mother objects that she can't possibly turn their pain into art—"I write fiction. This isn't fiction.... This is a nightmare of narrative slop. This cannot be designed"—but the story we are reading is indeed her story, quite cleverly designed. The flat, distancing third person is presented as a trick of self-preservation: "She wants only to hear about the sadness and emergencies of others." By the story's end, as The Baby is discharged from the hospital, Moore bluntly confesses her role in the drama:

> There are the notes.
> Now where is the money?

Moore presents the metafictional switches in point of view as not mere trickery, but essential for representing the deeply alienating experience of a beloved child's illness. The story is less about the tragedy itself (although Moore certainly schools us in the heartbreak of the pediatric oncology ward) than about how we talk about tragedy, about different ways of representing and encoding reality—the doctor's cold, Spock-like medical-speak; the other parents' stalwart optimism. The goal of art is to create empathy for others' pain, and Moore is game to try. But she also warns us (going into second person, as she also does in the story), "In the end, you suffer alone."

Letters, journals, found documents, ephemera, frame tales, and a human soul in exactly the shape of a frying pan

I plan to cram a lot into this section. But in a way the hodge-podge is appropriate for a discussion of writers' use of techniques related to collage: including in their narratives things that are jarring, that come from elsewhere, that move us out of the category of straightforward narration. These writers are like painters who hang paint-encrusted baby shoes off their canvases. They aim to challenge or expand the expectations for their medium.

The most normative of these collagist methods is the time-honored tradition of diary entries and letters—and, these days, e-mails and text messages. The documents have a documentary, "Exhibit A" quality. The writer merely collects the evidence. As well as allowing a sheen of honesty or transparency—I'm not slanting the tale, the author assures, you're getting it straight—such documents allow the writer to liven up the fiction's act with a variety of voices. These voices can be less literate, without the whole fiction having to take on misspellings and simple diction, which can be grating. They can introduce a contrasting voice (as we discussed with the blog posts in Adichie's *Americanah*). They can hint at the absurd detritus that fills a daily life: in *Where'd You Go, Bernadette?* Maria Semple treats us to e-mails and text messages on subjects as diverse as the frustrations of IKEA shopping and the indignation of inflated emergency room bills, the very kind of things a wife and mother might hope to avoid by vanishing. Diary entries and letters further allow the writer to smuggle in large swaths of backstory that, in third-person aligned, the primary character could not know.

The epistolary tradition goes back quite a while—without it, there's no *Pride and Prejudice*, since without Darcy's eloquent letter, Lizzie Bennet would be stuck with her misconceptions about him. A. S. Byatt's *Possession: A Romance* pushes the boundaries of this method. Two contemporary scholars fall in love as they uncover and research the romance of two famous nineteenth-century figures falling in love. The clandestine affair between the Victorian scientist (in a sexless marriage) and the poet (secretly a lesbian) unfolds for the reader bit by bit through masterfully paced clues, and the academics who discover the treasure trove of letters between their respective scholarly subjects must guard their secret because other, competing scholars are on their trail.

Needless to say, Byatt herself pens all of the letters with their archaic diction, as well as the nineteenth-century poems that the twentieth-century sleuths need to reinterpret in light of their discovery. We admire the breadth of her imagination, her erudition for fitting her invented characters into real literary and scientific history, and her sense of play, as well as her ability to do all that while advancing a lively, tense plot that brings not two but four protagonists compellingly to life.

Byatt has defended the choice to include an omniscient third-person narrator in key sections:

> I still receive angry letters from time to time from all over the world, saying these passages are a mistake—that I have cleverly told the story of the past through documents, diaries, letters, poems, and am breaking my own convention incompetently. But my decision was very deliberate . . . the third-person narrator has been much maligned in the

recent past—it does not aspire or pretend to be "God," simply the narrative voice, which knows what it does know. And I wanted to show that such a voice can bring the reader nearer the passions and the thoughts of the characters, without any obligation to admire the cleverness of the novelist. There is a nice irony about this—the writer and reader share what the critics and scholars cannot discover.

Note Byatt's emphasis: "without any obligation to admire the cleverness of the novelist." Third-person omniscience, she claims, just can accomplish some things that other points of view simply cannot.

But many contemporary writers in this tradition trash everything except the documents, often to great comic effect. There is a novel written only as a series of letters of recommendation from a downtrodden professor of creative writing at a mediocre college—*Dear Committee Members* by Julie Schumacher. And in *Hotels of North America* by Rick Moody, Reginald Edward Morse, a hotel reviewer at the august online publication Rate-YourLodging.com, not only provides hilarious reviews of an international series of hotels as diverse as The Plaza in New York and the Sand Trap Inn in Cannon Beach, Oregon, but thereby tells his entire antic life story. Moody maintains websites for both Rate Your Lodging and the character's ostensible Life Coach advice column, so the novel actually continues off the page in a satisfying, fiction-bleeding-into-fact kind of way.

How phenomenal for the author who hits on an original approach in this vein. Schumacher owns recommendation letters and Moody owns hotels, just as Jennifer Egan owns the idea of writing the climax of a novel as an extended PowerPoint presentation, as she does to end *A Visit from the Goon Squad*. One-of-a-kind, or at least decidedly first-of-its-kind: What writer wouldn't crave that? When it's good, it's very, very good. When it's bad, however, we can sense the writer trying hard to be original and, in our time-honored tradition as sniffing, hard-to-impress readers, we will just point out the other writers who have gotten there first, and/or better. There's also always the risk of the approaches dating as the technology does. Once texting becomes ubiquitous, this concept of writing a whole novel composed of texts seems less thrilling. Same might go for works of fiction that contain hyperlinks.

Fiction using this kind of device is usually more lighthearted. Not that serious subjects can't be addressed—drunkenness, divorce, depression—but the overall tone tends toward the parodic. *Erasure*, by Percival Everett, is about a "serious," "difficult" Black novelist, appalled by the Oprah-ization of Black literature—ridiculous representations of poverty and dysfunction like the current big bestseller *We's Lives in da Ghetto*. As a lark, he pens a parody of a "Black" novel under a pseudonym: *Fuck* by Stagg R. Leigh. The whole novel that begins with the narrator stabbing his mother, full of dropped gerunds and wantonly hilarious misspellings, is contained as a frame tale within *Erasure*, and by whole I mean every chapter, from Won, Too, and Free through Seben, Ate, etc. To the surprise of Serious Author Thelonius "Monk" Ellison, that "fake" novel also becomes a huge bestseller. How is Ellison to go on TV to promote the book? How is he to serve on a committee that is considering bestowing a major literary prize on *Fuck* as what his fellow judges call "a true, raw, gritty work. . . . The energy and savagery of the common black is so refreshing in the story"?

Everett creates Thelonius Ellison, who creates Stagg R. Leigh, except of course we know that Everett has really created them both. Ellison narrates the novel in first person, but is Ellison actually Everett? No, since *Erasure* spoofs not only the uproariously bad novel-within-a-novel but Ellison's postmodern pretensions as well. The reader never quite gets to the last figure in the novel's intricate Russian nesting doll. The Black writer, Everett suggests, is damned whether he does or doesn't conform to stereotypes of the Black writer. Except that Everett himself actually *does* escape the stereotypes by writing a novel that gives a range of very smart commentary on racial stereotypes in fiction, and that is both highly literary and highly readable.

One notable exception to the lighter-tone rule is George Saunders's novel *Lincoln in the Bardo*. Abraham Lincoln's son has died. Grief-stricken Lincoln visits the cemetery where his son is buried—a cemetery that serves as a kind of limbo for dead people whose souls have not yet departed for heaven (or hell), all of whom don't realize they're dead. (They call their coffins "sick-boxes," complain about their lack of visitors, and await with dread the arrival of the angels they call "the matterlight-blooming phenomenon.") The novel contains some zany, even slapstick elements as Saunders introduces the cast of dead and their backstories. One man, struck down before he could consummate his marriage, walks around with a permanent (notably huge) boner. Another man has tons of wildly waving eyes and hands, the better to ravish other men with—in real (lived) life, he never came out of the closet.

But the entire novel is narrated in a series of short excerpts from published (and invented) works on Lincoln, each properly "sourced," including the made-up ones, and then a kind of running transcript among the (invented) dead, each line of dialogue also attributed. It takes a while to gain footing in the novel and in fact, preventing a reader from getting quick, confident footing is surely part of the goal. One of the dead voices makes this point directly, when Lincoln's son first announces his discovery that they are all not merely convalescing, but in fact deceased:

Now look, Mr. Vollman said to the boy. You are wrong. If
what you say is true—who is it that is saying it?

Who is *hearing* it? I said.

Who is speaking to you now? said Mr. Vollman.

To whom do we speak? I said.

Indeed. Questions to be asked about every work of fiction,
and every narrator: Who says? To whom? Saunders mounts an
aggressive challenge against the conventional answers to these
questions.

In all of the examples above, the use of the documents to form a
narrative is not merely decorative, not done merely to be different
or get attention. The method is essential to the points the authors
want to make about disenfranchisement, lack of connection, the
frenetic or unsettled or random or often absurd feel of the characters' lives. In her sequel to *The Handmaid's Tale*, called *The
Testaments* (note the Biblical pun), Margaret Atwood includes a
series of first-person chapters identified as "Transcript of Witness Testimony 369B"—that witness being the daughter of Offred
from the last novel, the one stolen from her when Offred was
abducted and forced into reproductive slavery. She also includes
some surreptitiously written accounts by the villain of the last
novel, often communicating directly to us ("Here, my reader, I
owe you an explanation"). Atwood is self-conscious about who is
telling the story, to whom, because that is how we understand history: through the accumulation of individual stories.

Illustrations in narrative

Donald Barthelme began using whimsical black-and-white
drawings in his short fiction in the early 1970s. "At the Tolstoy Museum we sat and wept," begins his story in "At the Tol-

stoy Museum," which includes historical-looking lithographs of Tolstoy. "The Flight of Pigeons from the Palace" also has illustrations—anatomical drawings, architectural perspectives. These collagist elements function similarly to the cartoons in Monty Python skits: they completely disrupt the tone, like the big cartoon foot that enters at the end of *Monty Python's Flying Circus* to sploosh, because while it's clear they're supposed to provide documentary evidence, what they are evidence of is completely, delightfully *un*clear. The Barthelme story "The Photographs" begins:

> The attached photographs of the human soul (Figs. 1 and 2), taken by Pioneer 10, the first spacecraft to navigate the outer solar system, were made on December 14, 1973, as the craft was leaving the magnetic field of Jupiter. The "photographs" (actually coded radio signals from the device's nine foot dish antenna beamed back to earth) were, of course, incidental to the photographing of Jupiter itself, one of the mission's chief aims. They were made by Dr. Reginald Hobson, F.R.S., of Britain's Cavendish Laboratory, using Kodak Spectroscopic plates type IIIa-J baked for five hours at 65@ C. under dry N2 before exposure.

Very official-sounding, yes? Except that the "images" attached to the story aren't photographs at all but black-and-white drawings. "What are we to do with the bloody things?" Reggie demands about the images, which look, they've agreed, "rather like a frying pan"; the human soul is "downright ugly, to be perfectly frank."

"The Photographs" occupies a mere two pages in its issue of the *New Yorker*. For a much larger printing budget, try *Important Artifacts and Personal Property from the Collection of Lenore*

Doolan and Harold Morris, Including Books, Street Fashion, and Jewelry. Leanne Shapton is the author, but her name doesn't appear on the cover. Instead the "catalogue" is attributed to—

Strachan & Quinn Auctioneers
New York * London * Toronto

—and the book includes more photographs than text (in captions). Shapton's book certainly falls into the "First time ever used!" category of originality.

In terms of illustrated books, a writer has a whole other set of options in contemporary publishing: graphic novels. As a genre, they are now taken seriously and can cover a surprisingly wide variety of subject matters and tones, from the Holocaust (Art Spiegelman's *Maus*) to the indignities of caring for aging parents (Roz Chast's *Can't We Talk About Something More Pleasant?*).

Fashion in fiction, and food

All of the mixed-medium points of view discussed in the last section fit squarely under the banner of postmodern experimentation. I won't trouble you with an extended definition of postmodernism, which you can google, but here are two key elements of postmodernism. You'll see that in the use of collage and pastiche, especially—inserting borrowed or allusive elements into their narratives—all of these writers aim to disrupt conventional methods of storytelling. And in their playfulness about what they're willing to co-opt, they challenge the solemnity we saw in the modernism of Joyce et al. A work of fiction, postmodernists claim, can both enlighten and entertain. So distinctions between "high" and "low" art are pointedly disregarded (like that animated cartoon foot in the Monty Python skits, which actually looks very much like a foot in old works of art and was in fact "borrowed" from it; this kind of co-opting of classical elements is very common in postmodernism). Last, though certainly all of these writers do everything in their power to thwart overly simplistic thematic summaries of their work, the pastiche simply seems to tell a more true story. As Donald Barthelme noted about his own work:

> I'm fated to deal in mixtures, slumgullions.... The confusing signals, the impurity of the signal, gives you verisimilitude. As when you attend a funeral and notice, against your will, that it's being poorly done.

Saunders would insist, as Barthelme does, that laughter and mourning are not mutually incompatible—anyone attending an Irish wake knows that. In his essay about the Barthelme story "The School," Saunders wittily, wisely analyzes what makes us follow with delight each move Barthelme makes "because we find his courage thrilling." While essentially plotless, the story challenges our expectations on a line-for-line basis. Barthelme, Saunders claims, keeps us from ever being a step ahead of him. He exuberantly shatters expectations, in service of our delight.

The reminder that fiction can be brave, can take risks, is important. Bravery is the upside of showmanship. There are reasons to climb Mount Everest other than just because it's there. Once you set a lofty challenge, your inability to make it to the top will be a more glaring failure than if you set yourself a more modest one, and readers tend to be harder on works of fiction that aspire to originality than ones that exist squarely within traditional forms.

It goes without saying that you can have pizza one night and the most outlandish chef's concoction another night. Traditional fiction and experimental fiction can satisfy different moods.

Just because you enjoy George Saunders does not mean that you have to eschew Alice Munro.

One caveat about attempts to be original is that where one goes, imitators soon follow. Once a writer executes a daring new maneuver, the writers behind him will initially copy him, then try to one-up him. Soon that degree of difficulty (Double axel! Triple axel! Triple axel with reverse dismount!) is built into the Olympic competition. Critic Harold Bloom chronicles this inevitable process in *The Anxiety of Influence*. Once modernism arrives on the scene, with all of its high holiness about Art with a capital *A*, postmodernism follows, with its corrective, anarchical playfulness.

In the late 1960s and early 1970s, writers like John Barth, Robert Coover, and William H. Gass wrote dense, difficult works stressing formal experimentation. But later in the decade, fiction writers like Ann Beattie and Bobbie Ann Mason returned to a more straightforward, conventional narrative approach and a much less aggressively "artsy" voice. These writers added a twist, though: they detailed socioeconomic milieus of American consumer culture with sparse sentences, but with a specificity about objects and brand names that Hemingway, father of the sparse, would never have permitted himself. This style was called, jokingly, dirty realism, or Kmart fiction, or Diet Pepsi minimalism. Then, suddenly it seemed, no one was using brand names anymore, and much critical attention began to be paid to quite maximalist writers like David Mitchell, working with a style of omniscience that had theretofore been out of fashion for quite some time.

So we see fashion in point of view cycle and recycle as we do in—well, fashion. When bell bottoms return, it is generally with something new in cut, material, or length that assures you can't just get your old jeans out of the closet, but must buy new ones.

Speaking of length, along with the maximalists like Mitchell on one end of the spectrum, on the other end we have seen a surge of interest in flash fiction—very short stories that challenge by their refusal to develop complete plots with the standard rising action and conclusions. Flash fiction is not new. Here's one complete story from Franz Kafka's *Parables and Paradoxes*:

> Leopards break into the temple and drink to the dregs what is in the sacrificial pitchers; this is repeated over and over again; finally it can be calculated in advance, and it becomes a part of the ceremony.

That's "Leopards in the Temple." Whatever you expect from a story, it's probably not that. But then, once you've read enough flash fiction, this story exists within a firmly established tradition, exactly like those leopards that no longer fail to shock in the temple.

And then, you get Lydia Davis.

Here's her story "Spring Spleen":

> I am happy the leaves are growing large so quickly.
>   Soon they will hide the neighbor and her screaming child.

And here's another story, called "Example of the Continuing Past Tense in a Hotel Room":

> Your housekeeper *has been* Shelly.

Davis is not the first person to write very short stories, but man oh man are some of them short. And man oh man are there a lot of them—her *Collected Short Stories* runs 752 pages. And yet varied! Some even like normal stories, but many only a page long. Here's the beginning of a review of her collection *Can't and Won't,* by the ever-amusing critic Dwight Garner:

> Lydia Davis's short stories are difficult to describe, but people like to try. A friend of mine likens them to mosquitoes. Some you swat away, he says. Others draw blood.
>
> Dan Chiasson, writing in *The New York Review of Books,* has compared them to "radar blips that promise interstellar life" and "specimen creatures in jars." The novelist Kate Christensen, in *Elle,* said reading one is like reaching into a bag of potato chips and pulling out something else, "a gherkin, a peppercorn, a truffle, a piece of beef jerky."
>
> That gherkin line appeals to me. That's what we should say about Ms. Davis: She has a new book of her gherkins out. Her stories are briny and often delicious, after all, though also a bit impudent and stunted. You devour them as if they were on toothpicks.

Interesting that here, too, we reach for food metaphors—writers' voices and approaches described by how they taste. Maybe, for a change of pace, we should adapt wine connoisseurs' lingo, and discuss writers in terms of fruit, acidity, tannins. This novel seems to me a bit . . . corked.

Along with the Xtreme Brevity, Davis also adopts many of the methods of the epistolary, of ephemera (lists and found objects), and of collage that we've discussed in this chapter. She has put these existing elements together in a way that is distinctly her own, and now there can be only one Lydia Davis, as there is only one Donald Barthelme and, I suspect, only one George Saunders (although his trope of the bizarre, decaying theme park, begun in his collection *CivilWarLand in Bad Decline,* is currently much imitated in MFA programs across the land).

There are only so many points of view available to the fiction writer, and we have now discussed all of them. I hope you feel encouraged to see the wide range that can be achieved within those strictures. Think of it like one of those math problems about the number of ways you can seat a dozen people at a dinner party—so many combinations are possible. In this chapter alone, in the third-person plural section, we looked at Justin Torres's first novel: he writes in the collective "we," plus he writes from a childhood point of view; furthermore, the family he examines is Puerto Rican and from New York, and he has things to say about that identity and culture; plus the narrator is gay, and Torres has some things to say about that, too; plus his book is composed of a series of short, lyrical sections rather than in traditional, clearly interconnected chapters, borrowing from the style of a novel-in-stories that has also become popular. Slice-and-dice existing possibilities that way and you wind up with fiction that is your own.

It can be exhilarating when writers come up with a new approach to point of view. Their daring represents not just flamboyant attention seeking but a respect for our intelligence, an earnest desire to surprise and delight. But an absolutely new approach to narrative isn't necessary—there are ways to work within the established traditions to craft your own fiction. In order to write, you have to believe that no matter how many other books are on your shelf, the story you tell is yours and yours alone.

CHAPTER EIGHT

POINT OF VIEW IN FICTION VERSUS FILM

THINKING LIKE A CAMERA

When beginning writers aim to "create a picture" that comes alive on the page, they are often thinking in cinematic ways. The images unspool in the imagination as if they're already filmed. But there are essential differences between how emotion is communicated on screen and on the page. Let's review those critical differences, with particular attention to how they influence literary description—of anything from a character's appearance to key actions.

Most of us are deeply, if often unconsciously, familiar with the techniques that cinematographers use to create mood. We get that if we zoom in for a close-up of a knife in a killer's hand, an attack is imminent. We get that if a trembling child gazes up at a cruel old teacher, the low camera angle will make the teacher appear even more threatening, make the child seem even more vulnerable. We don't need to have explained how a handheld camera's jerky, blurred footage as the car tumbles over the cliff is meant to communicate the accident's lack of control. If *Jurassic Park* then zooms out for a long shot of the car tangled at the bottom of the ravine, its horn distantly blaring but no movement within, we fear the prognosis is not good, even before the T-Rex shows up.

When a beginning writer does a car crash, it tends to be more like a script. It is, for starters, a predominantly visual account. So in essence, the writer is thinking like a camera. At least he thinks he is. Alas, the writer is probably not a trained cinematographer, with depth of knowledge about lenses, lighting, camera angle, film stock. The writer does not have the benefit of a film editor's services. The writer does not get a score to swell the desired emotion (cue the shark-approach motif from *Jaws*).

Most significantly, the writer lacks an actor. We have no close-up of the actor's shocked face. We don't have an actor translating and amplifying the emotions with the full range of expression, gesture, and voice that are in his tool kit. If we had Keanu Reeves to watch the bus blow up in *Speed*, we can sense the full force of the explosion. The script merely serves as scaffolding for the director and actor:

THE BUS
explodes.

JACK
Half-turns as the shock wave knocks him off his feet. Car alarms wail. People run. The bus carcass burns, twisted metal and flaming plastic where Bob was. Jack moves forward on instinct, but there's nothing he can do and the flames force him back.

As Jack stares in shock, we notice a PHONE RINGING, getting louder as it filters into Jack's consciousness.

Suddenly it dawns on him and he turns, dreamlike, and walks to the phone. Picks up the receiver.

The actor has been given a nifty gesture right before the

explosion: he puts the cop's donut he has just bought for break-fast, and almost just forgot, on the roof of his car as he fumbles for the key to open his car door. So the script cleverly contrasts the ordinariness of the morning with the explosion that shatters it. Our hero may be a bit scatterbrained, and thus likeable, until the day requires SWAT—then he becomes a hero.

But *none of this works on the page as fiction*. It's too broad. And mind you, this is a *good* script, one whose writer actually knows how to think about an actor's gestures. That donut on the car roof (A cop! A donut! Of course!) gives us something effi-cient and essential about the character, and further establishes trust with the audience—lets us know that the filmmakers are quite aware that we've seen a cop or two, in a movie or two, and allows us that knowing chuckle. But then surprises us, shatters our preconceptions, just as Jack's morning is disrupted. In fact, the whole of *Speed* is a wink and nod to the action movie genre, our expectations for the force of mind-numbing action. *Slow down!*

There's one thing that fiction can do, however, that no advanced digital manipulations can match: penetrate an indi-vidual's consciousness. Film can create a tone, create raw imme-diacy, suggest a character's state of mind, often through what scripts call "a point-of-view shot"—showing us what the charac-ter sees through his subjective viewpoint, then showing us the character's response, often with a close-up of a facial expression. But film simply cannot put you inside a character's experience the way a novel can. Fiction still owns character, the complex investigation of mood and motive.

What could the fiction writer do that the novelist can't? In fic-tion, Jack could also have a past, and a future. Memories and hopes would intrude into his day. The filmmaker can only pro-duce memory, or "backstory," as the most blatant kind of fade-out or film stock change, or by having the character relate the backstory in dialogue to someone else. Jack would have stray impressions and associations—and those would be more than visual. They'd probably involve taste and texture and most importantly smell, that most reliable of memory triggers. The thoughts would not necessarily move in a straight line, either. They could meander or intrude, as thoughts tend to do.

Here is a pivotal scene from Jane Austen's *Pride and Prejudice* that shows how the visual imagery becomes part of the story—but not the whole story—and how the view of the landscape is much more internal, more subjective, than a film can duplicate.

Elizabeth Bennet, clever and spirited but not rich, has turned down a marriage proposal from Darcy, an eligible bachelor whom she loathes as irredeemably proud. Now, on a vacation with her aunt and uncle (who are lovely people but "in trade," and thus lowlifes by pre-Trump social standards), she gets a sneak tour of Darcy's grand estate. We can imagine how to shoot this: Lizzie gazes from her carriage as we get the establishing shot of the mansion appearing down the long driveway lined with trees; inside, we'll see many rooms stuffed with sumptuous goodies, some in close-up, like that ornate grandfather clock, which might sound a stately bong in the reverent hush. Cut to Lizzie Bennet's awed face. Film can do that quite capably. But film can't do this:

> The rooms were lofty and handsome. And their furniture suitable to the fortune of their proprietor; but Elizabeth saw, with admiration of his taste, that it was neither gaudy nor uselessly fine; with less of splendor, and more of real elegance, than the furniture of Rosings.
>
> "And of this place," thought she, "I might have been mistress! With these rooms I might now have been familiarly acquainted! Instead of viewing them as a stranger, I might have rejoiced in them as my own, and

welcomed to them as visitors my uncle and aunt.—But no. "
—recollecting herself,—"that could never be: my uncle and
aunt would have been lost to me: I should not have been
allowed to invite them."

This was a lucky recollection—it saved her from
something like regret.

A good actress can show Elizabeth looking impressed, and
wistful. If we've been with an actress for a spell, we'll be familiar
enough with her facial expressions and gestures to know how
to read her conflicted feelings. But it would be very hard for any
actress to capture the full impact of this moment, with Lizzie
still stubbornly clinging to the idea that she made the right decision by declining the marriage proposal. Austen's readers—not
Elizabeth herself—see how her own pride is still getting in the
way. It'll be particularly delightful for those readers, and con-
founding for Lizzie, when in the very next scene, Darcy, who
was supposed to be safely absent from the property, unexpect-
edly appears, and is quite cordial to the aforementioned uncle
and aunt.

The drama for the reader is seeing what the heroine sees, seeing *more* than she sees, and just as we risk becoming as over-
confidently opinionated as Lizzie herself, being as surprised as
she is by the turn of events at key moments. The scene is multi-
layered. It's hardly a mere inventory of luxury goods. What does
Lizzie know and when does she know it? What do *we* know and
when do we know it? Even a house tour becomes a puzzle when
it is shaded by the consciousness of an observer.

Note that a filmmaker couldn't solve this problem with a
voice-over. Screenwriters adapting novels often try to smuggle
in some of the author's key lines with this method. But having Lizzie face the camera to say anything at all would violate
the intense privacy of her reaction. It would also make the tone

more predominantly comical, as voice-overs often are (see *Clueless*, which changes the Austen novel *Emma*'s third person to a bubbly first person)—if they're not used to conveniently smuggle in whole ungainly chunks of backstory that on the page would be exposition (see *Terminator 2*). There is plenty of film criticism discussing when voice-over is effective, and when it comes off as merely a cheap trick. "Voice-over is like strong perfume," says critic Sarah Kozloff, "a little of it goes a long way."

Notice the phrase "thought she" in the Austen quote above, which serves as a hinge to bring us from the room into the heroine's head. Now look how Andre Dubus makes the move into the character's thoughts in the first two paragraphs of his novel *Voices from the Moon*. Dubus manipulates the image—both of what you see as a reader, and of what the protagonist sees:

> It's divorce that did it, his father had said last night. Those were the first two words Richie Stowe remembered when he woke in the summer morning, ten minutes before the six-forty-five that his clock-radio was set for; but the words did not come to him as in memory, as something spoken even in the past one night, but like other words that so often, in his twelve years, had seemed to wait above his sleeping face so that when he first opened his eyes he would see them like a banner predicting his day: *Today is the math test; Howie is going to get you after school.... It's divorce that did it*, and he turned off the switch so that the radio wouldn't start, and lay in the breeze of the oscillating fan, a lean suntanned boy in underpants, neither tall nor short, and felt the opening of wounds he had believed were healed, felt again the deep and helpless sorrow, and the anger too because he was twelve and too young for it and had done nothing to cause it.

Then he got up, dressed in jeans and tee shirt and running shoes, went to his bathroom where a poster of Jim Rice hung behind the toilet, gazed at it while he urinated, studying the strong thighs and arms (in the poster Rice had swung his bat, and was looking up and toward left field), and Richie saw again that moment when Rice had broken his bat without hitting the ball: had checked his swing, and the bat had continued its forward motion, flown out toward first base, leaving Rich holding the handle. This was on television, and Richie had not believed what he had seen until he saw it again, the replay in slow motion.

We know what the novel will be about, the effect of a divorce on a young boy: check. We also know what that boy is like: average ("neither tall nor short") but smart and sensitive. Also not self-pitying or obsessed: he's concerned about the dissolution of the family, but not so distraught that he can't let his mind wander to baseball. Dubus has assured us that he'll have access to Richie's thoughts, but he won't communicate them solely in the boy's limited diction or through the boy's limited perception—the grand length of that opening sentence certainly belongs to the author, not Richie.

In some sense, this is the most traditional of openings, right down to the ring of that alarm clock. But it's also lushly cinematic, with that reverse zoom shot to the overhead view of the boy in the bed. We see what Richie sees—but we also see Richie. (It's not Richie who labels himself "neither tall nor short," or suntanned. As we discussed in Chapter 5, it's very hard for first-person narrators to describe their own appearance.) When we contrast the prepubescent boy with the steroidally strong adult baseball player in the poster, we get something else: a heads-up from the author that this tale will involve coming-of-age.

Dubus's way of orchestrating the movement of the reader's attention owes a lot to film. But the basic idea of suggesting mood with a visual image goes way back—to every work of literature that begins with the weather, probably as forbidden a cliché now as the ringing alarm clock. When the narrator of Edgar Allan Poe's "The Fall of the House of Usher" approaches, on horseback, the doomed manse of the title on a "dull, dark, and soundless day in the autumn," a house that is in bad enough repair to signify the haunting depravity of the people within, he shudders as he surveys "the bleak walls—upon the vacant eye-like windows—upon a few rank sedges—and upon a few white trunks of decayed trees—with an utter depression of soul which I can compare to no earthly sensation more properly than to the afterdream of the reveler upon opium—the bitter lapse into everyday life—the hideous dropping off of the veil." We get it, Ed, even if we have no clue anymore what a sedge is! This will not be a lighthearted sleepover!

For the contemporary horror film aficionado, the heavy foreshadowing of the dark-and-stormy night, maybe scored with theremins, would count as overkill, but we must give Poe credit for helping to invent what has been copied so often as to become a B-movie standard. In a contemporary film, there's more likely to be a contrast between the unthreatening daily and the upcoming horror. *Poltergeist* happens not in Transylvania, but in the most sunny of suburban neighborhoods in southern California. Similarly, there's no doom and gloom in the weather forecast for the ritual stoning at the heart of Shirley Jackson's "The Lottery," which begins:

> The morning of June 27th was clear and sunny, with the fresh warmth of a full summer day; the flowers were blossoming profusely and the grass was richly green.

Just a typical fine day in American paradise. Mrs. Hutchinson arrives at the town square late—"Clean forgot what day it was," she says. Again, to a reader who has seen a few movies, the camera (or author's) intent focus on Mrs. Hutchinson at the back of the crowd is a not-too-subtle foreshadowing that she is a Person of Interest in the denouement to follow.

These days in horror films, the Sunny Day opener has become just as familiar as portentous clouds and thunderclaps. We know bad things are coming. That's fine for a genre film: when we go to see *Saw III*, we're not expecting *War and Peace*. It's a haunted house ride, less rickety but the same kind of cheerful shock.

While the Poe story is told in first person, and the Jackson in third person, the voice we hear—who we follow—is not the protagonist's, but the author's, who is constructing the tale. The approach is solidly authorial. The nature of the omniscience is part of what makes the stories seem old-fashioned. But there are still plenty of contemporary works that share Poe's use of a single, dominant tone. Here's how Cormac McCarthy introduces us to "the man" and "the child" in the first paragraph of *The Road*:

> When he woke in the woods in the dark and the cold of the night he'd reach out to touch the child sleeping beside him. Nights dark beyond darkness and the days more gray each one than what had gone before. Like the onset of some cold glaucoma dimming away the world. His hand rose and fell softly with each precious breath. He pushed away the plastic tarpaulin and raised himself in the stinking robes and blankets and looked towards the east for any light but there was none. In the dream from which he'd wakened he had wandered in a cave where the child led him by the hand. Their light playing over the wet flowstone walls. Like pilgrims in a fable swallowed up and lost among the inward parts of some granitic beast. Deep stone flues where the water dripped and sang. Tolling in the silence the minutes

of the earth and the hours and the days of it and the years without cease. Until they stood in a great stone room where lay a great and ancient lake. And on the far shore a creature that raised its dripping mouth from the rimstone pool and stared into the light with eyes dead white and sightless as eggs of spiders. It swung its head low over the water as if to take the scent of what it could not see. Crouching there pale and naked and translucent, its alabaster bones cast up in shadow on the rocks behind it. Its bowels, its beating heart. The brain that pulsed in a dull glass bell. It swung its head from side to side and then gave out a low moan and turned and lurched away and loped soundlessly into the dark.

McCarthy thrusts us right into the protagonists' grainy, stark postapocalyptic void. We will never actually get a name for the everyman and everychild. The language has a fairy-tale-like simplicity: "in the woods," "like pilgrims in a fable," "where lay a great and ancient lake." As in the Dubus, the point of view here is third person predominantly aligned with the character and his observations—but with the author able to swoop out to amplify, when needed, the characters' thoughts. Presumably the man would not use the words "glaucoma" or "granitic," but we believe that the man could dream the powerful visual.

McCarthy choreographs for the cinematographer, starting with the close-up on the hand on the breathing boy, going wider-angle as the man stands up from the tent and pushes open the tent, and then the long shot as he looks toward sunrise to try to discern the hour (he can't). But then—as in the Austen—we go interior, into the dream, which gets more airtime than the actual physical world and also includes specific instructions on how to film the light and shadow. Note how much of the account is not purely visual, quickly evoking all of the other senses. It's cold. The blankets stink. The cave is silent, the monster lurches silently, but the water in the cave sings on the rocks.

Although we follow the man and the boy, I'd contend that our primary relationship is with McCarthy, who is working squarely in a modernist tradition that calls attention to the prose itself, and to the magisterial skill of the author for evoking the world. The sophisticated reader may also get the literary allusion, in the last line, to the "rough beast" of W. B. Yeats's poem about apocalypse, "The Second Coming."

The monsters in this tale are the humans, who, after destroying the planet, begin to eat human flesh. In a climactic moment, our duo's road trip brings them dangerously close to the cannibals, who fortunately are out hunting when the pair stumbles upon the food storage locker in the basement. I won't quote the legendarily horrific passage here—so as not to be accused of spoiling *everything*—except to note that the description is richly cinematic. We follow the pair down dark steps and see only what they see, in the beam of a flashlight. The passage is informed by the Hitchcockian conviction that what's imagined and feared can prove more unsettling than what's clearly seen: why the monster in the first *Alien* briefly glimpsed in the darkness, flexing its horrid, clicking, goo-dripping jaws, is spookier than many of the overblown CGI creatures that followed in the sequels.

While McCarthy's imagery is gruesome, the language is simple, never melodramatic or overblown. People generally credit Hemingway with this development and it's true that Papa liked to keep things clean and well lit, with a lot of short words ("old," "man," "and," "the," "sea") and not too many of them, but the real granddaddy of this approach is Anton Chekhov. Here he offers feedback on a draft to his writer-pal Maxim Gorky in 1899:

> The descriptions of nature are artistic; you are a genuine landscapist. Except that the use of the device of

personification (anthropomorphism) when you have the sea breathe, the heavens gaze down, the steppe caress, nature whisper, speak or mourn—such descriptions render your descriptions somewhat monotonous, occasionally oversweet and sometimes indistinct; picturesque and expressive descriptions of nature are attained only through simplicity, by the use of such plain phrases as "the sun came out," "it grew dark," "it rained," etc.

Taking his own advice, Chekhov, in his story "The Lady with the Dog," cuts right to the chase in the first sentence to describe the object of Dmitri's interest at a seaside resort: "a fair-haired young lady of medium height, wearing a *beret*; a white Pomeranian dog was running behind her." Like a good scriptwriter, he leaves the casting to the professionals. See her as you wish, so long as you understand that like Dubus's neither tall nor short young boy, this woman is "in no way remarkable," so Dmitri's fascination with her surprises him; he has had other extramarital affairs, and does not get attached.

As he begins to fall for her, they walk by the beach, "and talked of the strange light on the sea: the water was of a soft warm lilac hue, and there was a golden streak from the moon upon it." As the couple begins to swoon, the moonlit ocean is romanticized, like the shots of the Brooklyn Bridge during first kisses in practically every movie taking place in New York City. But not much more is made of the scenery until Dmitri returns to Moscow and his loveless marriage—in winter.

Anyone who has taken a high school English course knows how to read seasons as symbolic: winter for death, spring for rebirth. Chekhov uses a single color—gray—repeatedly in the story. Anna has "gray eyes" that become "lovely gray eyes" as her suitor becomes enchanted. That, and her "slender delicate neck," are practically the only particulars we're given about her—and that little white dog, of course, as essential a marker for the story as Dorothy's dog in *The Wizard of Oz*, its white fur popping out in the first shot. When Dmitri goes in search of her, he takes a hotel room "in which the floor was covered with grey army cloth, and on the table was an inkstand, grey with dust and adorned with a figure on horseback, with its hand and its head broken off." When he stalks Anna at her house, he sees, across the street, "a long grey fence adorned with nails." At the story's end, as they confront the difficulties to come, he looks in the mirror and notes "his hair was already beginning to turn grey."

I personally do not want to grade the paper about what gray "symbolizes" here. It's true that gray isn't a bright, cheerful color, and also that it isn't black-and-white but indeterminate, as is this adulterous affair. But I'd argue that gray doesn't need to mean much more than that, except to help establish what, in a film, would be called the color palette—the general color temperature and look of the whole, which helps to create the mood and evoke emotions. Chekhov is just doing it efficiently, as Hemingway, in "Hills Like White Elephants," quickly sketches a lot of divisions as a couple drinks while awaiting their train at a Spanish train station—tracks, bead curtains, and many times there's shade on one side and sun on the other—to suggest the stark difference in opinion between what "the American" and "the girl" want to do about that nameless "procedure" they're euphemistically discussing to end an unplanned pregnancy. The palette in the Hemingway story is overlit, harsh, bleached, like the hills of the title. Even though they're at the beach, which ostensibly should offer sunshine, the palette in the Chekhov is misty, indeterminate. The adulterers don't really know how they'll go forth; in nineteenth-century Russia, it will be tricky. Yet the story resonates with us, still rings true, despite our wholly different culture and divorce rate.

In the Chekhov, as in the McCarthy, both the look and movement of what we observe is keyed to what the protagonist observes. It's a decidedly subjective account. This is a very simple idea in principle, but it takes some practice and patience to achieve. Here's a scene from Charles Baxter's story "A Relative Stranger," in which the narrator is about to meet the identical twin from whom he was separated at birth:

Going into a bar in the midsummer afternoon takes you out of the steel heat and air-hammer sun; it softens you up until you're all smoothed out. This was one of those wood-sidewall bars with air that hasn't recirculated in fifty years, with framed pictures of thoroughbreds and cars on the walls next to the chrome decorator hubcaps. A man's bar, smelling of cigarettes and hamburger grease and beer. The brown padded light comes down on you from some recessed source, and the leather cushions on those bar stools are as soft as a woman's hand, and before long the bar is one big bed, a bed on a barge eddying down a sluggish river where you've got nothing but good friends lined up on the banks. This is why I am an alcoholic. It wasn't easy drinking Coca-Cola in that place, that dim halfway house between the job and home, and I was about to slide off my wagon and order my first stiff one when the door cracked open behind me, letting in a trumpet blast of light, and I saw, in the doorframe outline, my brother coming toward me. He was taking his own time. He had on a hat. When the door closed and my eyes adjusted, I got a better look at him, and I saw what he said I would see: I saw instantly that this was my brother. The elves had stolen my shadow and given it to him. A version of my face was fixed on a stranger. From the outdoors came this example of me, wearing a coat and tie.

Notice, again, how the account is not just visual but involves

other senses: the smell of the bar, touch and texture ("padded light," bar stools "soft as a woman's hand"), sound ("air-
hammered," "sluggish"). Notice, again, how these observations
aren't offered in a list but all in a lump, so they can be taken in
as a unified impression. The fact that the bar isn't just described,
but described as "one of those bars"—you've been in them, you
know the type—is another important gesture here; you may recognize this establishment, but you, unlike him, might not view
the bar as a hard drinker. From the length of the sentence, we
get the narrator's relieved comfort in that bar. It's his irony, not
the author's, that we hear in the image of the friends on the other
side of the river. As an alcoholic, he knows life isn't a soft drink
commercial, or an episode of *Cheers*. Notice, too, how he has
directed the brother's dramatic entrance in that "trumpet blast
of light"—the visual and sound combined again. The brother is
wearing a hat. And a suit and tie—our narrator is more blue-
collar. We don't need to know the color of the suit, or the brand.

The device of directing the reader's eyes in terms of what the
character sees—giving us that POV shot—can be very powerful,
and works for descriptions of people as well as landscapes. Here
is how Flannery O'Connor in "A Good Man Is Hard to Find"
introduces The Misfit who has pulled up in a "big black battered
hearse-like automobile" (hint, hint) and is about to murder the
grandmother along with her entire vacationing family:

> The driver got out of the car and stood by the side of it,
> looking down at them. He was an older man than the
> other two. His hair was just beginning to gray and he wore
> silver-rimmed spectacles that gave him a scholarly look.
> He had a long creased face and didn't have on any shirt
> or undershirt. He had on blue jeans that were too tight for
> him and was holding a black hat and a gun. The two boys
> also had guns.

This reveal is similar to how the suffering people in the basement are unveiled in the McCarthy: O'Connor has saved the
guns for the end of the paragraph, while you'd think the fact
that the people in the car were all armed would be the first thing
you noticed. But it's the grandmother looking, and she proceeds
from head to toe. That The Misfit looks "scholarly" turns out to
be fitting, since he'll show quite the philosophical flare in his
upcoming rumination about crime sprees. The grandmother,
whom we know fancies herself quite the lady in how she dresses,
makes no observation about the fact that he's bare chested and
doesn't note that first either. His jeans are too tight because he
stole them from his last victim, as we'll learn shortly.

So why the flatness of the description? The children about to
be shot were shouting "in a frenzy of delight" as soon as they
had the accident that stranded them here, but the grandmother,
always so chatty and opinionated, has gone quite mute. She's in
shock! And that's important, because from here on in, she will
be stripped of the smug preconceptions that have made her so
annoying, so she can experience the moment of grace upon her
death that deeply religious O'Connor wishes to grant her.

Katherine Heiny, in *Standard Deviation*, doesn't simply tell
us that a particular dinner party was dull and went on way
too long. As the evening ends at last, "Elspeth had the deeply
reflective air of someone who had just seen a particularly sav-
age wildlife documentary, and Bentrup had taken on the seedy,
shellacked look of a late-night convenience store shopper." The
observations presumably belong to the quiet hubby who is the
novel's center of consciousness. In an act of generosity, Heiny
has bestowed her own saucy humor on her narrator.

Here's part of the first paragraph from Joy Williams's story
"The Visiting Privilege":

Donna came as a visitor in her long black coat. It was
spring, but still cool, and she never wore light colors, she
was no buttercup. She was visiting her friend Cynthia,
who was in Pond House for depression. Donna never had a
drink before she visited Cynthia. She shunned her habitual
excesses and arrived sober and aware, with an exquisite
sinking feeling.

Pop quiz: Whose point of view is this? I vote for free indirect discourse: "she was no buttercup" is clearly Donna's own diction,
as is the proud, slightly self-mocking, old-fashioned language
"shunned her habitual excesses." We know from the story's first
sentences that Donna is not terribly focused on Donna's well-
being, and that her "exquisite sinking feeling" upon entering the
clinic is weird and most likely inappropriate. Williams likes to
thrust us right into a situation without much mooring. That long
black coat, like the hats in the Chekhov and O'Connor stories,
is pretty much all we need to see of Donna making her grand
entrance.

The big production numbers

All of these examples (with perhaps an exception for futuristic
cannibalism) have considered fairly realistic scenarios, where
the description of an outfit or a blood-stained mattress gives you
what you need to know. What about visuals in plots with larger
casts and more mayhem—horror, science fiction, or even the violence of war, where we want a bigger picture than we can achieve
from one character's vantage point?

A writer can provide the equivalent of a pan shot of the carnage, as Richard Flanagan does in *The Narrow Road to the
Deep North*:

Then had come the rocks and dried pellets of goat shit and dried olive leaves of the Syrian campaign, slipping and sliding with their heavy gear past the occasional bloated Senegalese corpse, their thoughts their own as, far away, they heard the stutter and crack and crump of battles and skirmishes elsewhere. The dead and their arms and gear were scattered like the stones—everywhere, inevitable—and other than avoiding treading on their bloated forms beyond comment or thought . . .

A single protagonist could observe these things. Please note, however, that the moment a writer resorts to the equivalent of an overhead shot, going wide-angle to show how large the field of suffering is, you need an omniscient narrator. For some visuals, a film definitely has a leg up over fiction to objectively portray a large-scale scene or event: the sinking of the *Titanic*, the storming of the beach at Normandy. A third-person–aligned narrator or first-person narrator cannot observe himself from overhead.

A writer can, however, suggest the depth of the field of suffering by cleaving closely to what a single protagonist feels. In describing the experience of slavery, Toni Morrison favors narrowly subjective accounts. Paul D in *Beloved* recalls the horrors of being on a chain gang with forty-five other men who are kept bound together in leg irons, in cages in a ditch that floods in heavy rain:

In the boxes the men heard the water rise in the trench and looked out for cottonmouths. They squatted in muddy water, slept above it, peed in it. Paul D thought he was screaming; his mouth was open and there was this loud throat-splitting sound—but it may have been somebody else. Then he thought he was crying. Something was running down his cheeks. He lifted his hands to wipe away the tears and saw dark brown slime. Above him rivulets of mud slid through the boards of the roof. When it come down, he thought, gonna crush me like a tick bug. It happened so quick he had no time to ponder. Somebody yanked the chain—once—hard enough to cross his legs and throw him into the mud. He never figured out how he knew—how anybody did—but he did know—he did—and he took both hands and yanked the length of chain at his left, so the next man would know too. The water was above his ankles, flowing over the wooden plank he slept on. And then it wasn't water anymore. The ditch was caving in and mud oozed under and through the bars.

Look how much information Morrison gives the cinematographer here. The camera wants to be claustrophobically close, until the men break free together from the cages—"For one lost, all lost"—when we are given a broader vision of the other slaves struggling through the torrents of mud in unison. What you couldn't get on film is the skillful move into Paul D's thoughts that Morrison achieves with "When it come down, he thought, gonna crush me like a tick bug." Nor could you get the rhythms of rising panic in "how he knew—how anybody knew—how anybody did—but he did know—he did," a phrase that both accelerates the men's escape, and changes the time register to "he never figured out," letting us know how indelibly this critical moment will survive in his memory. So the scene is, simultaneously, both totally trapped in the frantic present and also in the future, which is the larger thematic claim Morrison is making about how the institution of slavery haunts both the slaves and the country.

This is a scene that demands to be read. Things happen on the page that can't happen on screen. Of course, a skilled actor can involve you in feeling for Paul D's suffering, and a good director can create cinematic analogues for the complex emotions about freedom that the novel portrays (director Jonathan Demme goes so far as to use insects and butterflies, not in the novel, as visual metaphors). But creditable a job as Oprah Winfrey does portraying the fierce female lead, she's still Oprah Winfrey. A viewer's double awareness of both the character and the actress playing her in Real Life changes the dynamic. Janet Maslin's review of the movie in the *New York Times* ends, "In so ambitiously bringing this story to the screen, Ms. Winfrey underscores a favorite, invaluable credo: read the book."

Beloved is a faithful adaptation of the novel. Stanley Kubrick's 1980 adaptation of *The Shining* is decidedly not. Many of the movie's most iconic visuals do not exist in Stephen King's novel about an off-season caretaker and family snowbound in a haunted hotel. There isn't an elaborate, towering topiary maze for Jack to freeze to death in, and Wendy, the wife, is not the useless, weepy mouse in the novel that she is in the movie. The illustrious scene where Wendy defends herself against her crazy husband with a baseball bat went through 127 punishing retakes—the highest number ever for a scene with dialogue, according to *Guinness World Records*—and Kubrick endlessly insulted actress Shelley Duvall on set. No wonder she was crying.

"[The movie] is so misogynistic," Stephen King complained in an interview with Andy Greene for *Rolling Stone*. "I mean, Wendy Torrance is just presented as this sort of screaming dish-rag." He was quite outspoken about his displeasure with the film:

> I think *The Shining* is a beautiful film and it looks terrific and as I've said before, it's like a big, beautiful Cadillac with no engine inside it . . . the character has no arc in that movie. Absolutely no arc at all. When we first see Jack Nicholson, he's in the office of Mr. Ullman, the manager of the hotel, and you know, then, he's crazy as a shit house rat. All he

> does is get crazier. In the book, he's a guy who's struggling
> with his sanity and finally loses it. To me, that's a tragedy.
> In the movie, there's no tragedy because there's no change.

King demands that we feel for Jack's slipping sanity. Despite the supernatural element, his novel is still deeply character focused. Much less so Nicholson's portrayal of Jack, which is incongruously comical, and in fact the entire tone of the movie diverges wildly from the tone of the novel—so much so that afterward, King demanded script, director, and cast approval before he would sell movie rights.

But is "different" necessarily "bad"? There isn't really another horror movie with a tone like that of *The Shining*, simultaneously broadly comical and terrifying. You could claim that the blend of humor and horror in that 1980 film set a tonal bar for many horror films to come, which seem to knowingly mock their own outlandish premises at the same time as they ask us to lose ourselves in actual terror.

Finally, the film doesn't really belong to the characters. It belongs to Kubrick himself—he is what film critics call an "auteur director," in control of every line of dialogue, shot, costume, and set decoration in his film's mise-en-scène.

We've often asked in these pages who you "hear" while reading a book—the character or the author. Same goes for a movie: in a Kubrick film, you mostly hear Kubrick. Even the stars are mere extras. As another auteur director, Alfred Hitchcock, was widely known to say of his cast: "All actors are cattle." (Or, as he later corrected, "I never said all actors are cattle; I said all actors should be treated like cattle.") You will admire Kubrick or not. But you know who your relationship is with.

For all his fame and popularity, Stephen King is surprisingly unegotistical. His characters are actually given star billing. In *On Writing: A Memoir of the Craft*, King confides that when rewriting, "For me, the most glaring errors I find on the re-read have to do with character motivation." He's always concerned with making sure their actions track and make sense. They're not puppets.

Can a movie be, as we've seen a work of fiction can be, *both* focused on deep empathy for particular characters, *and* have a strong, auteur-like directorial presence? Definitely. Look at Roman Polanski's *Rosemary's Baby*, about a poor woman forced to bear Satan's child, due to a deal her evil, selfish husband made with some devil-worshipping neighbors. This movie is superior to the Ira Levin novel on which it's based. Naturally we must give Levin credit for coming up with the whole concept, not to mention the plotting of every scene and practically every line of dialogue. But it's Polanski who makes the New York apartment building where the action takes place a memorably terrifying maze, from its too-thin walls to its dark basement laundry rooms. And it's Polanski who films Rosemary—present in virtually every scene—in such a way that we feel her vulnerability during pregnancy. Levin tells us; Polanski shows us. (The film critic Penelope Gilliatt called the film "gynecological Gothic.") Polanski is a master at giving ordinary details an extraordinary strangeness. Polanski makes the apartment building itself a character in the story, an objective correlative as strong as the decaying house in "The Fall of the House of Usher." This is an effect much harder to achieve in a work of fiction.

A great novel may be the hardest to make into a great movie. There's more nuance to lose. A novel with an original story line or set of characters, but one that is less dependent on language or tone, gives both the director, and the actors, more room to invent.

As we have seen, even in a matter as simple as describing a character's outfit in a piece of fiction, issues of point of view come into play. We want an author to direct our attention to what matters, in a way that helps us to fully experience what's happening.

The first step is first and foremost to encourage our empathy. But in some cases, authors can also subtly guide us to understand things the character isn't yet aware of, or question the character's vision and version of events. Furthermore, in the tone of the description—the length of the sentences, the diction, the nature of the imagery—the author establishes a voice for himself as well. Even in a story that follows a character's perceptions quite closely, we're aware of the author. As we'll discuss in our revision chapter, weaknesses in drafts often result from miscalculations of this tricky balance of attention. The author may have failed to spend the time to fully enough imagine the character's experience of the events. Conversely, the author may follow the character through the doorway *too* ploddingly.

On the simplest level, if a writer takes our time with a description of a hat, we have to know why the hat is revealing. There's no reason, really, to tell us that before the man walks into the bar he grabs the doorknob and turns it. We know he has to get into the room by putting one foot down, then the next, before he gets to the bar to say "A double and make it snappy." The description can't be there so the writer can rev up his motor to figure out what's going to happen in the next scene. Let's give Chekhov the last word:

> You understand what I mean when I say, 'The man sat on the grass.' You understand because the sentence is clear and there is nothing to distract your attention. Conversely, the brain has trouble understanding me if I say, 'A tall, narrow-chested man of medium height with a red beard sat on green grass trampled by passers-by, sat mutely, looking about timidly and fearfully.' This doesn't get its meaning through to the brain immediately, which is what good writing must do, and fast.

CHAPTER NINE

ON REVISION

PITFALLS IN POINT OF VIEW

You'll notice that I haven't given you summaries at the end of each chapter, a bulleted list of things for you to consider about each chosen point of view, and once you cross everything off you'll be good to go, like you were packing for vacation. Issues about point of view are too complicated for that kind of color by number. There are simply too many variables. Instead, I hope that I've given you a way to think about who tells the story as the central question at the heart of any piece of fiction.

I would stress that these are questions for a revision. A writer can't be the stern overseer of his impulses on the first draft. It's paralyzing. That initial instinct that comes to you about how to tell the tale should be respected and coaxed. But on subsequent drafts, a writer needs to scrutinize more deeply. Each wrong step that you confront and attempt to fix is useful, and improves your initial instinct when you go to the next thing you write, even if the final draft is still not salvageable.

A lot of knowledge comes from close reading—the kind we've engaged in over the course of our time together. Not just admiringly inhaling the whole bouquet, but identifying every scent note like some nostril-flaring perfumer. Close reading shows you how much the chosen point of view inflects every choice about voice, diction, sentence rhythm, tone, description.

Here are some regularly occurring point-of-view problems, with suggestions about how to address them during the rewriting process.

Kill default omniscience

The single most common problem I see with first drafts is with writers who automatically adopt an omniscient point of view. As we discussed in Chapter 3, omniscience is still the approach that seems safest and most sanctioned. So we get a lot of first sentences like this (think of it as a game of Mad Libs, and fill in the blanks):

> [Name] looked up at the [noun establishing location] and [verb]. "[Line of dialogue, ending with exclamation point!]"

Could be "Sarah looked up at the bartender's neck tattoo of a bird in flight and giggled. 'Good move, dude!' she thought," often followed by the report of a gesture—"swirling the straw in her mojito." Or considerably more somber: "Private Second Class Marvin T. Jones tried to focus in the infirmary's dim light on the patient moaning in the bed next to his. God, his leg. Gone. Christ, it was Fred! Marvin's own pain began to throb in his arm, or what he thought was his arm, and only then did he realize. . . ."

An opening of this type is meant to thrust us right into the action, introduce the protagonist, give essential information about the location, and draw in the reader to the stakes. All writers have been warned not to waste time lingering too long on setup, to be compact and efficient, but the trouble is that this kind of opening is *so* standard, so without personality, that it simply doesn't give us enough to work with. Actually, it doesn't give us anything, except:

> I am writing a story!
> The story is about Sarah/Marvin!
> Sarah/Marvin lost her/his boyfriend/arm!

Third-person narration needs to have a voice and introduce the author as well as the characters. We need to have a clearer sense of the writer's relationship with the characters, and if the writer has chosen an omniscient point of view, we need to see that he has some authority and oversight, and some personality or credibility as a reporter, as well as some real access to the character's thoughts. First paragraph of *A Beautiful Truth* by Colin McAdam:

> Judy and Walter Walt Ribke lived on twelve up-and-down acres, open to whatever God gave them, on the eastern boundary of Addison County, four feet deep in the years of rueful contentment. Judy was younger than Walt, her dreams had an urgent truth, and five years had passed since they removed a cyst from her womb that was larger than a melon. Her uterus collapsed and for a year she awoke to formaldehyde dawns feeling sick and lonely and hopeless, no more chance of a child.

See the difference? See that the narrator has a posture toward his protagonists? "Up-and-down acres" and "formaldehyde dawns" let us know what to expect from McAdam as a soulful interpreter of his characters' problems. So, too, here, in "Wolf of White Forest" by Anthony Marra:

> No one could explain why the wolves returned in the early years of the newly formed Russian Federation. Biologists arrived with honorifics and plastic binders, departed with unpaid hotel bills and findings so disparate it was a wonder they could agree a wolf had four legs, two eyes, and one nose. Some blamed an irregular cycle of population growth and decline. Some blamed global warming and intense logging of woodlands to the distant southwest. Most blamed their mothers, for one thing or another. Vera had her own theory, but no one thought to ask her.

Given the number of choices in point of view available to contemporary writers, a writer who chooses omniscience better have a good reason. She had better show that her viewpoint has range, reliability—*something* other than what the characters themselves would know, if they were allowed to tell the stories themselves.

Notice that both of the first paragraphs quoted above demonstrate the mastery of temporal distance we've discussed. The narrators know their characters' whole stories. They are starting *in media res*, as it were: Judy is already barren, her operation five years ago, and she's about to adopt not a baby but a chimp (which you know from the flap copy); the wolves are already taking over Russia, and Vera is about to interact with them (how being enough to bring us to the next paragraph). So it is in the middle of the story of a life, not a single day or event.

One more example, and if you're going to start with a scene, it should actually be powerful:

As they were leaving the Mumbanyo, someone threw
something at them. It bobbed a few yards from the stern of
the canoe. A pale brown thing.

"Another dead baby," Fen said.

He had broken her glasses by then, so she didn't know
if he was joking.

Where (or what) is the Mumbanyo? Who is Fen? Who is "she"?
And wait, why did Fen break her glasses? In *Euphoria*, Lily King
plunges you immediately in a third-person–limited point of view
of her protagonist, a Margaret Mead-like anthropologist, who is
on a boat speeding away from the last tribe they've studied. She
has malaria, and is not only half-blind without her glasses but
quasi-hallucinating. She's going from something, and to something, and both ports are compelling mysteries.

We'll discuss methods for addressing weaknesses in third-
person limited momentarily, but I've found that the kind of
layering of time frame we see in the examples above is one of
the hardest things for beginning writers to achieve. The story
unfolds in the writers' minds, and they lay it out for us as it
comes to them. More experienced writers know how to think
further ahead in the narrative, like chess players plotting past
the next move. That larger panorama is immediately evident. So
it's not just a range of characters—we can tell right away above
that McAdam, Marra, and King will all segue into points of view
aligned with their protagonists—but a range in timeline. We are
not myopically limited to focusing on the cocktail being stirred
or shaken at that moment.

Temporal distance can be achieved in the rewriting process.
Think of it as making a good sauce or stew: you want to cook all
of the ingredients down together until they are rich and thick,
not just stir them together and slop them on the plate. And this

often involves another skill that I find less experienced writers are not as supple at wielding, which is crafting good exposition—the language a writer uses to set the scene, give background information, or otherwise set up what is to come.

Summary versus scene

Obviously, key scenes in a work of fiction need to be seen, not merely heard about. But not *every* scene needs to be spelled out step-by-step. If Sarah, above, is about to go home with the bartender with the bird neck tattoo after he finishes his shift, we can jump into bed with them, or even skip to the postcoital disappointment. Then the writer can keep the great details about the pickup scene and not tell us every little thing, as Kristen Roupenian does at the beginning of her story "Cat Person": "Margot met Robert on a Wednesday night towards the end of her fall semester. She was working the concession stand at the artsy movie theatre downtown when he came in and bought a large popcorn and a box of Red Vines." In a way, this opening is very close to the Sarah-at-the-bar opening we rejected a couple of pages ago. It starts with the standard name and location, and then gives us the standard line of dialogue as an opening gambit: "That's an . . . unusual choice," she said. "I don't think I've ever actually sold a box of Red Vines before."

But then Roupenian pivots very quickly to a third-person-aligned point of view, adding temporal distance: "Flirting with her customers was a habit she'd picked up back when she worked as a barista, and it helped with tips. She didn't earn tips at the movie theatre, but the job was boring otherwise, and she did think that Robert was cute. . . ." With this swift shift, the author dangles both Margot's past (her barista job) and her future (whatever is going to happen with Robert). It amounts to a promise from the writer that she knows the whole arc of the relationship, and that it's going to be worth our time.

Same with the example from Lily King. She immediately establishes the nature of her oversight as being inextricably tied to the observations of her protagonist, Nell. So King simply cannot write the phrase "Nell's husband, Fen," because it would disrupt the alignment. Nor can she write a phrase like "he had broken her glasses by then—another act of wanton, drunken violence" or anything making use of a more intrusive omniscient narrator. But King *has* established (1) that she knows Nell intimately, and (2) that she will tell us the most important parts. The opening chapter of *Euphoria* is a great example of temporal distance and compression—the techniques that allow Marion Winik in a *Newsday* review to declare, "This novel is as concentrated as orchid food, packing as much narrative power and intellectual energy into its 250 pages as novels triple its size."

Writing good exposition is actually a skill that *can* be practiced discretely. Take a whole scene from your story or novel. Let's say it's five pages, chronicling the party at which Harry and Sally first met. Now take a highlighter and look ruthlessly at what's notable in that scene. What lines of dialogue, what descriptions? It's as important to pause to admire what works as what doesn't—if something gives you a flush of pleasure, seems just right for no reason you can pinpoint, if you even felt that as you were writing it, ask yourself why. Cook down to one solid, meaty paragraph of "backstory" and choose the most powerful, revealing details—and if none are that powerful or revealing, back to the drawing board to reimagine the scene.

Now experiment with its placement in the story. It doesn't have to be the first scene, even if it is the first meeting. You can also save some details that seem like TMI in that compressed paragraph for later garnish—if Sally noticed the crisp creases in Harry's soft periwinkle blue shirt at that party (one of her favorite colors), and thought admiringly that he must use a dry cleaning service, thus be a grown-up with a real job, she can remember that shirt at a future point in the story, right before the divorce, when the last straw for her is him throwing the shirt on the floor after work, because he's not willing to expend the energy to get it *into* the laundry basket.

Then, on a subsequent rewrite, you can come up with a less clichéd revelation of the woe that is this particular failing marriage than the husband's inability to pick up his dirty socks, or put his glasses in the sink, or put the toilet seat down. (More on such details momentarily.)

If I could choose the one aptitude that really separates the seasoned writer from the less experienced one, it would be the ability to accomplish this kind of scene compression. It affects the whole shape of the story as well as the power of individual scenes. What tends to happen is that on a first draft, the writer begins a work by spelling out every single detail—first meeting, first date, what are people wearing, what color is their hair, what did he say, what did she retort, their shirts, taking their shirts off, consummation—so by the time he gets to the divorce, there's just not enough time or space left. "Whoops. Fifteen pages already, and my story is due to the workshop group by tomorrow, and anyway it has been made clear to me that no one publishes stories longer than fifteen pages anymore, especially by new writers. Time to introduce the divorce lawyer. . . ." What we get are imbalances of focus. The stories are top-heavy.

That's when a rewrite can boldly get rid of whole scenes, compress them to exposition, and *really* start *in media res*.

Let's look at another method for combating that pesky default omniscience.

"Then he lit a cigarette": stage directions

A hilarious line from the Martin Amis novel *Money*:

> "Yeah," I said, and started smoking another cigarette. Unless I specifically inform you otherwise, I'm always smoking another cigarette.

Weaker fiction is full of stage directions used to punctuate dialogue, especially in third person. People shake their heads. They smile, grin, and nod. They raise eyebrows and roll their eyes. They put their hands on their hips, cross their arms, stamp their feet. They slam doors or tiptoe out of rooms. They drink. They rattle their ice. They blow on their coffee. Sometimes they get really creative and let one finger idly circle the edge of their glass.

And they smoke. They smoke a lot. Updike once said that he lit a cigarette, and then had his character light a cigarette, whenever he was stuck. The cigarette was a substitute for thought—it's basically the foot twitching on the gas pedal, to keep the motor of the narrative from stalling out.

One can argue that when a writer has characters constantly sipping coffee, stirring, looking away, picking up the fork, twirling the fork, clearing their throats, and smoking, it's usually the case that nothing much is going on. Each new match the character strikes leaves the character and the reader in a meaningless cloud of smoke.

This is one area where literary fiction and commercial fiction diverge decidedly. Commercial fiction is full of such gestures; literary fiction rarely allows them. The gestures in commercial fiction are the equivalent of instructions for the actor in a screenplay—except that only amateur writers of screenplays include such things; professionals have the respect for actors to keep such instructions to the barest minimum. They don't go in for a lot of stomped feet and sighs. It is the actor's job to figure out how to communicate the emotion that should ostensibly be clear from either the dialogue itself, or from what's happening in the scene. About a character who has just been rear-ended, the writer does not need to tell us that she yelped in surprise.

So on a rewrite, the author can get out that highlighter again and mark every single stage direction, making sure that each one is a *telling* gesture, one that really reveals character or adds something else of value. If it doesn't add something, cut it. Conversely—another exercise you can try discretely—see whether you can make it more meaningful by being sure that the observation about the gesture is convincingly, imagistically rooted in the perceptions of an observer. From Charles Baxter's story "Westland":

> I took her to a fast-food restaurant and sat her down and bought her one of their famous giant cheeseburgers. She held it in her hands familiarly as she watched the cars passing on Woodward Avenue. I let my gaze follow hers, and when I looked back, half the cheeseburger was gone. She wasn't even chewing. She didn't look at the food. She ate like a soldier in a foxhole. What was left of the food she gripped in her skinny fingers decorated with flaking pink nail polish. She was pretty in a raw and sloppy way.

What makes this passage work is the narrator's obvious fascination with the strange, ostensibly homeless young woman he's treating to lunch as a humanitarian gesture. It isn't filler. Through his judgments, we learn as much about the narrator as about the woman he's describing: he's attracted to her, even though he clearly thinks she's beneath him. We can tell as well that she's more interested in the lunch than the man across the table. The narrator doesn't know all this, of course—another example, like the ones we saw in our chapter on first person, of the author knowing more than the narrator knows. The sense of humor, however—the jaunty rhythms of the description of her eating, along with the image of the soldier in the foxhole— belong to the character himself.

Many contemporary writers have sounded the death knell of the gesture used as a spacer, shim, or grout for dialogue (pick your construction metaphor). Often, the descriptions come with a little postmodern disclaimer, a sense that the writer wants to challenge conventional means of storytelling, including this very device. Here's a paragraph from *Lolita*, complete with the requisite smoker, in which both Nabokov and Humbert Humbert campaign against "deadly conventionality":

> There was a staircase at the end of the hallway, and as I stood mopping my brow (only now did I realize how hot it had been out-of-doors) and staring, to stare at something, at an old gray tennis ball that lay on an oak chest, there came from the upper landing the contralto voice of Mrs. Haze, who leaning over the banisters inquired melodiously, "Is that Monsieur Humbert?" A bit of cigarette ash dropped from there in addition. Presently, the lady herself—sandals, maroon slacks, yellow silk blouse, squarish face, in that order—came down the steps, her index finger still tapping the cigarette.
>
> I think I had better describe her right away, to get it over with.

This passage acknowledges directly to the reader that the literary convention of presenting a character, and dwelling on the first meeting, is just that, a convention. So, too, all of the moving in and out of doors, hot and cold—pure, meaningless stage direction. "And staring, to stare at something, at an old gray tennis ball that lay on an oak chest": the line mourns the fact that prose must be filled with stuff, and that the stuff is old and gray and useless as that misplaced tennis ball. And yet the paragraph is great fun, and Nabokov manages, *still*—despite mocking the convention—to use it to effectively convey Humbert's disdain for his landlord's tawdry American pretention.

Of course, Nabokovian self-conscious playfulness is far from the kind of fiction in which stage directions usually appear, like our Dan Brown example from *The Da Vinci Code*, the first chapter of which is full of tilted heads, eyes opening wide, turned gazes, and so on, as the gunshot flies and the mayhem begins. But in literary fiction, even in a reasonably realistic accounting, it's important for the details to be fresh, surprising, and used to establish character. Look at this paragraph from *The Corrections*, in which Jonathan Franzen shows us two lovers on Ecstasy at an academic conference (Chip is Melissa's professor), complete with the requisite cigarettes and, yes, stage directions:

> He took Melissa down on the cigarette-divoted carpeting of Room 23 without even shutting the door.
>
> "It is so much better like this!" Melissa said, kicking the door shut. She yanked her pants down and practically wailed with delight, "This is *so* much better!"
>
> He didn't dress all weekend. The towel he was wearing when he took delivery of a pizza fell open before the delivery man could turn away. "Hey, love, it's me," Melissa said into her cell phone while Chip lay down behind her and went at her. She kept her phone arm free and made supportive filial noises. "Uh-huh ... Uh-huh ... Sure, sure ... No, that's hard, Mom ... No, you're right ... that is hard ... Sure ... sure ... That's really, really hard," she said, with a twinkle in her

voice, as Chip sought leverage for an extra sweet half inch of penetration. On Monday and Tuesday he dictated large chunks of a term paper on Carol Gilligan which Melissa was too annoyed with Vendla O'Fallon to write by herself. His near photographic recall of Gillian's arguments, his total mastery of theory, got him so excited that he began to tease Melissa's hair with his erection.

Hysterical, is it not? And look how clearly you know that Franzen is mocking these characters, much as he enjoys sharing the very specific details of their drugged rutting in Room 23. Here, he doesn't eschew the machinery of the conventional novel. In the Nabokovian spirit, he ups the ante, mocking the very conventions he's employing, while also determined to make them work to propel both the characters and the reader to their literal and figurative climaxes. Except here it's multiple climaxes: the paragraph builds, then piles on s'more. Less isn't more for Franzen. More is more.

Of course, there are writers who attack the problem of the stage direction in a very different way. They keep their descriptions spare, their prose lean, the plate and palate Japanese. There's nothing stray or extraneous. That's an approach, too. But whether exuberant or spare, all successful writers must acknowledge the "then-she-lit-a-cigarette" problem and try to find a way to make the convention fresh, or totally sidestep it.

So look at every rolled eye and raised eyebrow in your work, every hand on every hip, and ask yourself: Who watches the character do this? Does the reader need to see this? Am I falling into a lazy default omniscience? Is there any way I can make the gesture more meaningful, more revelatory? If not, can I just get out my big black Sharpie and cross it out?

Try doing one draft of a rewrite, of either story or chapter, and cut out 10 percent. In a fifteen-page story, there has got to be a page and a half of hot air. If you can resist looking back at the previous draft, you might not even notice the loss. Once you clear away some of the less evocative imagery, some meaningless stage directions, it's easier to see what's missing—and what's really excellent.

What would Jesus (or your character) do?

A fiction writer's most important tool isn't technical. It's profound interest in other people. Fiction writers collect stories. Put them in a crowded restaurant and they're going to eavesdrop on the conversation at the table next to them. On a plane, on their way to the bathroom, they zoom right in on the woman alone in the middle seat of a row, quietly sobbing as she arranges a line of tiny gin bottles. Part of the interest is not so noble and can be gossipy, even a tad rapacious—the writer as scavenger, thief, or plagiarist of potential plots. But the best writers bring to their imaginations a talent for empathy. As George Eliot averred, "The only effect I ardently long to produce by my writings, is that those who read them should be better able to imagine and to feel the pains and the joys of those who differ from them in everything but the broad fact of being struggling, erring human creatures."

In one way, the fiction writer shares with the journalist an ability to ask the right questions. To get the subjects talking, to make the subjects feel valued. Anyone who has done research for a novel knows that people really like to talk about what they do. Good fiction writers not only listen, but listen well. They let the subjects go on and not necessarily in a straight line, because what's most important may not be the first detail offered (in fact, rarely is).

Often a writer who's stuck needs to do more research, either through reading or direct interviews, to nail a character. One fine student novel-in-progress featured two contrasting protagonists, one a young male computer programmer fresh out of college on his first job and one an underpaid, illiterate, haggard, middle-aged maid at his office building. Guess which character in the young male writer's story was more convincing. In essence, he was seeing the domestic worker from outside, even when he was purportedly writing from her point of view. This isn't just a question of getting the details correct, though that's important—I actually met my husband after a draft of my second novel had a character "laying Sheetrock," not hanging it, and someone suggested that if I was going to write about a character involved in construction, maybe I should visit a construction site. On the other hand, you can fall into a black hole of research. For my novel *Love Bomb*, I arranged to hang out with a SWAT team while they did their drills, and I certainly learned a lot about what 99 percent of movies get wrong about SWAT, but really, I was just spinning my wheels. I did not actually need to know *quite* that much about SWAT. (It was, at that moment, just more fun than writing.)

The most important thing to remember is that when you're in a third-person–aligned point of view, the character, not the narrator, makes the observations. And the observations should never be rote, should reveal character and/or motive.

So: snow has fallen in your story. Please, please, I beg you with my whole heart, don't use the phrase "a blanket of snow." If your character lives in a cold clime, and you're writing in a third-person–aligned point of view, the character will know all those zillion Eskimo words for snow. At the beginning of *Winter's Bone*, Daniel Woodrell introduces his heroine as she looks at her neighbor's meat left out to cure:

Snow clouds had replaced the horizon, capped the valley
darkly, and the chafing wind blew so that the hung meat
twirled from the jiggling branches. Ree, brunette and
sixteen, with milk skin and abrupt green eyes, stood bare-
armed in a fluttering yellowed dress, face to the wind, her
cheeks reddening as if slapped and slapped again.... She
smelled the frosty wet in the looming clouds, thought of her
shadowed kitchen and lean cupboard, looked to the scant
woodpile, shuddered. The coming weather meant wash
hung outside would freeze into planks, so she'd have to
stretch clothesline across the kitchen above the woodstove,
and the puny stack of wood split for the potbelly would not
last long enough to dry much except Mom's underthings
and maybe a few T-shirts for the boys.

This is classic omniscience, with a segue into third-person
limited. We could have used it as one of our cinematic landscape descriptions in Chapter 8: Woodrell sets a scene of stark,
unforgiving poverty in the Ozarks. If we were completely in
third-person aligned, the character would not note her own shud-
dering, or the color of her flimsy, faded dress, or certainly not her
own "abrupt green eyes" (my favorite description in a paragraph
that is, for my taste I confess, a little adjective heavy). When
Woodrell dips into Ree's thoughts, however, he knows what
snow means to her. It's not postcard pretty. It's not sleigh bells
as she rides to Grandma's for Christmas dinner. As I've stressed
throughout this book, he has got all the senses involved: smell,
sound, and touch, as well as sight, and it's great that the *pre-
monition* of snow serves as the novel's opening. Once he moves
to Ree's thoughts, Woodrell just writes "the potbelly," not "the
single potbelly stove that served as the family's only source of
heat"—you can't say that in third-person aligned.

Learning that distinction takes some practice, and also takes spending the time to get past the cliché of that blanket of white snow—the clichés always being the first things that come to mind until you dig deeper. If clichés are unfortunate in omniscient narration, they're unforgivable in third-person aligned. As an exercise, I often ask students to share something about their mothers in the kitchen. It is first going to be something obvious that is annoying: her copper pots gleam, she's such a neat freak that she alphabetizes her spices. But then someone comes up with something really revelatory, which makes me see a specific mother bustling or sashaying as mistress of her domain. Same exercise can be done with describing a blind date where the person across the table is unattractive to the observer. He chews too loud, chews with his mouth open, talks while he chews, she has spinach in her teeth, she plays with her hair too much. Standard-issue. But after some work, out comes the equivalent of Madame Bovary's disdain for the way her husband Charles's spoon clacks against his teeth when he eats soup. "She ate like a soldier in a foxhole." "She held the burger in both hands"—well, of course she did, how else are you going to hold a burger?—but as observed by that protagonist, it makes her look like a squirrel with a nut, somewhat feral. A woman who knows her husband inside out, as Nell knows Fen in *Euphoria*, reads him precisely, with an anthropologist's accuracy:

> Fen had his back to her but she could see the expression on his face just from the way he was standing with his back arched and his heels slightly lifted. He would be compensating for his wrinkled clothing and his odd profession with a hard masculine glare. He would allow himself a small smile only if he himself had made the joke.

One technique that helps to generate truly fine, aligned observations is to grant your protagonist full, deep intelligence, rather than holding back all of the insight for your authorial self. There are successfully rendered naïve or intellectually challenged characters in fiction (*The Color Purple! Flowers for Algernon!* Faulkner!), but I often see a character in beginning writer's fiction made to be "typical," and thus lesser than the writer. A bad speller. A broad accent with mispronunciations. Easy to mock. Excellent writers choose characters as interesting and insightful as they are. Although Greer is shit-faced ("actually, I'm only pee-faced") at a typical frat party, at a typical college's weekend, away from her longtime boyfriend and about to be raped, Meg Wolitzer in *The Female Persuasion* lets her character own the clever description when she talks about her dorm at the party:

> She told him she lived in Woolley, and he said, "You have my sympathy. It's so depressing there."
>
> "It really is," she said. "And the walls are the color of hearing aids, am I right?" Cory, she remembered, had laughed when she'd said that, and told her, "I love you." But Darren just looked at her again in that irritated way. She thought that she even saw disgust in his expression. But then he was smiling again, so maybe she had seen nothing. The human face had too many possibilities, and they just kept coming in a fast-moving slide show, one after another.

There's no reason at all for us to spend time with Greer unless Wolitzer can make her lively and engaging for us. Wolitzer never describes her from outside. Greer knows she isn't conventionally beautiful but believes that "she still looked appealing in a very specific way, small and compact and determined, like a flying squirrel." Greer owns the image. It's Greer who reports that the blue streak in her hair "had been added at home with a drugstore kit in eleventh grade. She'd stood over the sink in the upstairs bathroom, getting blue all over the basin and the rug and the shower curtain, until in the end the room looked like the set of a slasher film on another planet." Notice, too, the layering of time frame here: we are both "in scene" and summarizing past events.

A writer can wind up seeming unappealingly selfish if she keeps all of the clever lines and observations for herself. It's as bad as a boss taking credit for a subordinate's work. You know how in Woody Allen movies, all of the characters are stand-ins for Woody Allen, with his gestures and inflections? A film or TV character with a persona can certainly inhabit the persona over and over to fine effect, as, say, Larry David does in *Curb Your Enthusiasm*. But Larry David's wife and friends don't talk exactly like him. The other characters provide some necessary foil and contrast. If we're going to be stuck in one mind on the page, it's probably time to consider first-person narration.

"But it really happened": working with autobiographical material

This is a large enough subject for another book, but it's worth acknowledging that the calculus in determining the proper closeness, or distance, from a protagonist gets considerably more difficult when that protagonist is the author himself. It's harder for the writer to know what's interesting. It's also harder to know where to start. The TMI problem we discussed in the first-person chapter becomes much more attenuated.

Often a writer will separate herself from the character, make the character clearly Other. It makes the writing easier by increasing the objectivity. So while Chinelo Okparanta grew up in Nigeria, her character Ijeoma in *Under the Udala Trees* is *not* her. Instead she uses her own past to help build a credible character. "My mother watched her father die in the war, the same way my protagonist does," Okparanta told an interviewer. She also notes that she "grew up with people always reciting these proverbs to me. Between that and all these Bible verses and Bible quotes, I thought that it would be fun to just play around with it in the novel." Note the concept of *play* in that quote: pieces of the experience are her own, but she has enough distance from the material to provide shape.

In this example, for me at least, the author fails to manifest enough distance from the character. In *Parachutes and Kisses*, Jong's protagonist is, like Jong herself, a best-selling novelist, Isadora (star of Jong's bestseller *Fear of Flying*), and struggles to find time to write amid her other responsibilities:

> One writes along in blissful, or paranoid, solitude. One feels vaguely masturbatory about one's work; and if one is a woman, the whole world conspires to reinforce that notion, calling one "narcissistic," "self-absorbed," "self obsessed" (as if Picasso were not, as if James Joyce were not, as if all artists were not maddened narcissi falling into their own reflections—the drowning in self being one of the conditions for transcending the self).

Despite the formal "one," it seems pretty clear that this *apologia* applies to Jong herself, and comparing herself to Picasso may not be the best approach for one trying to avoid being accused of narcissism.

So should Jong have made her heroine something other than a best-selling novelist? A heart surgeon? Perhaps, but sometimes such transpositions create other conundrums, because each detail you change—either to protect the innocent (or the guilty, who might sue you for libel), or just for a little disguise—changes the character, and thus risks making that character's actions or even thoughts less coherent. If you're a writer and make an autobiographical character a painter instead, the character must now *think* like a visual artist.

Sometimes, too—in the tradition of "truth is stranger than fiction"—things that really happened in Real Life simply don't work on the page. One coincidence too many, or too many tragedies in a row, so the reader feels numb, or . . . well, so very many things can go wrong.

The one quality that a writer of autobiographical material must possess is an ability to either laugh at oneself, or be critical of oneself—maybe even harshly critical. We discussed humor as a key skill for writing in first person. Both Iris Owens and Tama Janowitz have produced heavily autobiographical portraits of single women negotiating bad love affairs with characterizations that are scathingly, almost jubilantly, self-mocking. In *Absurdistan*, Gary Shteyngart shows humor as well toward his experience as a Russian immigrant; he's willing to portray himself (and his stand-ins) as clueless dweebs.

And unfunny experiences? Kathryn Harrison considered incest as the subject in several novels, but found that the transformations required to fictionalize her story resulted in plots that felt somehow dishonest; she has told interviewers that this led her to write the memoir *The Kiss*, about her incestuous affair with her father. When the memoir came out, some critics accused her of being sensationalistic to pen a bestseller. I consider that deeply unfair. In neither the fiction nor the memoir does she paint herself as a blameless victim. That's partly what makes the memoir so powerful. It's bleached clean to the bones of self-pity and self-pleading.

Harrison has used other aspects of her own past to write historical fiction. Her novel *The Binding Chair, or: A Visit from the Foot Emancipation Society* is about women suffering the pain and indignity of bound feet in China at the turn of the century. Her grandmother was living in Shanghai at exactly that time.

Obviously, the novel isn't *about* her grandmother—who was Jewish, *sans* bound feet—but Harrison uses some of the exotic stories she'd heard about the period in composing the story. That's a productive approach a writer can take when using personal narrative: don't make them the *only*, or even the main, story. Imagine outward, past the self. You may have had cancer, but so have other people. Maybe you had to be there to know this about a treatment:

> A hematologist sunk a bore into the bone above Jack's ass in order to extract a core of marrow—the doctor, a gaunt and elegant-looking man, putting all the grunting muscle into it of someone undoing the frozen lugs of a car wheel. When he was done he showed Jack the prize: an inch-long spongy cylinder, not white as Jack had expected but red. The doctor's hairline was droppletted from the exertion; and the young nurse-assistant, who'd told Jack before it began that the procedure was all new to her too, looked greenish afterward. Jack still was sore when he sat.

But Feld is not Jack. Feld just generously bestows the character with his insights, his insider knowledge.

I teach a course called Truth and Lies: Autobiographical Fiction and Fictional Autobiography, in which we look at writers who have considered the same themes in both memoir and fiction. Danzy Senna has discussed being biracial in both fiction (*Caucasia*) and memoir (*Where Did You Sleep Last Night?*). Rick Moody addresses alcoholism in both fiction (*The Ice Storm*) and nonfiction (*The Black Veil*). Certain issues will haunt certain writers, come up repeatedly in their work, and examining the approach to the material in different genres can be very productive. In some cases, a manic or intricate plot, full of invented others, allows the writer to use what he knows about a subject, as it does for Frederick Barthelme in his novel *Bob the Gambler* (as opposed to his memoir about his own addiction, cowritten with his brother Steven Barthelme, *Double Down: Reflections on Gambling and Loss*).

Not every writer excels at both fiction and memoir. The skill sets are not identical, mainly because of differences in the first person: in Chapter 5, we discussed how a first-person narrator is ultimately *not* the author, whereas in a memoir, he is. But the well-crafted literary memoir, as opposed to the Famous Person Tell-All, has become such a popular and accepted genre that a reader might ask, if a writer's goal is to tell his own story, why he doesn't just go ahead and do so.

A very good reason why not can be found in the novel *Asymmetry*. Although it is widely known that the author, Lisa Halliday, had a relationship with the novelist Phillip Roth when she was a young woman working at Roth's literary agency, the affair between a writer and the much-older literary legend chronicled in *Asymmetry* is also not Roth. As Halliday put it to an interviewer, "Yes, some people are going to think of Philip Roth, but Ezra Blazer is a work of fiction. The entire book is an amalgam of details and impressions derived from experiences both romantic and platonic that I've had over the years, plus a healthy dose of research and imagination." The novel comprises three completely different sections, one considering a wholly imagined and very different character (different sex, different ethnicity), and it's not until the end that you realize the sinuous way in which the three narratives connect. *Asymmetry* quite directly considers the question of how we transform life into fiction:

> About the extent to which we're able to penetrate the looking-glass and imagine a life, indeed a consciousness, that goes some way to reduce the blind spots in our own.

It's a novel that on the surface would seem to have nothing
to do with the author, but in fact is a kind of veiled portrait
of someone determined to transcend her provenance, her
privilege, her naivete.

Again, we see a writer asking hard questions about her own character, as well as the limitations of her own self-knowledge and
literary skill. A novelist, one character in *Asymmetry* asserts, "is
forever bound by the ultimate constraint: She can hold her mirror up to whatever subject she chooses, at whatever angle she
likes—she can even hold it such that she herself remains outside its frame, the better to de-narcissize the view—but there's
no getting around the fact that she is always the one holding the
mirror. And just because you can't see yourself in a reflection
doesn't mean no one can."

It's worth mentioning that Halliday wrote *Asymmetry* when
older, that affair with Roth long in her past—another example
of how temporal distance helps create critical distance. I think
I can state with confidence that no one in the first flush of a love
affair should write about it—or in the first tide of fury at the end
of that affair, either. Divorce lawyers will ask clients to write
a short summary of their marital disputes to help with cases,
and often get long, wild screeds full of spewed hatred *IN CAPI-
TAL LETTERS, BOLD, ITALICS ***AND*** UNDERLINED!!!* But
that's why you hire a lawyer—to craft the narrative that most
effectively and efficiently makes your case. I suppose a good editor can serve some of the same purpose.

Change the point of view, change the point

We've tried this technique repeatedly in these pages, and I stand
by it as a useful method for examining point-of-view choices.

Change them.

See whether a critical passage makes more sense, or less, in a different point of view.

Take any passage quoted in these pages and try it in another way. Does it work? Why or why not?

Sometimes it's completely obvious how central the point of view is to the story being told. From the first line of Carver's "Cathedral"—"This blind man, an old friend of my wife's, he was on the way to spend the night"—you know that the story simply has to be told in first person. It cannot be:

> Bub was not relishing the forthcoming visit from an old friend of his wife's, because the man was blind.

Look at the difference between these lines in first person—

> I wasn't enthusiastic about his visit. He wasn't anyone I knew. And his being blind bothered me. My idea of blindness came from the movies...a blind man in my house was not something I looked forward to.

—and the third-person–aligned translation:

> Bub was not enthusiastic about his visit. The blind man wasn't anyone he knew. And his being blind bothered Bub. Bub's idea of blindness came from the movies...a blind man in his house was not something Bub was looking forward to.

Granted, that's a stunningly clumsy translation. Nevertheless, we see how central it is that the protagonist communicates with us directly as first person requires. "He wasn't anyone I knew" expresses perfectly the narrator's lack of interest in his wife having friends of her own, without saying so directly. "My idea of blindness came from the movies" gives the tongue-in-cheek insight to the character, not the author. Anything along the lines of "Bub's ideas of blindness came from the movies" completely disrupts the identification and posits a judgment by the author. If the author just tells us outright how narrow and bigoted Bub is, there's much less incentive for us to spend time with the character.

Nor could Cheever's "The Swimmer," told in third-person (mostly) aligned, be in first person:

> Beyond the hedge I pulled on my trunks and fastened them. They were loose and I wondered if, during the space of an afternoon, I could have lost some weight. I was cold and I was tired and the naked Hallorans and their dark water had depressed me. The swim was too much for my strength...

We would never stand for a first-person narrator withholding information until the end of a story in the way that first person requires here. We wouldn't even stand for him making us follow him through the various backyards. Also, he doesn't sound depressed here. Or drunk. He sounds kind of ... literary. This is a case where the writer introduces us to a limited Other, and we count on the writer to reveal the character little by little, in an elegant striptease.

We've discussed how making an earnest effort to see the world through a character's eyes can deepen a work. However, sometimes a work needs more of an authorial presence. Try the beginning of the Chekhov story we discussed in Chapter 3, without Chekhov's judgments about Gurov. If Chekhov did not inform us that "It seemed to him that he had been so schooled by bitter experience that he might call them what he liked, and yet he could not get on for two days together without 'the lower race,'" why should we read about every detail of Gurov and Anna's affair?

The lack of any kind of voice for the writer can be felt most acutely in drafts of long novels with multiple characters, or in historical novels where the reader is told every detail of every character's progress. It's clear why we might want to witness a wedding, or an arrival at Ellis Island, but a reader might ask, "Do I really need to know how Sam got the mortgage on his house in 1934?"; "Is there a reason why I have to go shopping with Melissa in 1976 and see every dress she rejected to wear to her job interview?"; "Do we even need to see the interview—can't we just go directly to the first day on the job?" These are situations where authorial direction—a sense of why the scene is worth including—can be important at the beginning of chapters or at key moments where the reader's interest might flag. Think of it as the chapter's elevator pitch. You may want to be quiet as a narrator, not too intrusive, but you still need to alert a reader why the story needs to be told.

Outlining can be helpful not only in determining the movement of plot but determining tone and voice. If you force yourself to write one or two sentences, *only*, to summarize each chapter of a novel in progress on a rewrite, you might see (1) whether anything of significance has happened in the chapter, and (2) whether you've made clear what the significance is. Sometimes that process can reveal not only whole chapters that can be cut or combined but ways that you can make thematic connections for the reader—ways you might not have been aware of on a first draft. You can use the same technique for sections of a short story, to coldly assess how the narrative is moving.

I know that everyone derides the concept of the elevator pitch as shallow and sensationalistic. And it's true that the two-line book descriptions in Publishers Marketplace often follow this "pitched-as" concept, "Pitched as *Sex in the City*, but in Tehran."

"Pitched as *The Road,* but with sorority sisters." Silly as those examples are, you can't sell a novel without being able to make clear why someone should buy it, how your book would be both attractive to readers who appreciated similar books (that "readers have also looked at" on Amazon) and appealingly original. That kind of summary can even help you to clarify why *you're* interested in a plot development or description.

First drafts often just follow the action in a scene, without direction or compression. The emphasis, the *point of view* as it were, often gets retrofitted on subsequent drafts. For that reason, in my experience, the beginnings of stories and novels always require the most revision. Further along in a project, as you gain confidence, your voice becomes firmer, your first instincts better. So you're often returning to the beginning, to revise with the full knowledge you don't have until later in the writing process.

Ending with endings: famous last words

Because we've focused on fictional beginnings in this book, and efficient, small samples of prose, we haven't discussed the entire progress of stories and novels. But effective endings, too, involve decisions about point of view. Readers expect to know by then how to feel about the events recounted. They may know more than the character himself knows; they may not even be told how the character feels.

We've quoted both novels and short stories in these pages, but in the matter of endings, the two genres decidedly diverge. By the time you've spent hundreds of pages with a character, you expect to leave knowing their fate—even if the ending doesn't get them to the very end of life. Does the narrator of *Then We Came to the End* keep his job? Does the anthropologist in *Euphoria* get the credit she deserves for her brave research? Does

Madeleine, the woman in Jeffrey Eugenides's *The Marriage Plot*, wind up with the man who has obsessed about her since college? Short stories, on the other hand, often cover events in a much narrower time frame, often a single day or even a single dinner party. Very few contemporary stories involve the curve of an entire life, the way Tolstoy's "The Death of Ivan Ilyich" did. So the question the reader asks is why they're hearing about the event to begin with—what makes the event or events worthy of attention?

Let's look at a couple of violent deaths in short fiction, and see how the endings involve point-of-view decisions.

In "A Good Man Is Hard to Find," Flannery O'Connor takes a character who is so typical that she does not even deserve a name, who is utterly predictable in her smug beliefs, not to mention manipulative and selfish, and by the end of the story has you feeling ways about the old lady that you would never expect. This is a story that undergoes a startling tonal shift as the family on their vacation, kids bickering in the back seat, meets a ruthless killer—it starts as *National Lampoon's Vacation*, and ends as *The Road*.

Similarly, in "Bullet in the Brain," Tobias Wolff takes Anders, a smug, narrow man—"a book critic known for the weary, elegant savagery with which he dispatched almost everything he reviewed"—and very quickly has him shot during a holdup, thereafter leaving the bank and literally *entering his brain* for the man's last thoughts, which involve, of all the incongruous things, childhood baseball, and some kid's weirdly ungrammatical Southern slang. In some sense Wolff's story overtly riffs on O'Connor's famous story with its bloody ending—and, too, on "An Occurrence at Owl Creek Bridge," Ambrose Bierce's story about a Civil War soldier being hanged, in which we learn only at the end that the whole vision of his escape has been *in his head*. Like so many of the examples we've discussed here, the

story is not just about sudden death but how fiction best confronts and makes sense of such an event—about, finally, how fiction captures our thoughts and teaches us about the world.

Michael O'Donoghue, in his famous *National Lampoon* magazine parody of self-help guides called "How to Write Good," suggests that all stories end with this line: "Suddenly, everyone was
run over by a truck." ("If the story happens to be set in England,
use the same ending, slightly modified: "Suddenly, everyone was
run over by a lorry.") Especially in short stories, however, which
often cover a single event or even a smaller slice (in the case
of Elizabeth Tallent's "No One's a Mystery," a single car ride),
the conclusion can involve a change of heart or a new insight.
James Joyce called these shifts in perception epiphanies. The
workshop formulation is to demand that no matter how trivial
or indecisive the events recounted, by the end of the story, the
character has to "grow or change." Charles Baxter argues in his
essay "Against Epiphanies" that the glint of the Sudden Real-
ization has become such a shopworn method for exiting a short
story that it has lost much of its power to shine for us.

Still, there are moments of exquisite, deeply satisfying recognition at the end of great stories, and the nature of the recognition will change depending on the magnitude and nature of the
events recounted. Let's look at just one example, from a story we
discussed earlier in this chapter.

The unnamed first-person narrator of Raymond Carver's
"Cathedral" gets drunk and stoned with a blind dinner guest.
That's the plot, pretty much in its entirety. Since the story happens during a single night, too fast for wholesale personality
changes, the narrator isn't likely to emerge from this experience ready to volunteer at a hospital or learn Braille. But he does
smoke some weed and chat with the blind man after the wife
goes to bed, and closes his eyes to draw that cathedral with his
guest. The story's famous last words:

But I had my eyes closed. I thought I'd keep them that way for a little longer. I thought it was something I ought to do.

"Well?" he said. "Are you looking?"

My eyes were still closed. I was in my house. I knew that. But I didn't feel like I was inside anything.

"It's really something," I said.

But *what* is it? Or are the narrator's final words just the bland equivalent of "Oh, wow"? This ending has been analyzed as being both epiphanic and anti-epiphanic. The narrator has been unmoored from the comfort of his preconceptions. That's reading "not being inside anything" in a positive light, almost as if he has achieved a transcendental moment. Nevertheless, it's not a deep connection with the blind man he's experiencing with "I didn't feel like I was inside anything." He's still detached, isolated—and under the influence. But . . . maybe a little less isolated from his fellow man than before? Maybe, realistically, our changes have to come in small increments? The ending manages to be both climactic and open-ended.

Despite the Carver narrator's simple diction, we're aware of Carver behind him, cleverly crafting the story of an Ordinary Man. The metaphor of the cathedral—man's greater, soaring aspirations, as opposed to his earthbound life—is not the narrator's. The metaphor about "the blind leading the blind" belongs to Carver, not the narrator. So does the clever twist of the final-not-final epiphany-non-epiphany. Carver speaks over his first-person narrator's head here to his readers. He certainly shows a bemused sympathy with his protagonist's narrow-mindedness, but the real relationship here is not between the two stoned men. Although the story is written in first person, it still forges a relationship between the writer and us. Carver has given us everything we need to write a paper about this story: this story is to the great literature (and amazing architecture) of the past as this beer-guzzling, bigoted man is to, say, Odysseus. Contemporary American life isn't exactly spiritual, but we can still achieve small moments of grace.

So, in fact, Carver *can* address the reader. In this case, the epiphany belongs more to us than to the character, although for the record, that is not what Carver himself thought:

> Well, the character there is full of prejudices against blind people. He changes; he grows.... He puts himself in the blind man's place. The story affirms something. It's a positive story and I like it a lot for that reason. People say it's a metaphor for some other thing, for art, for making.... But no, I thought about the physical contact of the blind man's hand on his hand.

Here we reference the aforementioned intentional fallacy. Whatever initial idea sparked Carver's imagination, those larger themes are there, and the reader is entitled to note them. After all, Carver had the men watch a documentary on the building of the great cathedrals of Europe. He didn't have them watch *Jaws*, and draw the pointy teeth in the shark's open mouth.

A very informal survey, to be sure, but most novelists will tell you their endings require much less torturous fussing and revision than the beginnings. By the end, they know what they're doing, where they're going.

Story endings are trickier, and in my experience, the failures tend to go in two diametrically opposed directions. The first is an overly obvious summing up of the story's themes. The obvious model for this kind of ending is James Joyce—he invented the Epiphany Ending, after all. So when the young narrator of "Araby" arrives at a neighborhood bazaar he couldn't wait to attend, and it turns out to be tawdry and unsatisfying, he tells us:

Gazing up into the darkness I saw myself as a creature driven and derided by vanity; and my eyes burned with anguish and anger.

But it's hard to get away with quite that bold and florid an authorial declaration in a contemporary short story, and writers who attempt to do so often seem pompous, or a little silly. Indeed, they often err in the other direction, ending with Carveresque or Hemingwayesque lines of dialogue that are meant *both* to seem like something that would be said, *and* sum up the situation in a provocative way, like the ending of "Hills Like White Elephants":

"Do you feel better?" he asked.
   "I feel fine," she said. "There's nothing wrong with me. I feel fine."

There's really no trick to getting that perfect combination of casual and final in a last line of a short story. It just takes work to make the ending seem both delicate, and definite. In the lines above, you certainly know that the pregnant girl about to go for her "procedure" is not fine at all. Hemingway doesn't have to tell you.

By the time you get to the ending of a great story or novel, your view of the characters and situations has expanded, like one of those sponge animal capsules that bloom when placed in water. I hope that the same thing has happened to your understanding of point of view in fiction.

Let's end this chapter—and our book—with a couple of great last lines from novels. I will appropriate them, postmodern collage-style, without attribution, so as not to be accused of any spoilers, although, as I've said repeatedly, I don't believe in spoilers, except about the final scores of seventh games in NBA final matchups.

After all, tomorrow is another day.

It is a far, far better thing that I do, than I have ever done; it is a far, far better rest that I go to than I have ever known.

The knife came down, missing him by inches, and he took off.

I never saw any of them again—except the cops. No way has yet been invented to say goodbye to them.

But now I must sleep.

Are there any questions?

. . . and his heart was going like mad and yes I said yes I will Yes.

EXERCISES

Chapter Two

Look at the opening of one of your own stories or novels and list everything a reader could know from just those couple of sentences. Do we get a clear idea about the main issue facing the protagonist, as well as the fiction's plot, setting, theme? Do we hear the author's distinctive voice?

Try the opening from a piece of your own fiction in a different point of view. Does it change the tone or meaning? How?

Choose a key passage in your fiction and identify how the diction and sentence rhythms are identifiably your own. Is there a recognizable, quintessential voice? In other words, what writing are you particularly proud of, and why?

What can we know about the novel or story to come, merely from your title? Does the title set up expectations? How is the title *Moby Dick* different from "What We Talk about When We Talk about Love"?

Chapter Three

Write an efficient bio-sketch to introduce your protagonist. Try to make your omniscient evaluation of the character bold and authoritative. Is he a bully after having been a fat kid who was bullied himself? Does she lie about her nationality and college degree at each job interview? Gain your readers' trust by proving that you know your subject definitively.

Introduce your character with a single distinctive physical detail. Rather than a police report of height, weight, hair color, and so on, what is the character's most defining feature?

Write a simile or metaphor that shows off your own vantage point toward the story and introduces your own style and sensibility as a writer. Experiment with injecting such an observation at a surprising point in the narrative and ask how the authorial presence enhances, or detracts from, the story's tension by allowing the narrator to speak this directly.

In a key scene, have your narrator provide temporal distance to enhance his reliability—in other words, imply that the narrator knows how the story ends, even if the characters do not.

Chapter Four

Experiment with the injection of free indirect discourse into a third-person account. Can you make it clear when the voice or perception is the character's own, rather than the narrator's?

Observe how free indirect discourse subtly shifts, or reinforces, the intended effect.

Write about a character who isn't a philosopher, or a poet—one who feels deeply, and is observant, but isn't necessarily articulate. How will you represent those feelings in third-person aligned? Does the character require a stream-of-consciousness approach? Can you capture the fullness of the feelings without seeming to condescend to the character?

Experiment with creating multiple third-person–aligned characters for your narrative who offer contrasts to your primary protagonist. If your character is a jewel thief, what might you gain by exploring the theft from the vantage point of the jeweler who faceted the stone? The frail widow who needed to sell the ring to fund her assisted living? The worker in Sierra Leone who first mined the diamond? Ask whether those viewpoints are too "on the nose" or, contrarily, provide surprise and liveliness.

Next, experiment with how you stage the sections on the various characters. Does it enhance the suspense if you pull back before the jewel heist to explore a character with a very different trajectory?

Chapter Five

In your character's voice, write a first-person justification for an obviously immoral or unsavory act. Let your character plead his case directly to the reader, and make it as convincing as you can.

Then experiment with the placement of the defense—is it more compelling, or less so, if it's delivered before the account of the act itself?

Write an observation or assertion in your first-person narrator's voice that a reader will question—and make sure your reader "hears" you making a point. What does the account gain by having the author subtly communicate to the reader in this way?

Make it clear to your reader how your protagonist looks, *without* having that character look in a mirror.

Write a passage that makes your first-person protagonist like-able, by the way that narrator comments on another character or situation. In other words, tell us about your character indirectly, through his evaluation of others.

Try a key section in your fiction in both present tense and past tense. Does the past tense require an older, wiser judgment from your protagonist? Or does the simple fact of past tense imply that the narrator has "moved past" the events?

Chapter Six

Experiment with describing something that a child wouldn't have the vocabulary for, making sure you don't restore to a "faux-naif" voice in which the child sounds overly wide-eyed and winsome.

Take a crucial scene from your fiction and see how it's different when related as the age the child is when it happens versus as an adult looking back on the event.

Write a passage from an animal's point of view that makes use of what we know about that animal's perceptions. How does something smell to an animal with a superb sense of smell? How does prey look on the ground to a flying owl?

Chapter Seven

Write the opening of a piece of your fiction in third or first person as a second-person narrative. Is it now disarming? Does it involve the reader more, or distance the reader from the action?

Now try the fiction as a collective voice. How does the narrator's "we" speak of a group identity?

Insert a "found document" into your fiction—a newspaper article or letter. How does that change the voice? Would a series of such documents be an interesting way to advance your plot? You can even experiment with having major plot revelations happen through the insertions—for example, if your character is divorcing, and selling off all of his possessions, the "ephemera" could be eBay ads, each of which triggers a specific memory.

Find a newspaper article that tells a fascinating story (for example, man forces woman to drive getaway car as he robs bank, on their first date), and think about what point of view you would use to tell the tale.

Chapter Eight

Try to create the equivalent of a "POV shot" in film by having your characters' observations about an event be highly subjective.

Take a scene in your fiction that is predominantly visual, and add the other senses—texture, taste, smell—that fiction can explore so much better than film.

Try staging a climactic scene in your fiction by having the focus move from a larger, wider shot of the event (the battlefield, the chaos after the earthquake) to a much narrower focus (your own character's injury).

Chapter Nine

Find a clichéd stage direction in your story—a raised eyebrow or hands on hips—and try to find a gesture that is actually revealing about the character.

Take a scene from your fiction that you fear may go on too long, and try to compress it into one paragraph of solid, rich exposition. If the scene was a five-page account of a dinner party, see how that party looks if recalled—and with only the most significant encounters or lines of dialogue remaining.

Look at an autobiographical detail from your work that involves a revelation you feel queasy about. Is there a way to change the plot to be less true to life—without violating the fiction's believability? What happens if your sixth-grade teacher suddenly becomes an airline pilot? What would you need to know about that pilot to penetrate his point of view?

Take a scene from your fiction in third person, and ask whether you can forcefully change the observations from being in a standard omniscience to a third-person–aligned point of view. What would your character know, what would your character observe, that showcases his particular view of the world? Focus on senses other than sight.

Think about how you're using exposition. Is there a key scene in your fiction that might be more powerful if it were compressed and summarized? Conversely, is there a scene that is merely summarized that might be more powerful if we heard the dialogue, or followed the action more step-by-step?

ACKNOWLEDGMENTS

First, much gratitude to Ellen Levine at Trident Media, and Jill Bialosky and Drew Weitman at W. W. Norton, for shepherding this project to print. Copyeditor Nina Hnatov and project editor Rebecca Munro made essential contributions as well.

Thanks to these writers and friends who read drafts of the manuscript and provided helpful amendments: Tyler Hoffman, William Fitzgerald, Jay McKeen, Susan Coll, Rachel Pastan, James Marcus, Michael Deagler, and Stephanie Manuzak.

Thanks to all the Rutgers-Camden MFA students who have taken my craft class in point of view. They've helped me fine-tune these arguments and provided many useful examples and counterexamples.

AUTHORS AND WORKS CITED

Adams, Richard. *Watership Down*. New York, Macmillan, 1974.

Adichie, Chimamandah Ngozi. *Americanah*. New York: Alfred A. Knopf, 2013.

Adler, Warren. *The War of the Roses*. New York: Warner Books, 1981.

Albert, Elisa. *After Birth*. Boston: Houghton Mifflin Harcourt, 2015.

Alvarez, Julia. *In the Time of the Butterflies*. Chapel Hill, NC: Algonquin Books of Chapel Hill, 2010.

Amis, Martin. *Money: A Suicide Note*. New York: Penguin Books, 1986.

———. *The Rachel Papers*. New York: Alfred A. Knopf, 1974.

Atwood, Margaret. *The Handmaid's Tale*. Toronto: McClelland and Stewart, 1985.

———. *The Testaments*. New York: Nan A. Talese/Doubleday, 2019.

Austen, Jane. *Emma*. Edited by Stephen M. Parrish. 2nd ed. Norton Critical Edition. New York: W. W. Norton, 1972.

———. *Pride and Prejudice*. Edited by Donald Gray. 3rd ed. Norton Critical Edition. New York: W. W. Norton, 2001.

Auster, Paul. *Timbuktu*. New York: Henry Holt, 1999.

Baker, Nicholson. *The Mezzanine*. New York: Vintage Books, 1990.

Banks, Russell. *The Lost Memory of Skin*. New York: Ecco, 2011.

Barnes, Julian. "The Saddest Story." *Guardian*, June 6, 2008.

Barthelme, Donald. "The Photograph." In *The Teachings of Don B.: Satires, Parodies, Fables, Illustrated Stories, and Plays*. Edited by Kim Herzinger. New York: Turtle Baby Books, 1992.

———. "The School." In *Sixty Stories*. New York: Putnam, 1981.

Barthelme, Frederick. *Bob the Gambler*. New York: Houghton Mifflin Harcourt, 1997.

———. "Shopgirls." In *Moon Deluxe*. New York: Simon & Schuster, 1983.

Barthelme, Frederick and Steven Barthelme. *Double Down: Reflections on Gambling and Loss*. New York: Mariner Books, 2001.

Barthes, Roland. *The Pleasure of the Text*. Translated by Richard Miller. New York: Hill and Wang, 1975.

Bartlett, John. *Bartlett's Familiar Quotations*. New York: Little, Brown, 2012.

Baxter, Charles. "Against Epiphanies." In *Burning Down the House*. New York: Graywolf, 2004.

———. "A Relative Stranger." In *A Relative Stranger*. New York: W. W. Norton, 1990.

———. "Gryphon." In *Gryphon: New and Selected Stories*. New York: Pantheon Books, 1998.

———. "Westland." Ibid.

Begley, Adam. "Guardian Review: Timbuktu by Paul Auster," *Guardian*, May 29, 1999.

Bell, Madison Smart. *All Souls' Rising*. New York: Pantheon, 2000.

———. *Master of the Crossroads*. New York: Pantheon, 2000.

———. *The Stones that the Builder Refused*. New York: Pantheon, 2004.

Bender, Aimee. "Separation Anxiety." *New York Times*, September 16, 2010.

Bierce, Ambrose. "Occurrence at Owl Creek Bridge." In *Fiction 100*. Edited by James H. Pickering. 10th ed. New Jersey: Pearson Publishing, 2012.

Bloom, Harold. *The Anxiety of Influence: A Theory of Poetry*. New York: Oxford University Press, 1973.

Booth, Wayne C. *The Rhetoric of Fiction*. Chicago: University of Chicago Press, 1983.

Borges, Jorge Luis. *Labyrinths*. Edited by Donald A. Yates and James E. Irby. Preface by André Maurois. New York: New Directions, 1962.

Boswell, Robert. *Tumbledown*. Minneapolis, MN: Graywolf Press, 2014.

Bowles, Paul. *The Sheltering Sky*. New York: New Directions, 1949.

Boyle, T. C. "Sorry Fugu." In *T. C. Boyle Stories*. New York: Viking Press, 1998.

———. *Tortilla Curtain*. New York: Viking, 1995.

Brodesser-Akner, Taffy. *Fleishman Is in Trouble*. New York: Random House, 2019.

Bronte, Emily. *Wuthering Heights*. Edited by Alexandra Lewis. 5th ed. Norton Critical Editions. New York: W. W. Norton, 2019.

Brown, Dan. *The Da Vinci Code*. New York: Doubleday, 2003.

Bushnell, Candace. *Sex and the City*. New York: Atlantic Monthly Press, 1996.

Byatt, A. S. *Possession*. Modern Library Edition. New York: Random House, 2000.

Cahalan, Rose. "17 Great Books on the Border to Read Instead of *American Dirt*." *Texas Observer*, Jan. 23, 2020.

Camus, Albert. *The Stranger*. Translated by Stuart Gilbert. New York: A. A. Knopf, 1946.

Carver, Raymond. "Cathedral." In *Cathedral: Stories*. New York: Alfred A. Knopf, 1983.

Charles, Ron. "Marilynne Robinson's 'Lila:' an Exquisite Novel of Spiritual Redemption and Love." *Washington Post*. September 30, 2014.

Cheever, John. "The Country Husband." In *The Stories of John Cheever*. New York: Alfred A. Knopf, 1978.

———. "The Swimmer." Ibid.

Chekhov, Anton. "The Lady with the Little Dog." In *Anton Chekhov's Short Stories*. Selected and edited by Ralph E. Matlaw. 1st ed. Norton Critical Editions. New York: W. W. Norton & Company, 1979.

Choi, Susan. *Trust Exercise*. New York: Henry Holt and Company, 2019.

Christie, Agatha. *And Then There Were None*. 75th anniversary ed. New York: William Morrow, 2011.

Cleland, Lance. "Tumbledown: An Interview with Robert Boswell." *Tin House*, September 16, 2013.

Coetzee, J. M. *Disgrace*. New York: Viking, 1999.

Cohen, Leah Hager. *Strangers and Cousins*. New York: Riverhead Books, 2019.

Cohn, Dorrit. *Transparent Minds: Narrative Modes for Presenting Consciousness in Fiction*. Princeton, NJ: Princeton University Press, 1978.

Conrad, Joseph. *Heart of Darkness*. Edited by Paul B. Armstrong. 5th ed. Norton Critical Edition. New York: W. W. Norton, 2016.

Coover, Robert. "The Babysitter." In *Pricksongs & Descants*. New York: Dutton, 1969.

Crichton, Michael. *Jurassic Park*. New York: Alfred A. Knopf, 1990.

Cummins, Jeanine. *American Dirt*. New York: Flatiron Books, 2020.

Davis, Lydia. "Example of the Continuing Past Tense in a Hotel Room." In *Collected Stories of Lydia Davis*. New York: Farrar, Straus and Giroux, 2009.

———. "Spring Spleen." In *Collected Stories of Lydia Davis*. New York: Farrar, Straus and Giroux, 2009.

DeMaupassant, Guy. "The Necklace." In *Fiction 100*. Edited by James H. Pickering. 10th ed. New Jersey: Pearson Publishing, 2012.

Diaz, Junot. "This Is How You Lose Her." In *This Is How You Lose Her*. New York: Riverhead Books, 2012.

Dickens, Charles. *A Tale of Two Cities*. Edited by Robert Douglas-Fairhurst. Norton Critical Edition. New York: W. W. Norton, 2020.

Doctorow, E. L. *Ragtime*. New York: Random House, 1975.

Doerr, Anthony. *All the Light We Cannot See*. New York: Scribner, 2014.

Donoghue, Emma. *Room*. New York: Little, Brown, 2010.

Dostoevsky, Fyodor. *Notes from Underground*. Translated by Michael R. Katz. 2nd ed. Norton Critical Edition. New York: W. W. Norton, 2000.

Dubus, Andre. *Voices from the Moon*. Boston: D.R. Godine, 1984.

Egan, Jennifer. *A Visit from the Goon Squad*. New York: Alfred A. Knopf, 2010.

Elie, Paul. "How Racist Was Flannery O'Connor?" *New Yorker*, June 15, 2020.

Eliot, George. *Middlemarch*. Edited by Bert G. Hornback. Norton Critical Edition. New York: W. W. Norton, 1977.

Ephron, Nora. *Heartburn*. New York: Knopf, 1983.

Erdrich, Louise. *The Round House*. New York: Harper, 2012.

Eugenides, Jeffrey. *The Virgin Suicides*. New York: Farrar, Straus and Giroux, 1993.

Everett, Percival. *Erasure*. Hanover, NH: University Press of New England, 2001.

Faulkner, William. "A Rose for Emily." In *Fiction 100*. Edited by James H. Pickering. 10th ed. New Jersey: Pearson Publishing, 2012.

——. *As I Lay Dying*. New York: J. Cape, H. Smith, 1930.

Feld, Ross. *Only Shorter*. San Francisco: North Point Press, 1982.

Ferrante, Elena. *My Brilliant Friend*. New York: Europa, 2016.

——. *The Lost Daughter*. New York: Europa, 2008.

Ferris, Joshua. *Then We Came to the End*. New York: Little, Brown, 2007.

Fitzgerald, F. Scott. *The Great Gatsby*. New York: C. Scribner's Sons, 1925.

Flanagan, Richard. *The Narrow Road to the Deep North*. New York: Alfred K. Knopf, 2014.

Flaubert, Gustave. *Madame Bovary*. Translated by Margaret Maudon. London: Oxford World's Classics, 2008.

Flynn, Gillian. *Gone Girl*. New York: Crown, 2012.

Foer, Jonathan Safran. *Extremely Loud and Incredibly Close*. Boston: Mariner Books, 2005.

Ford, Madox Ford. *The Good Soldier*. New York: Vintage Books, 1951.

Fowler, Karen Joy. *We Are All Completely Beside Ourselves*. New York: G. P. Putnam's Sons, 2013.

Franzen, Jonathan. *The Corrections*. New York: Farrar, Straus and Giroux, 2001.

Garner, Dwight. "A Bowl of Cherries Left to Dry in the Sun." *New York Times*, April 2, 2014.

Gay, Roxane. "Review of *My Absolute Darling* by Gabriel Tallent." Goodreads, September 6, 2017.

Gibson, William. *Pattern Recognition*. New York: G.P. Putnam's Sons, 2003.

Gilman, Charlotte Perkins. "The Yellow Wallpaper." In *Fiction 100*. Edited by James H. Pickering. 10th ed. New Jersey: Pearson Publishing, 2012.

Greene, Andy. "Stephen King: The Rolling Stone Interview," *Rolling Stone*, October 31, 2014.

Greenidge, Kaitlyn. "Who Gets to Write What?" *New York Times*, September 24, 2016.

Greer, Andrew Sean. *Less*. New York: Little, Brown, 2017.

Groff, Lauren. *Fates and Furies*. New York: Riverhead Books, 2015.

Gruen, Sara. *Water for Elephants*. Chapel Hill, NC: Algonquin Books, 2006.

Haddon, Mark. *The Curious Incident of the Dog in the Night-Time.* New York: Doubleday, 2003.

Hale, Benjamin. *The Evolution of Bruno Littlemore.* New York: Twelve, 2011.

Halliday, Lisa. *Asymmetry.* New York: Simon & Schuster, 2018.

Heckerling, Amy. *Clueless.* Los Angeles, CA: Paramount Pictures, 1995.

Heiny, Katherine. *Standard Deviation.* New York: Alfred A. Knopf, 2017.

Heller, Joseph. *Catch-22.* New York: Simon & Schuster, 1961.

Hemingway, Ernest. "Hills Like White Elephants." In *Men Without Women.* New York: C. Scribner's Sons, 1927.

Hosseini, Khaled. *The Kite Runner.* New York: Riverhead Books, 2003.

Ishiguro, Kazuo. *Never Let Me Go.* New York: Alfred A. Knopf, 2005.

Jackson, Shirley. "The Lottery." In *The Lottery and Other Stories.* New York: Farrar, Straus and Giroux, 2005.

Jagernauth, Kevin. "Stephen King Says Stanley Kubrick's *The Shining* Is 'Like A Big, Beautiful Cadillac With No Engine Inside It.'" *IndieWire,* February 3, 2016.

James, Henry. *The Portrait of a Lady.* Edited by Robert D. Bamberg. Norton Critical Edition. New York: W. W. Norton, 1975.

Janowitz, Tama. *Slaves of New York: Stories.* New York: Crown Publishers, 1986.

Johnson, Adam. *The Orphan Master's Son.* New York: Random House, 2012.

Johnson, Denis. "Car-Crash While Hitchhiking." In *Car Crash While Hitchhiking and Emergency: Two Stories.* New York: Picador, 2020.

Jones, Thom. "Cold Snap." In *Cold Snap: Stories.* Boston: Little, Brown, 1995.

Jong, Erica. *Parachutes and Kisses.* New York: Signet, 1985.

Jordan, Peter. "Chekhov's Letters." *TSS Publishing,* July 7, 2019.

Joyce, James. "Araby." In *Dubliners.* New York: B. W. Huebsch, 1916.

———. *Portrait of the Artist as a Young Man.* New York: B. W. Huebsch, 1916.

———. *Ulysses.* Modern Library Edition. New York: Random House, 1946.

Kafka, Franz. "Leopards in the Temple." In *Parables and Paradoxes.* New York: Schocken Books, 1961.

———. *The Metamorphosis*. Edited by Mark M. Anderson. 1st ed. Norton Critical Editions. New York: W. W. Norton & Company, 2015.

Kertesz, Imre. *Fatelessness*. Translated by Tim Wilkinson. New York: Vintage International, 2004.

Kesey, Ken. *One Flew Over the Cuckoo's Nest*. New York: Viking Press, 1962.

Kincaid, Jamaica. *Annie John*. New York: Farrar, Straus and Giroux, 1985.

King, Lily. *Euphoria*. New York: Atlantic Monthly Press, 2014.

King, Stephen. *On Writing: A Memoir of the Craft*. New York: Scribner, 2000.

———. *The Shining*. Garden City, NY: Doubleday, 1977.

Kirn, Walter. "My Hard Bargain." In *My Hard Bargain*. New York: Alfred A. Knopf, 1990.

Koepp, David. *Cold Storage*. New York: Ecco, 2019.

Kozloff, Sarah. *Invisible Storytellers: Voice-Over in American Fiction Film*. Berkeley: University of California Press, 1989.

Kubrick, Stanley. *The Shining*. Burbank, CA: Warner Home Video, 1980.

Kakutani, Michiko. "Woman Caught in the Paradox of Being Adrift and on a Journey." *New York Times*, September 28, 2014.

Kushner, Rachel. *The Flamethrowers*. New York: Scribner, 2013.

Kwan, Kevin. *Crazy Rich Asians*. New York: Doubleday, 2013.

Lee, Harper. *To Kill a Mockingbird*. Philadelphia: Lippincott, 1960.

Lethem, Jonathan. *Motherless Brooklyn*. New York: Doubleday, 1999.

Levin, Ira. *Rosemary's Baby*. New York: Random House, 1967.

Levy, Ariel. "Nora Ephron: Everyone's Arch and Insightful New Best Friend." *New Yorker*, June 18, 2017.

Mantel, Hilary. *Wolf Hall*. New York: Henry Holt, 2009.

Márquez, Gabriel Garcia. *One Hundred Years of Solitude*. Translated by Gregory Rabassa. New York, Harper & Row, 1970.

Marra, Anthony. "Wolf of White Forest." In *The Tsar of Love and Techno*. New York: Hogarth, 2015.

McAdam, Colin. *A Beautiful Truth*. New York: Soho Press, 2013.

McCann, Colum. *Let the Great World Spin*. New York: Random House, 2009.

McCarthy, Cormac. *The Road*. New York: Alfred A. Knopf, 2006.

McDermott, Alice. *Charming Billy*. New York: Farrar, Straus and Giroux, 1998.

McEwan, Ian. *On Chesil Beach*. New York: Nan A. Talese/Doubleday, 2007.

McInerney, Jay. *Bright Lights, Big City*. New York: Vintage Contemporaries, 1984.

McLaughlin, Emma and Nicola Kraus. *The Nanny Diaries*. New York: Griffin, 2003.

Messud, Claire. *The Woman Upstairs*. New York: Alfred A. Knopf, 2013.

Mishima, Yukio. "Patriotism." In *Short Fiction: Classic and Contemporary*. Edited by Charles H. Bohner. New York: Prentice-Hall, 1994.

Mitchell, David. *Cloud Atlas*. New York: Random House, 2004.

———. *Ghostwriter*. New York: Random House, 2000.

Modiano, Patrick. *Suspended Sentences: Three Novellas*. Translated by Mark Polizzotti. New Haven, CT: Yale University Press, 2014.

Moody, Rick. *The Black Veil*. New York: Back Bay Books, 2003.

———. *Hotels of North America*. New York: Little, Brown, 2015.

———. *The Ice Storm*. New York: Back Bay Books, 2002.

Mooney, Ted. *Easy Travel to Other Planets*. New York: Little, Brown and Company, 2015.

Moore, Lorrie, "Two Boys." In *Like Life: Stories*. New York: Vintage Contemporaries, 2002.

———. "People Like That Are the Only People Here: Canonical Babbling in Peed-Onk." In *Birds of America*. Picador: New York, 1988.

Morrison, Toni. *Beloved*. New York: Knopf, 1987.

Munro, Alice. "Amundsen." In *Dear Life: Stories*. Alfred A. Knopf, 2012.

———. "Haven." Ibid.

———. "In Sight of the Lake." Ibid.

———. "To Reach Japan." Ibid.

Nabokov, Vladimir. *Lolita*. 50th anniversary ed. New York: Vintage, 1989.

O'Brien, Edna. *Girl*. New York: Farrar, Straus and Giroux, 2019.

O'Brien, Tim. "The Things They Carried." In *The Things They Carried*. New York: Houghton Mifflin Harcourt, 1990.

O'Connor, Flannery. "A Good Man Is Hard to Find." In *A Good Man Is Hard to Find*. New York: Harcourt, Brace, 1955.

O'Donoghue, Michael. "How to Write Good." Workable Web Solutions.

O'Hara, J. D. "Donald Barthelme: The Art of Fiction." *Paris Review*. Issue 80, Summer 1981.

Okparanta, Chinelo. *Under the Udala Trees*. New York: Houghton Mifflin Harcourt, 2015.

Olsen, Tillie. "I Stand Here Ironing." In *Tell Me a Riddle: A Collection*. Philadelphia: Lippincott, 1961.

Owens, Iris. *Hope Diamond Refuses*. New York: Knopf, 1984.

Ozick, Cynthia. "The Shawl." In *The Shawl*. New York: Alfred A. Knopf, 1990.

Parker, Dorothy. "Big Blonde." In *The Portable Dorothy Parker*. New York: Viking, 1957.

Parker, Ian. "Edna O'Brien Is Still Writing About Women on the Run." *New Yorker*, October 7, 2019.

Poe, Edgar Allan. "The Cask of Amontillado." In *The Collected Tales and Poems of Edgar Allan Poe*. Modern Library Edition. New York: Random House, 1992.

———. "The Fall of the House of Usher." Ibid.

Polanski, Roman. *Rosemary's Baby*. Paramount Pictures, 1980.

Proulx, Annie. *Brokeback Mountain*. New York: Scribner, 2005.

Pynchon, Thomas. *The Crying of Lot 49*. New York: Perennial Library/Harper & Row, 1966.

Robinson, Marilynne. *Lila*. New York: Farrar, Straus and Giroux, 2014.

Roth, Philip. *The Human Stain*. Boston: Houghton Mifflin, 2000.

Roupenian, Kristen. "Cat Person." In *You Know You Want This*. New York: Scout Press/Simon & Schuster, 2019.

Russell, Karen. "Engineering Impossible Architectures." *Tin House*, December 11, 2012.

———. "St. Lucy's Home for Girls Raised by Wolves." In *St. Lucy's Home for Girls Raised by Wolves*. New York: Alfred A. Knopf, 2006.

Russo, Richard. *Empire Falls*. New York: Alfred A. Knopf, 2001.

Salinger, J. D. *Catcher in the Rye*. Boston: Little, Brown, 1951.

Salter, James. "Last Night." In *Last Night: Stories*. New York: Alfred A. Knopf, 2006.

Saunders, George. "The Perfect Gerbil: Reading Barthelme's 'The School.'" *McSweeney's*, no. 24, 2007.

———. "Victory Lap." In *The Tenth of December: Stories*. New York: Random House, 2013.

———. *Lincoln in the Bardo*. New York: Random House, 2017.

Schulman, Helen. "Russell Banks Imagines a Paroled Sex Offender's Future." *New York Times*, October 7, 2011.

Schumacher, Julie. *Dear Committee Members*. New York: Doubleday, 2014.

Semple, Maria. *Where'd You Go, Bernadette?* New York: Little, Brown, 2012.

Senna, Danzy. *Caucasia*. New York: Riverhead Books, 1998.

———. *Where Did You Sleep Last Night?* New York: Farrar, Straus and Giroux, 1999.

Shapton, Leanne. *Important Artifacts and Personal Property from the Collection of Lenore Doolan and Harold Morris*. New York: Farrar, Straus and Giroux, 2009.

Shepard, Jim. *The Book of Aron*. New York: Alfred. A. Knopf, 2015.

Shteyngart, Gary. *Absurdistan*. New York: Random House, 2006.

Smith, Zadie. *White Teeth*. New York: Random House, 2000.

Spencer, Scott. *Endless Love*. New York: Knopf, 1979.

Spiegelman, Art. *Maus: A Survivor's Tale*. New York: Pantheon Books, 1986.

St. John, Emily. *Station Eleven*. New York: Alfred A. Knopf, 2015.

Sterne, Laurence. *The Life & Opinions of Tristram Shandy, Gentleman*. Modern Library Edition. New York: Random House, 1950.

Svorecky, Josef. *The Bass Saxophone*. Translated by Kaca Polackova-Henley. Toronto: Anson-Cartwright Editions, 1977.

Tallent, Elizabeth. "No One's a Mystery." In *Time with Children*. New York: Collier Books, 1988.

Tallent, Gabriel. *My Absolute Darling*. New York: Riverhead Books, 2017.

Tawada, Yoko. *Memoirs of a Polar Bear*. Translated by Susan Bernofsky. New York: New Directions Publishing Corporation, 2016.

Tolstoy, Leo. *Anna Karenina*. Translated by Louise and Aylmer Maude. Edited by George Gibian. Norton Critical Edition. New York: W. W. Norton, 1970.

———. *War and Peace*. Edited and with a revised translation by George Gibian. New York: W. W. Norton, 2001.

Torres, Justin. *We the Animals*. Boston: Houghton Mifflin Harcourt, 2011.

Twain, Mark. *The Adventures of Huckleberry Finn*. Edited by Thomas Cooley. 3rd ed. Norton Critical Edition. New York: W. W. Norton, 1998.

Updike, John. "A&P." In *Pigeon Feathers and Other Stories*. New York: Alfred A. Knopf, 1990.

———. *Rabbit, Run*. New York, Knopf, 1960.

Vida, Vendala. *The Diver's Clothes Lie Empty*. New York: Ecco, 2015.

Waldman, Katy. "*Fleishman Is in Trouble* Turns the Marriage Novel Inside Out." *New Yorker*, June 27, 2019.

Wallace, David Foster. *Infinite Jest*. New York: Back Bay Books, 2006.

Whitehead, Colson. *The Underground Railroad*. New York: Doubleday, 2016.

Williams, Joy. "Taking Care." In *Taking Care: Short Stories*. New York: Random House, 1982.

———. "The Visiting Privilege." In *The Visiting Privilege: New and Collected Stories*. New York: Alfred A. Knopf, 2015.

Winik, Marion. "Powerful *Euphoria* Reimagines Margaret Mead." *Newsday*, June 19, 2014.

Wolff, Tobias. "Bullet in the Brain." In *The Night in Question and Other Stories*. New York: Alfred A. Knopf, 1996.

Wolitzer, Meg. *The Female Persuasion*. New York: Riverhead Books, 2018.

Wood, James. *How Fiction Works*. New York: Picador, 2008.

Woodrell, Daniel. *Winter's Bone*. New York: Little, Brown, 2006.

Yeats, W. B. "The Second Coming." In *The Collected Poems of W. B. Yeats*. New York: Scribner, 1997.

Yost, Graham. *Speed*. Directed by Jan de Bont, Los Angeles, CA: Twentieth Century Fox, 1994.

PERMISSIONS